D1118744

Blues Before **Sunrise**

Steve Cushing

Foreword by Jim O'Neal

Blues Before **Sunrise**

THE RADIO INTERVIEWS

University of Illinois Press

Urbana and Chicago

©2010 by the Board of Trustees
of the University of Illinois
All rights reserved
Manufactured in the United States of America
1 2 3 4 5 C P 5 4 3 2
∞ This book is printed on acid-free paper.

Library of Congress Cataloging-in-Publication Data
Blues before sunrise : the radio interviews / [compiled by]
Steve Cushing ; foreword by Jim O'Neal.
    p.   cm.
Includes index.
ISBN 978-0-252-03301-8 (cloth : alk. paper)
ISBN 978-0-252-07718-0 (pbk. : alk. paper)
1. Blues musicians—United States—Interviews.
2. Blues musicians—United States—Biography.
I. Cushing, Steve.
II. Blues before sunrise (Radio program)
ML394.B646   2010
781.643092'273—dc22   2009027102
[B]

Contents

Foreword

JIM O'NEAL

(*Cofounder,* Living Blues Magazine)

The story of the blues is one that we historians have discussed, documented, and analyzed for decades. But the story that Steve Cushing presents in *Blues Before Sunrise* is that all too rare account that can be told only by the people who lived the blues and told most genuinely in their own words, in language of the blues. For an art form that also serves as an oral history of a culture in song, what better way could there be to get a people's perspective on the blues?

One of the key components of a compelling story can be not only who tells it but also who's listening. In Steve Cushing, the storytellers of *Blues Before Sunrise* found an eager and willing ear, one who knew and appreciated their music and their struggles, and one who was willing to simply listen and let the stories flow, just as he learned to accompany many bluesmen as a drummer on the Chicago club scene. His *Blues Before Sunrise* radio show has provided a public outlet for the artists' stories and music to be heard across the country. For some of these artists, this was surely their one and only radio interview.

While a typical blues radio show host might be chasing down the hottest touring and recording acts of the moment, Cushing took his explorations of the blues back to its roots, finding artists whose long-ago "tours" might have consisted only of performing at one plantation or country juke joint after another, or whose recording careers might have been over and done in one or two sessions—as well as artists like Alberta Hunter and Tommy Brown who once had tastes of commercial success in the show-business end of the blues. But even their eras of the blues were nothing like the contemporary blues scene of the 1980s and '90s, when these interviews were done. This is a history that won't repeat itself. This is a world that today's listeners and readers will never know.

Little Hudson, a Chicago bluesman whose story might never have been chronicled at all had his name not been preserved for posterity on a rare single on the highly collectible J.O.B. label, was, at sixty-six, the youngest of this book's subjects at the time Cushing taped their respective interviews. The irrepressible Alberta Hunter was the oldest, at eighty-nine. Even though most of the artists had retired from music at some point, several heeded the call to perform again when a new generation of listeners took interest in their old recordings and learned that the singers were still around and able to be coaxed back onstage. No doubt some of those listeners heard these artists first on *Blues Before Sunrise* radio.

The blues, of course, isn't just one story. It's a swirling sphere of stories from the underworld, populated by a vast array of characters, each with their own interpretations of music and society and their own reasons to sing, play, or produce the blues. The *Blues Before Sunrise* cast has no big stars who are household names like B. B. King or Muddy Waters, although some of the singers here were quite successful in their day. But most spent their careers at street level, scuffling for whatever they could make playing blues bars, juke joints, street corners, or southern country picnics, and, more often than not, having to look outside their music to find ways to support themselves.

And that in itself is crucial to understanding the blues, which is much more than the standard musical history of the major recording artists who made the classic hits. While many blues artists aspired to stardom, others were happy just to be able to play for friends and neighbors; others struggled their whole lives to make it and never did; some relegated blues to the background and played other kinds of music that their listeners would pay for; some gave it up for the church or a job with a steady paycheck; some made their way by gambling, hustling, bootlegging, or any means other than working for the big boss man. The erstwhile blues singers variously toiled not only in the traditional blues day jobs of picking cotton and working in factories; one ended up as bus driver, another as an electronics technician. We also meet a preacher, a nurse, a nursing home owner, and the owner of a laundry business. And some continued to play the blues to help make a living, although for none of them was music a sole lifelong means of support.

The denizens of the blues underworld most often circulated within a marginal fringe of an already marginalized black subculture in a segregated country where, in the music business and in daily life, they were subject to prejudice, discrimination, and swindling. Denied respect and rights by white society, blues singers also found themselves castigated by the churchgoers of their own communities who condemned them for singing "the devil's music." They learned to do whatever it took to make it. If they couldn't beat the system, they'd beat each other out of what they could. As blues producer Cadillac Baby recalls here from many years of experience, "You had to maneuver and hustle. It kept you shifty."

If the tales in this book meander and stray from musical topics at times, it only serves to remind us that these slices of life are the raw ingredients from which a blues artist constructs his art. Blues was both a means of survival—in an emotional and spiritual sense if not always a financial one—and a declaration of "the facts of life," as the blues' most noted songwriter, Willie Dixon, was fond of saying. It was Dixon who also said that a blues artist's songs were shaped by his "raisings and surroundings." So here we discover whiskey-making recipes, lessons on "riding the blinds," superstitions and folk tales, pimps and prostitutes, treatises on rules of conduct (in the nightclub, on the road, or in the hobo jungle), stories of dealing with the power structure, whether personified by a lawman like Two-Gun Pete from Jody Williams's memories or by the syndicate figures Tommy Brown knew.

But the musical life is still the focus, and we have musicians' anecdotes about one another, tales of their exploits together, their travels and gigs and recording sessions, boasts and toasts, and homegrown analyses of their own and others' musical styles and acumen. The first-person stories of *Blues Before Sunrise* traverse a winding geographical patchwork that brings stories of the blues together from across the country. Several of the life sagas follow the "deep blues" migratory trail from the rural South to Chicago (or in Yank Rachell's case, to Indianapolis), but the collection also encompasses Grey Ghost's itinerant career as a Texas piano pounder, the fifties R & B circuit traveled by Georgia's Tommy Brown, who later made a name for himself as a comedian, the big-city vaudeville and cabaret era of Alberta Hunter, and the multifaceted musical journey of Jesse Thomas from Louisiana to Texas and California and back. With Tommy Brown we even sidetrack up to a striptease joint in Alaska.

We can also follow the transition in blues from the pre–World World II "Ancient Age" to what Steve Cushing has designated "Postwar Glory" as the music moved from acoustic sounds and rural settings to electric instruments and urban environments. Some of the artists were able to participate in, and even help to formulate, the "Postwar Glory," the exciting years when amplified Delta blues filled the streets of Chicago's South and West sides. But for the four Chicagoans interviewed here, the glory of that era was short-lived and was scant in comparison to the fame and accolades accorded the bigger names in Chicago blues like Muddy Waters and Howlin' Wolf. Uncle Johnny Williams and Little Hudson left the blues life; so did Jody Williams for many years, although he did make a comeback highly applauded by hard-core aficionados. John Brim remained an intermittent presence on the scene.

The last three interviews take us to another fascinating sphere of the blues, that of the promoter, producer, and disc jockey. Mississippi-born Cadillac Baby, self-proclaimed "Chiseler from Manchester" in one of his comic routines, shared a background similar to the blues artists he booked at his nightclub and recorded for his label, whereas New Yorker Ralph Bass was a Jewish/Italian hepcat so drawn to the world of African American blues, soul, jazz, and gospel that he became a part of it. Bass would always leave interviewers wanting more, telling them "I'll have it in my book." Sadly, that book was never completed, which makes his reminiscences here all the more valuable. Richard Stamz, once one of the most popular and powerful radio personalities on the Chicago rhythm-and-blues scene, may have faded into obscurity with the public, but never in his own mind. His oratory portrays the drive it took to wheel and deal in the era of independent commercial radio, from the nuts and bolts of advertising sales to the inside scoop on payola.

Blues Before Sunrise leaves us, in the end, with both a broader and a deeper appreciation for those who have lived the life of the blues. Steve Cushing continues to beat the drum, on the bandstand and behind the microphone, for those whose voices deserve to be heard.

Thank you, Steve.

Acknowledgments

Special thanks to the interviewees who sat patiently and shared generously: James "Yank" Rachell, Jesse Thomas, Alberta Hunter, R. T. "Grey Ghost" Williams, John and Grace Brim, Jody Williams, Rev. Johnny Williams, Rev. Hudson Shower, Tommy Brown, Ralph Bass, Narvel "Cadillac Baby" Eatmon, and Richard Stamz.

Thanks also to the following friends: Al Brandtner, Vicki Haas, Illinois Slim, Bob Koester, Ken Kowalski, Jim O'Neal, Tary Owens, Maryann Price, Robert Pruter, Bruce Powell, Mike Rowe, Dick Shurman, Kurt Swanson, Bessie Thomas, David Waldman, and Frank Zirbel.

And thanks as well to the staff at the University of Illinois Press, including Laurie Matheson, Joan Catapano, Breanne Ertmer, and Cope Cumpston.

Introduction

Blues Before Sunrise was first broadcast in June 1980. For the first ten years it was a local-only program broadcast on WBEZ, the public radio station in Chicago. In 1990 the program went into national syndication and today is heard on seventy-five stations across the nation. The focus of this award-winning program is on the first fifty years of recorded blues, starting with the very first blues record, "Crazy Blues" by Mamie Smith, recorded in 1920. When historians and musicologists refer to blues as "America's root music," it's the blues recorded during this period to which they refer. These recordings serve as the basis for most of American popular music, including jazz, gospel, rhythm and blues, soul, and rock 'n' roll. Each week the show explores, preserves, and popularizes the various genre and eras of the blues. Imagine walking through the rooms that house the record collection at the Smithsonian Institution, the walls lined from floor to ceiling with shelves of blues records—blues from every era and stylistic school ever known. *Blues Before Sunrise* is the program that pulls the records off the shelf and plays them for you, profiling the figures—seminal and obscure—that shaped this music; helping to breathe life into these neglected pioneers of popular culture, tracing their development and highlighting their relevance through the decades. *Blues Before Sunrise* is not just another record show; it's a cultural treasure trove, the program where every week is Black History Month!

In addition to playing records from this historic era, over the years I've made it a part of the program mission on *Blues Before Sunrise* to talk with the people who've made the music. Throughout its history this program has presented extensive, in-depth interviews with literally scores of blues people, including singers and players, record producers, managers, and deejays. These bluesmen and blueswomen have fascinating stories to share about their lives and careers, their recordings, and the bygone world that spawned the blues. These stories are humorous and dramatic and help bring to life this largely undocumented chapter of African American heritage.

This book is a collection of twelve of the interviews/oral histories that were originally broadcast on the *Blues Before Sunrise* radio program. In almost every case the interviews selected for this book are definitive—the best, most informative conversations on record with each of these candidates. The interviewees in the "Ancient Age" section are all artists who recorded before World War II. With the deaths of Robert Jr. Lockwood and Henry Townsend in 2006, the interviews found in this section may be the final word from their generation. Over the next decade, the final few survivors of postwar Chicago blues will be gone as well. I hope this simple portfolio will ensure that the life stories that accompany their music will be preserved in full bloom for coming generations.

Part One **Ancient Age**

Yank **Rachell**

The mandolin is a rare instrument in the world of blues. Throughout the entire history of this music there have been only a handful of blues mandolinists of note. Yank Rachell and Charlie McCoy were the preeminent mandolinists during the prewar years, and Johnny Young was the lone postwar blues mandolinist. The mandolin remains popular in bluegrass and old-timey music, but has reached a virtual dead end in blues.

Pete Crawford made this interview with blues mandolinist Yank Rachell possible. Pete had formed one of those symbiotic relationships that many aspiring young white players had with veteran black bluesmen in the early 1960s, a tradition that continues to this day. Yank taught Pete how to play guitar in accompaniment to his mandolin and hired him to play gigs and recording sessions as his accompanist. Pete, in turn, hustled club and festival gigs and provided reliable transportation. The two worked together for many years. I don't recall if I approached Pete or if Pete approached me, but he arranged the interview and then drove me down to Yank's house in Indianapolis, a four-hour drive from Chicago.

Yank Rachell (*back*) with Sleepy John Estes. Photo courtesy of Yank Rachell.

As I recall, there were a couple of problems in doing this particular interview. First, when we set up the recording equipment in Yank's living room, his young grandson sat in. He was about six years old and didn't seem to understand that he couldn't sing or speak while we were recording. It didn't take Yank long to shag him out of the room, since he wouldn't be quiet, but try as we might we couldn't get rid of him. There were more doors in that room than on an advent calendar, and this kid popped through each one of them. Every time the kid reappeared, we would stop recording while Yank scolded him out of the room. This went on for most of the first hour.

Another difficulty for me was that Yank spoke with a unique dialect. I usually had no problem understanding what was said when black musicians spoke, having spent a decade on Chicago's South and West sides. Yank, however, had a very high-pitched, very nasal, rapid-fire manner of speaking. During this session I had a hard time following the conversation. I can be grateful that Yank was a natural storyteller—and that Pete, having heard his stories for many years, requested Yank's best anecdotes.

This interview took place on September 27, 1984. Yank Rachell died on April 9, 1997.

■ ■ ■

Well, I was born in Brownsville, Tennessee, way out in the country, you know. My daddy was a farmer. He got this farm, raised cotton and corn. So I didn't know nothing else but that. When I got larger, I heard about the city. "Daddy, let's move to the city." He said, "I ain't eating them wasps nests." He called light bread "wasps nests." Say, "I ain't eating them wasps nests, no light bread." Daddy said, "I'm gonna stay here and raise me some corn. Then I'd have some meal and eat some cornbread. And raise me some sow bosom." Talking about a hog. All right. Well, we stayed there. Planted cotton and corn and sorghum. All that junk, you know.

So we used to have an old radio with a horn on it. You'd hear them talk. When we didn't have one, we'd go to people's house and listen to it. So we decided we wanted to play some music. I did—me and my brothers—the three of us. So my brothers and I met some girls, schoolgirls. We wasn't trying to court them. We were too young trying to court them. But they had a guitar. They would lend it to us. And we'd go home and try to play. We couldn't play nothing, but we had an uncle, he could play. And I had a cousin, he could play. So my uncle, he lived in the city, and he'd come out in the country on a weekend. And he'd teach us how to play something on the guitar. Well, we three learned how to play the guitar.

Well, my older brother, he passed away. That left me and the baby boy. So I was going down the road one day. Wasn't no street then in them times. I was about eight years old. Man sitting on a porch playing a mandolin. One of them old gold mandolin with stripes on it, you know. I went by his house. I knew him. My mother and father knew him well. His name was Ollie Row, I never will forget. I said, "Mr. Ollie, what is that you got there?" He said, "A mandolin, son." I say, "Yeah?" I said, "I'd like that." And he said, "Let me sell it to you." "Let me see it." Say, "I believe I could play." I hit a lick or two. "Let me sell it to you, son." I said, "I ain't got no money. How much you want for it, Mr. Ollie?" "Five dollars." Five dollars was a lot of money then—I'm eight years old. Five dollars—I ain't never saw five dollars, I don't reckon. I said, "I ain't got five dollars. I'll trade you a pig for it." He said, "All right. Go get the pig." Well, he knew the value of a pig, but I didn't. So I didn't care. My mother and father had a lot of pigs and things. I went home, went to the barn. Got me a tow sack—"croaker sack," they call it. I put the pig in there and went 'round the thicket to the man's house. They didn't live far from us. And I gave him the pig and he gave me the mandolin. Well, that's all I wanted. I wasn't thinking about nothing else. So I came home with it.

There's one thing in the world to try to learn how to play a mandolin. If you can't play it, it'll run you crazy. Dinging, dinging, dinging. I couldn't play nothing. He didn't show me anything. So I carried it out. Every evening I'd come from school, I'd grab it. My daddy, he didn't like it. "Boy, get out of here with that fuss. Go to bed." "All right, I'll go to bed." When he'd leave, I'd get it. I'd be so glad when that old man leave home I didn't know what to do, because I want to play on that mandolin. So he didn't let us do much playing on it. He'd go off, we'd play. I'd hand it to my brother and he'd hand it back to me. Hand it to him. Then one day, my mother, she didn't say nothing much that morning. She's sitting there sewing, piecing a quilt or something. She said, "James." I said, "Ma'am." She said, "Where's the pig?" I said, "I don't know." She said, "I ain't seen that pig in a day or two." I said, "I ain't either, Momma." I know where the pig was; the man had the pig. She said, "Go out there and see if you can find him." I said, "Yes ma'am."

She hadn't never said nothing to me about playing the mandolin. She was good about it. I went out there to the barn and stayed about five minutes, or ten minutes, because I was in a hurry to get back to play on the mandolin. The old man was gone, you know. I come back. "You see him, James?" I said, "No, I ain't seen that pig *nowhere*." I picked the mandolin back up. I wasn't interested in any pig. So she said, "What is that thing you got there anyway? What is that?" I said, "It's a mandolin." "Mandolin?" I said, "Yes, ma'am." "Where you get that thing?" I said, "I got it from the man down the street, down there at the road." She said, "How'd you get it?" Now, in them days you better not steal anything—you do and you'll be dead, because they'll kill you. They didn't allow you to steal where I come from. "Did you steal that thing, boy?" I said, "No, Momma. I didn't steal it." She said, "How'd you get it?" I said, "He let me have it." "Who was it?" "The man down the street." She said, "How come he let you have it?" I said, "He let me have it." So she said, "Uh-huh—you *stole* it."

We had a tree out there in the yard. We lived right in the bottom, the edge of a bottom. She went and got every switch off that tree—looked like that tree withered. She come right back grabbing them switches. She said, "You're gonna tell me something about that mandolin, about that thing you're playing." She said, "Pull your clothes off." I commence to sniffing and crying, you know. She say, "I ain't gonna whup them clothes." She said, "I bought 'em and I ain't gonna whup 'em now—I'm gonna whup you." I commenced to crying, you know. I said, "Momma," I said, "I traded the pig for it." She said, "I ought to kill you." She said, "No, never mind, I ain't gonna do nothing to you." She said, "You know what? This fall when we kill meat, and we're gonna sit down and eat the meat, and you eat that thing what you got, that mandolin." (*laughs*) So I didn't care. I didn't care no way. So she wouldn't whup me.

So finally a guy come along named Willy Newborn. He was a mandolin player and a guitar player, too. Well, I played around with him, so he could play a mandolin. Well, he couldn't play too good, but he could play some. He would tune it. And so I learned to play it, you know. I just listened to him. So I learned to play it. A lot of times something comes to me, I didn't make it up, but I would learn how to play it then. We walked ten miles just to play them old country dances, you know. So I went with him one night. I played with him. A man gave me two dollars. I come on back. "That man's crazy paying me to play!"

I was the fool; I had never made no money, you know. I said to myself, "That man's crazy." I come on out. Said, "Momma, here's what I made." "Uh-huh," she say, "well, you better keep it, because you ain't gonna get no meat this fall." (*chuckles*) Well, I kept on playing; then my brother, he learned to play it. I'd play a piece and he'd play a piece—I'd play a piece and he'd play a piece. Well, my uncle had to teach me how to play a little on the guitar. So we'd team up. He played the mandolin and guitar. He'd play the mandolin, I'd play the guitar. Then he'd play the guitar and I'd play the mandolin. So we grew up like that.

We played that way until my brother Davey Boy passed. Oldest boy died first, but he had learned how to play, too. The three of us could play. So I'd play and play, them old country suppers. In the fall of the year, that's when you'd make some money—from gathering that cotton down there, you know. They'd gather cotton. They'd carry the cotton to the gin and gin their cotton. A lot of people don't know how that was, but they'd make money like that. So one night a man asked me, he say, "Yank?" I said, "Yes." His name is Charlie Barnes. He said, "How about playing something?" I said, "I ain't got no guitar, Mr. Charlie." He said, "I'll buy you a guitar." I said, "All right."

Sure enough, he bought me an old guitar. And I went to his house. Started on a Thursday night. Thursday, Friday, and Saturday I played for him. Different people would come from different places. So I didn't know Sleepy John then. I was living on the north side and he was living on the south side of town. But actually he heard about me—they gonna bring him in there to play guitar against me, you know. Of course, John never did do nothing but flail a guitar. But I used to pick one. So we'd come down to the house, full, you know. Old John coming out—looked like an old sleepy man. Sat down, you know. I looked at him. I said, "This old guy, I'm gonna run him out from here playing tonight." He played some and I played some. And so we played around there and played around. So he liked how I played and I liked how he played. So that's why we teamed up together, right then and there, at that man's house. So we both were playing guitars.

Well, I could play a mandolin. So I quit playing guitar and played mandolin and left him on the guitar. So Sleepy John and I went playing together. And we'd play every fall. People come asking for you. And they'd have a fish fry on a Saturday night. Friday and Saturday night. The women would be in the kitchen. They'd pull the table across the middle door. And you'd go out and they would serve you, you know, in the kitchen there. Fish and K-wives—they call 'em hog chitlins. They'd have that moonshine whiskey out there. And we'd be playing out there in the country night, drinking that moonshine, guys fighting. Shooting out the lamp and breaking windows and things. One night, guys got to fighting and I run into the stable with a mule. Well, that guy was shooting pistols. So me and John played and played.

Well, we went to Memphis then, me and him. We sat down on the street playing one day. A fellow come by named Jab Jones. He was a piano player, Jab Jones. He say, "You sure can play. You play good enough to make records." He said, "There's a man from New York here now making records. Why don't you come on and see if we can make some records with him." I said, "Where's he at?" "He's on Shore and Beale." We said, "Well, we'll meet you up there tomorrow then." We was lying, but after all, we did go up there. The guy was there.

Man name of R. S. Peer—big, fat, fine-looking white guy from New York. RCA Victor, that's who recorded us. This boy, Jab, carried us up there. He said, "Are these the musicians?" He said, "Let me hear you." We played, me and Sleepy John. He say, "Yeah, I can use you."

In them times they didn't have no tape; they had wax. And that wax was expensive—you couldn't mess that wax up and erase it like you do this tape anyway. So we practiced up a little and we got together and we made the record. "Goin' to Brownsville, Take the Right-Hand Road." That was our home, in Brownsville, you know. "*I ain't gonna stop walking till I get in sweet mama's door.*" John and I made that up. Next thing was the "Divin' Duck Blues." I made that. We three made the first recording together in 1929. Well, the man paid us. That man give us nine hundred dollars. Lord have mercy! I never had seen that kinda money in my life, because I had just come off the farm, you know, youngster. I said, "That man's crazy giving us all this money!" I'm the fool. (*chuckles*) Three of us got three hundred dollars a piece, now. Well, my God, in 1929—three hundred dollars! Good God almighty.

We went down on Beacon Street, me and John did. We bought some of them old suits. They had a lot of them old secondhand suits and shoes down there. We bought three whole suits. Hired us a taxi to go to Arkansas. Kept the man over there a week, riding us around. The money come easy. Riding us around. Come back to Memphis. Well, I supposed to come to Brownsville. I bought a wristwatch and I had to pawn my wristwatch to have enough money to come to Brownsville on the bus. Now, that was the fool I was. (*chuckles*) So I goes to Brownsville.

After a while the record come out—ooh, it sounds so good! So many people'd be in front of the main record store the police had to stand there, you know, and make them let people get by. They had the street blocked. "That's John Adam and Yank Rachell. John Adam and Yank. Boy, they got some records out." And you couldn't get by the street. The police had to make 'em get out of the way. A man named Arthur John. He had a little old music store there. And he said, "That record brought you a half a million dollars." A half a million dollars. And we got about three hundred dollars royalty.

So I got married. Commenced to raising a family. I got four kids—two boys and two girls. So John want me to go. I couldn't go then. I said, "John, I can't go. I got to stay here with my family." John loved to go. He'd pick up anybody could play a harp or something. So then he went around. Hammie [Nixon] used to follow. Then he took Hammie. So him and Hammie teamed up together playing. Him and Hammie played a long time together. Well, when my family kinda grew up, I met up with Sonny Boy [John Lee Williamson aka Sonny

Boy Williamson I]. Sonny Boy and I teamed up. It was twenty-five miles from Brownsville to Jackson, Tennessee. Sonny Boy's home was in Jackson. Well, I would go to Jackson. I met a friend over there; he could play. So I'd go out and play with him. Because I didn't know where John was, you know. I'd catch the bus and go to Jackson. So there's this little old Sonny Boy on a bike. He'd follow me around on his bike. "Let me play with you. Let me play with you." I looked at him; I said, "All right. Next time."

So I went over there one evening. People giving a dance out there in the country. From Jackson. I carried Sonny Boy out there with me. He got down and got to playing that harp and singing. Man want to whup him about his wife. He sure could play harp and sing. So we come on back. I had a call to New York. I put out that "Squeaky Workbench Blues." A guy up in New York called us. Called me and Dan Smith and B. Johnson. I wouldn't carry Sonny Boy. He just had started. He wasn't good enough back then. We played up there in New York. Come back. Well, Dan Smith, who went with me up there, he come on back to Jackson; I come on back to Brownsville. Jackson a bigger place than Brownsville, Tennessee. Jackson is a city. Pretty nice city. So he was up there woofing about how he had been recording, but people didn't know how much money he made. He even had some rubber [fake] money. And he's up there in a club, talking about how much money he made in New York. He had never been nowhere before. So they saw some money, sure enough. But it was rubber money, but they thought it was real money—they killed him. Robbed him. Killed Dan Smith.

Well, then I went to playing with Sonny Boy. Me and Sonny Boy started playing together. Sonny Boy got so good, we went recording. We went to St. Louis and we met Walter Davis. And Walter Davis, he met us playing with Lester Melrose. We played some and Lester Melrose wanted us to record for him. Well, we're living down South. So he sent Walter Davis down there every spring to pick up me and Sonny Boy, and we'd go to Chicago and record. We were staying with Tampa Red. Tampa Red had a big house. All the musicians come out to the city, why, he had a place for them to stay. The company was paying him, you know. We'd go up there to Tampa Red's and stay. He had an old dog—I never will forget it—drank more beer than a man. You didn't give him some beer, he'd bite you—he would! Tampa played at a tap right across the street from his house. He had an old parakeet. Tampa's wife, she'd give the bird a note. He'd put it in his mouth and go to the tap. That damn bird would fly over there to Tampa! Right over Lake Michigan—that's one place, one studio we was in where I made "Lake Michigan Blues." We was in a studio right, I don't know, about the ninth or tenth floor. Everything set up when you get there. Piano and everything. Two, three fifths of whiskey. Lester Melrose had that, because Sonny Boy ain't gonna play unless he got him some whiskey—not play good. So every studio we went to, they set up. Well, that's why we recorded. Sonny Boy and I in Illinois. I think we went to Joliet, Illinois, once. Walter Davis. So we'd go up there every year. Every spring come out with a new record, you know. We said, "Well, Big Bill [Broonzy] and them gonna record." We'd say, "Well, let us go record, too." And so, "We gonna put out something that they ain't got." Something like that, you know. We enjoyed that. Every summer, me and Sonny Boy would.

Then Walter Davis started to playing with us. Me and Walter Davis and Sonny Boy. Sonny Boy loved to drink and Walter Davis didn't drink. Me, him, and Walter Davis, coming to Chicago, and Sonny Boy's mother was coming on down with us, and Big Joe Williams. We'd all come to Chicago. Sonny Boy and Walter Davis got to arguing. They got to arguing. Wasn't either of them scared of [the] other, as far as that goes. But Joe Williams had a little pistol in his dashboard. And I got the pistol because I didn't want either one of 'em to shoot the other. I took and put it in my pocket. So Walter and Sonny Boy got out. They wants to kill one another. After a while I got them quieted down. But both of 'em called themselves mean when they get a drink. Of course, Walter Davis didn't drink, because Walter had done killed a man in St. Louis. He killed a guy one night. A fellow come at him with a knife, one Mother's Day night. Old Walter Davis kept a .45 on his arm, in a scabbard. And the guy kept on coming on him with the knife. He said, "Get back now, mister, if you want to see Mother's Day," he say, "get back." Fellow kept on at him. He killed him—and got out of it! So I knew Walter would do that. And I didn't want him and Sonny Boy to kill one another. So that's the only trouble I had with Sonny Boy. He'd get drunk, clown some. After that I came back home. Sonny Boy wanted to live in Chicago. So he didn't have no wife, got no children. "Yank, let's go to Chicago and live." I said, "No, I can't go. I can't leave my children there." He went to Chicago and come back to Jackson, "Come on, man. I'm making plenty of money up there. Come on, let's go." I said, "No, I can't go." I said, "My children are little. I can't go off [and] leave them." So he went back up there.

Well, my father-in-law was a preacher. He would go to Jackson, Tennessee, from Brownsville. He come back, he tell me, he say, "Yank." I'd say, "Yeah." He said, "Sonny Boy got killed." I said to myself, "This preacher don't know what he talking about." But it was the truth. Sonny Boy got killed. He was friendly. He was friendly but he loved to drink. He'd drink, he was friendly as could be. But he wasn't no scaredy guy. So he trailed down at the club and he got ready to come home—he got him a cab. Well, some guy was watching him. He was naturally a country boy, out of Jackson, Tennessee. He had a diamond ring on. I think he'd gambled and won three, four hundred dollars. So these guys caught the cab he caught. But he wasn't thinking. He's half drunk, you know. He got in the cab and they got in the cab with him. He got out; they got out. When they got out, they knocked him down and jumped on his chest. They took his ring and his money. And he staggered up to the door, rung the doorbell, and told his wife—she's named Lacey Belle. He said, "I made more money tonight than I ever made in my life. But I'm hurt, I'm sick." She run out and called an ambulance. It came and he died before he got in the hospital.

Well, then, when John come back, we started to playing back together. When he'd come in, I'd go with him. But I still played them old country suppers until I left there forty years ago. People come lined up at our house, want us to play for them, you know. But John would tell four or five different people, "Yeah, I'll play for you Friday night." Friday night come, all of them would be looking for us. We had to hide. I said, "John, don't lie to the people. You can't play for everybody." So one night we was supposed to play for a man. Another guy was going to pay us more money and we went there. We got there, the guy come there with a pistol. "God damn it, you supposed to play for me." John made the trade; I didn't. He wouldn't always tell the truth. "God damn it. You gonna play for me." So the man we were playing for, he said, "No, they ain't going nowhere." He said, "If you don't get away now, I'll kill you." So he left. So that stopped John from doing that.

Me and John and them used to go play, and he'd get drunk and go and jump on all the musicians that were there. We'd go to a place they call Across the Line. But those were different guys. And John would go down and get on his side, because they'd give him whiskey. He'd go down and get drunk and going to fight us—cuss us out, do everything. Shot a shotgun in the house. He'd be the terriblest man you ever seen. Moonshine—we'd drink that white whiskey and we'd play out in the country. Little old police used to be in Brownsville, call[ed] Charlie Smith. He wasn't no taller than that little boy than he'd try to arrest you. So I was playing and I went outdoors. They used to sell whiskey in a little flat, they called it. It wasn't quite a half a pint. He'd come and try to catch you. It was a dry state. Tennessee used to be a dry state. If they catch you with some whiskey, they'd send your ass to jail. So Charlie Smith was crawling under the house. I happen to spy his head. I had the bottle up. I spied him. He come running out from under that house. And I say, "Ahgalump!" Throwed the bottle down! (*chuckles*) That made him so mad. "Where's that whiskey?" I say, "I ain't got no whiskey." "I seen you with some." "Well, I ain't got none now." "I'll catch you." He never did catch me with no whiskey. Dad gum it! And we would watch for him. Charlie Smith. Every country dance he hear about, he'd be there. Little old low fellow, this little old guy out there trying to hustle something up. He wasn't doing nothing but watching black folk, you know. Stay around there and try to arrest them.

And he had a son. We call him Spec, Speckle Face—young kid. I was living right at the fairground in Brownsville. I worked for a man that had a café, Frank Richard. So Spec said, "Yank?" I said, "Yeah." "Fair going on. Can you sell some whiskey?" I said, "Yeah." He got some whiskey I reckon his daddy done took. He brought me two kegs of this Kentucky whiskey. He said, "You sell it and I'll give you half the money." I said, "Yeah." Well, my father-in-law's house was right there at the fairgrounds. I slipped the whiskey under his house. I said, "Well, they ain't gonna come to the preacher's house for whiskey." I stick the whiskey down in there. I sold whiskey.

So one night I missed work at the café because I was selling that whiskey up there. Well, the little man I was working for at the café, he was mad, you know, because I took off. He had never want me to get off. I said, "Mr. Sadler, the fair's in town; it's the last night and I'm going. I ain't gonna work tonight." So I missed that night, but I sold a lot of whiskey. The guy at the fairground, they done called down, told me to bring him some whiskey. He knew I had it. So I load up my pocket and I went down. Tip Arnold was the sheriff, high sheriff up there. So some guy told the police, "Yank got some whiskey. He coming yonder there now."

Well, I had a cousin that had a job in the hotel. She said, "Yank, don't go to the front gate, because the highway patrol are around there." She says, "Go in the back gate." Soon as I got out of the car, one old black guy standing there, drinking it down. Old George Crew. I told him I had some whiskey, which I did. Carrying about five half pints. He said, "Well, Yank, if they catch you, they won't catch this one." And he drank it down, you know. Well, just as I got out of the car, here comes old George Hunter, deputy. Coming down, I'm just walking. "You give me that God-damned whiskey before I bust your God-damned head." I said, "Well, now, I got some whiskey, but—" He said, "I know you went bootlegging around here." I said, "No, I wasn't bootlegging. I come by a place, some guy was there and I scared him. He run off and I put it in my pocket." I was telling him a lie, you know. I said, "I put it in my pocket." "Oh, you God-damned liar. I ought to knock your head off." I said, "You can arrest me, but don't you hit me. Don't you hit me with that stick, Mr. Hunter. I tell you that now." "God damn, I'm gonna arrest you." I said, "All right, you can arrest me." So he arrested me. Put me in the car right in the middle of the fairgrounds, where all of them could come around. They're looking. I'm sitting in the backseat.

(*chuckles*) People all knew me around there. "What they got—Yank?" "Yeah, Yank's in the car." "What they got him for?"

You know what I had? I had eight hundred dollars on me. I thought he was gonna search me, but he didn't do it. That's why he was silly, I reckon. I had a Prince Albert tobacco box. I used to smoke Prince Albert tobacco. And I had that money in my right pocket. I was sitting in the backseat. I was steady punching them dollar bills down in that Prince Albert box so if they searched me they wouldn't catch a lot of money on me to prove that I was selling whiskey, you know. I punched them right down, right tight. He made me sit there with him till the fairground got ready to close up. I'm still sitting on behind him; he ain't searched me or nothing. But he carried me on uptown to jail.

The next morning he say, "You want me to call Frank?" I said, "Yes, sir, call Mr. Frank." That was my boss man, you know. "Frank, I got one of your niggers up here." "Yeah, God damn it. He didn't come to work last night. That's what he gets! I'll be up there directly. God damn it, that's what he gets for not coming to work." So I stayed in jail about three hours. Then he came. "Let him out." He had to come up with fourteen dollars. He paid the man fourteen dollars. Well, the boss man thought I didn't have a penny; I had that Prince Albert box full of hundred-dollar bills, you know. He paid and got me out. "Get in, Rachell. Let's go down to the café." I said, "All right." He said, "God damn it, if you had been at work last night, you wouldn't been in jail." I said, "Yeah, I took off last night." He said, "God damn it, see, you wouldn't come to work; that's the reason they locked you up. I had to come get you." I said, "Yeah." We went on down there; he opened the café door. We went in and sat down. I said, "How much was that, Mr. Frank?" "Fourteen dollars." I said, "Well—" I pulled out that Prince Albert box and commenced to pull that money out. He said, "Where'd you get all that money from?" I said, "I didn't work last night. That's where I got that." (*laughing*) I said, "Here's your money." He says, "You smart bastard, you. Hell, I don't much blame you for not working last night!" First time I ever been in jail. Didn't stay there long. That's what I went for. I had to have me some of that money. And so then that little old police, his son, he was scared to ask me for half the money, because I was in jail and he figured I would tell them, you know, that he furnished the whiskey, which he did. So I had all that money. Man, I had me about eight hundred dollars. I had all of it. And I still had a case of whiskey to sell—he never did ask me about that whiskey.

I was staying on a man's farm. They had the old '34 V8 Ford out then. Of course, you may not remember the '34 Ford. It's just like a Cadillac now. I lived on the man's farm. We had a big dairy farm. That's where I raised most of my kids at. I raised four kids on this farm. Robert Thornton was his name. I lived out in the country; he lived in town. I'm on his farm because I was milking the cow, capping orange juice up, and sending it off in the morning. So I said, "Mr. Robert, I needs a car." He'd call you "son." "Aw, son, you don't need no car." "Yes, I do." "Well, I'll see about it." He'd drive on off—whistled all the time. Drive with his hand out there. Plenty of money—had a big farm out there. So finally he bought this car.

We had a little place uptown we would go play, me and my brother, some old guy called Fish Dock, George Fish Dock. Every Saturday in that place would be so full. We'd be in there playing, playing, playing. So my brother, he lived out in the country a little piece. He had a Model A Ford and I had a V8 Ford. He said, "I got some whiskey at home." He was making his white whiskey. "Why don't we go out and get some?" We took a break. Told the man, I said, "Well, we gonna take a break. We be back." So my brother got in his Model A and I got in my car. Load of us went down there, you know. We got a drink and we come back. It was so good. Went back and got some more, I did.

So this white guy, his gate opened right there at the highway. He lived in the house by himself. Tom King. Big old tall fellow. Some pretty gals lived on his farm. I was going with one of them. He said, "Yank." I said, "Yes, sir." "What's that gal's name you go with here on my farm?" They just had moved out. "Her name's Betty." "I'm gonna talk with her." I said, "Okay. Help yourself." He said, "Will you help me?" I said, "No, I help myself—can't help you." So I went down to get some more whiskey. I come back, he stopped me. He said, "Don't you pass here no more, driving that car that fast." He said, "These tires are ragged, and don't you come by here driving that fast." I said, "Well, I got to go around, Mr. King." I said, "I'm playing uptown now. I got to go back." "Well, I'm going that way and I ain't gonna drive but thirty miles an hour, and you better not pass me." I said, "If you ain't driving no more than that," I said, "I *got* to pass you." And I laughed. (*chuckles*) I said, "I got to pass you, Mr. King." I was feeling good, too. I said, "If you ain't driving no faster than that, now, I'm gonna have to pass you." Then he says, "If you do, I'm gonna whip your damn brains out." I went down and got another drink of that corn [liquor]. Sure enough, I come on back, he's driving a Chevrolet on gravel road. I run up behind him. I said, "Toot, toot." He didn't do nothing. I got to a little place and I shot by him. That V8 Ford. (*makes car noises*) Gravel and everything.

But just before you get to town is the fairground. You go up on the fair then go into the town. I said, "I better stop down here, because if I get up there, he may wanna start some stuff. And I ain't gonna let all of 'em jump on me." So I stopped like I was working on the car. He drove up there on the other side.

"God damn it, nigger. I thought I told you not to pass me." I said, "Yeah, I told you I was in a hurry, I had to come by." He said, "I'm gonna whup you." He got out of the car. Used to have them old jack handles. He got out and he got his crank, started towards me. I got out of my car and reached in the dashboard, you know. He didn't know what I had. Come on the other side of the car, stood there. He say, "You got a pistol, ain't ya?" I said, "No, I ain't." I said, "I ain't got nothing. You can't see one." I said, "But you ain't gonna hit me with that iron." He said, "That's all right. I'll get you when you get to town." I said, "All right. I'm coming up there." He went on to town. So I drove on to town behind him, where we met my boss man. He's whistling. (*whistles*) Drive his car and whistle all the time. Mr. Thornton, he had fast eyes to the bunch of them. "Hey, Mr. Robert." "Hi, Mr. King." "Say, that nigger of yours on down there, he attempted to draw a pistol on me." "Who? Yank?" "Yeah." He said, "What'd he do?" "I told him not to pass me. I know that the tires are ragged and everything. He driving that car, and he tear up them tires and things." He said, "Well, Mr. King, I bought him the car. He stays with me." And he say, "It's all right." "Yeah, but he tried to 'tempt me." He said, "How?" Said, "I had this iron. I was gonna whup him. But he wouldn't run. He must have had a pistol." "Well, Mr. King, you don't understand. He don't have to let you hit him with no iron or nothing like that." "That's all right. I'll get him." He say, "All right, Mr. King, I'll talk with him."

So the man come on down to my house. "Yank, what's the matter with you and Mr. King?" I said, "Nothing." I say, "I passed him and he wanna whup me with an iron." He say, "I don't blame you, son, for that. Don't let him whup you with an iron." He said, "If you're scared tonight, come on down to my house." I said, "I ain't scared." So I stayed there. So my wife kept on saying, "Yank, why don't you leave for a while, because they may come in and try to do something to you. And you'd be asleep. You know how they do. They may do something to you." So I said, "All right." I went to St. Louis. I went to St. Louis and stayed there 'round about two years. When I come back, he's the first sucker I saw! Sitting up there. He said, "Oh yes, God damn it, you're back." I said, "Yes, sir, I'm back." "Well," he say, "which way you going?" I said, "I'm going straight down the road." He said, "I'm coming on down there and we gonna get this settled." I said, "All right, sir." He come on down there. He stopped. "Come here." I went over there. He said, "I ain't got nothing against you, boy. Damn it, you're a damn fool. I ain't got nothing against you. But I did want to talk with that yellow gal." I said, "Well, they out there. They was on your farm, you talk with them." I said, "I can't tell them nothing for you." So me and him was all right. Didn't have no more trouble with him. But, I'm telling you, boy, they could be rough down there. There's some rough characters in Brownsville, Tennessee. That's the reason I left there—because they was pretty tough on people. Specially black folks, you know.

While you were in St. Louis, did you know Robert Jr. Lockwood?

We stayed in the same house together. We used to room together. And he had an old gal. He'd come home and she whup him every night. We was crazy then, because he'd say, "Let's go. Let's go over to Brooklyn." We'd go over in Brooklyn, Illinois. I say, "Well, I ain't got no mandolin." He said, "Come on. I'm gonna win enough money to buy you a mandolin." Sure enough, he went over there and won enough money and bought me a mandolin. But, man, I like to got killed. You talk about two fools turning around, going back. Me and him drank a fifth of whiskey, trying to walk over the river on the streetcar line. And we were drunk. We hadn't got too far when we were gonna cross the river. When we got to the river, we wasn't paying too much attention. I was on this side going there, and he's on that side. And me and him were talking. Didn't look down, like a fool. And I went down, my hat flew all in the river. He's talking. He looked around. "Where you at?" And I was way down there on that crawl piece. If it hadn't been for that, I'd got drownded.

Yeah, I been knowing Robert Jr. I was with him the year before last in St. Louis. Peetie Wheatstraw, he was in Brooklyn, Illinois. He was't necessarily in St. Louis. I met him and Too Tight, a guy called Too Tight Henry [Castle]. He play twelve-string guitar. Fingernails that long (*gestures*) on one of his hands. But they got killed. One morning they were coming from somewhere. Train killed them. Killed Peetie Wheatstraw and Too Tight. Well, I never did get to play with Peetie, but I saw him with his long head. He played good. Didn't do much laughing at Peetie Wheatstraw, because he had his own style. So many people now try to whoop like him. (*sings*) A lot of them try to do that now. They say that, though. Yeah, I used to play in Brooklyn, Illinois. I saw all those guys. Probably very few musicians I don't know. I met them, anyway.

Yeah, I met right smart musicians in St. Louis. Henry Townsend, call him Mule. You know him? He pretty nice little musician. Him and his wife sang together. Yeah, I met quite a few of them. A lot of them I done forgot. It's been a good while when I was up there. Twenty-some years I was up there. I had a kid go to school in St. Louis. I came in '57. Well, Scrapper [Blackwell] got killed right when I got here [Indianapolis]. Me and him were supposed to go to Chicago to record for Bob Koester. And that's the first time I met Scrapper. And we recorded—went to go to record one Sunday, a boy killed him. I never did see Leroy [Carr], because Leroy was dead when I got there.

How about these other guys? Shirley Griffith and J. T. Adams. They were both here.

Oh, yeah. Me and Shirley played together till he died. J. T. and I played together. J. T. died the year before last—last year, I think. Yeah. Shirley Griffith and J. T. was playing together when I came here. So I had never seen him. So Shirley come to my house one day; somebody told him I was here. I thought he was a preacher, all dressed up. He played, had me play him a piece, too. I say, "Yeah." He said, "Come on. Go with me up to my friend's house. I'm on my way over to J. T." But they had been playing around. But they hadn't been out of town nowhere. So I played. Then we went to Iowa—Des Moines, Iowa. Iowa City. I went with them up there, two, three times. So me and Shirley played lots together. Shirley died and then me and J. T. played a lot. Then his hand got so he couldn't do nothing with it. He couldn't do anything. But he was a nice guitar player, J. T. was.

How about Pete Franklin? Was he from around this place?

Yeah, Pete was from here. He's a tough guy. Piano and guitar. Play the piano. Play Leroy's stuff. And played Scrapper's stuff on the guitar. I wanted to get ahold of one of his old records, but his sister says she had a tape of him, but I never got it yet. He drank himself to death—wine. Died the year before last.

Jesse **Thomas**

Jesse Thomas was one of about half a dozen prewar blues singers I had the opportunity to interview as they appeared at the University of Chicago's famed Folk Fest. The resident blues expert on the festival selection commit-

Jesse Thomas. Photo by Al Brandtner.

tee was David Waldman, who over the years did a wonderful job of ferreting out the best of the surviving prewar blues singers. Among the other old-timers that Dave recruited to appear in the fest were Grey Ghost, Jack Owens, Mose Vinson, R. L. Burnside, George McCoy, and Lavada Durst. I'd come out to see them perform at the festival and at its adjoining workshops and to make arrangements to interview them for the radio program. Despite the limited budget, Jesse was excited with the travel and the performance opportunity and appeared excited to do this interview, because as a Shreveport, Louisiana, resident he listened to my program each week (*Blues Before Sunrise* probably does a more thorough job of covering Louisiana than any other state in the union, since it's broadcast on more radio stations there).

The major dividing line in the world of blues is World War II. There's prewar blues—blues performed and recorded before the war—and postwar blues—blues performed and recorded after the war. If you were to give a thumbnail sketch of the differences between prewar and postwar blues, the two major differences would be these: prewar artists generally performed and recorded in a solo setting and on acoustic instruments, while postwar artists performed and recorded in an ensemble format on amplified instruments.

Jesse Thomas is part of a lonesome blues genre comprised of musicians who were essentially prewar stylists who performed and recorded in the years following World War II. They played a prewar style, performed and recorded largely as solo artists, and spent most of their time performing and recording in an acoustic setting—*no* amplification. Those who did use amplification used only the most basic setups: an electronic pickup on an acoustic guitar coupled with a small amplifier that had only basic settings—on/off and volume—no tone, no treble, no bass, and so forth. Other members of this particular genre include Smokey Hogg, Frankie Lee Simms, Country Jim, and first and foremost Lightning Hopkins. Unfortunately, this genre holds limited appeal to a contemporary listening audience that is used to music with a strong beat.

Within this genre, Jesse's music holds a special place. His playing and ambiance were unique, exquisite, and ethereal. His stated technique of trying to make his guitar sound like a saxophone coupled with the setting of his amplification produced a sound found few other places in the realm of blues. Despite the quality of his music, however, his career was a litany of disappointment and poverty—a life in pursuit of show-business glory—undermined by bad breaks, bad decisions, and bad timing.

This interview was conducted on February 15, 1992. Jesse Thomas died on August 15, 1995.

■ ■ ▪

When were you born and where?

I was born February 3, 1911, in Logansport, Louisiana. That's a small town south of Shreveport, Louisiana—about forty miles from Shreveport. On the highway going from Shreveport to Houston, Texas. Right on the line of Texas.

How many in your family?

There were thirteen of us.

In that lineup of thirteen, where were you?

I'm twelfth. (*laughs*) Almost to the end!

Any of the brothers and sisters still alive?

No, they're all gone now.

What did your parents do?

They were farmers in the small town of Logansport—sharecroppers, at that time they were called sharecroppers—and we all were raised in the country, on the farm. What we raised mostly was cotton, but we raised some corn. Then we had vegetable gardens that we would raise food for ourselves, but the cotton was for sale. It was commercial. That was how we made our living. We would plant cotton and raise cotton, and we would tend it, and that was our income. But the corn was what we used to feed our cows, chickens, and hogs, mules, horses; and the vegetable garden we raised vegetables for ourselves, but the cotton was for sale.

What was your first exposure to music?

Well, we were from a musical family. My father he played violin, and my brothers they kept an old guitar around the house most of the time. And they played it and I just watched them play. And by me having musical talent I learned to play guitar around the house there when I was about seven years old. And I would slip away from home and go around those places where I could hear music. My daddy was something else— What used to hurt me—what he would do to us, he didn't want us to go around nightclubs, or what they call barrelhouses, where people would go, and dancing and drinking and playing music, but I wouldn't want to be bad and I didn't want to drink. All I wanted to do was go 'round that barrelhouse—I didn't even care to go inside. I wanna stand close to where the piano was, where I could hear the piano, because I always wanted to be a piano player, and I love music and I wanna hear music. So I'd slip away from home sometime to go where music was playing, and my daddy didn't like that. Sometimes we could get a whipping for going around places like that. And I guess you've heard that back in those days they called the blues and stuff like that was devil's music, you know. And if you played the blues and didn't play a gospel tune, you was working for the devil. And that's what my daddy didn't like. He thought that would make us be bad boys; we would do it anyway.

Did your family have a strong church background?

Yeah. Especially my mother and people and neighbors around us—and our older sisters, you know, they were. But even if we didn't visit church regular, we had to kinda stay in line with those other church people. And wouldn't violate too much what they didn't believe in, like playing music and singing this and singing that. In other words, we weren't allowed too much to play music, but we would slip and do it anyway.

Did the rest of your family do anything with music?

My older brother, he was named Willard Thomas, and he made records under the name Ramblin' Thomas. He came to Chicago in the late 1920s and made records. And he got pretty famous on a record playing on the same label, Paramount label, as Blind Lemon Jefferson.

How old were you when your older brother made those records?

I was sixteen years old.

Did the fact that your brother managed to make records provide any special incentive?

Well, I was glad for him and that gave me the information. I found out that you could get on record and you could make money playing music. Up until then neither one of us had made any money amount to anything playing music. And I always played because I knew how, and when we were at home we played for fun with different friends, you know.

Was Willard still at home when he made those records?

He was off on his own, traveling around. He was in Dallas at that time, and they sent him up here to Chicago and [he] made records, and he came back to Dallas after he made the records, and he was traveling around playing music by himself.

Did it make a stir at the house when Willard got on the records?

Oh, yeah, it was exciting, you know! The idea that he went off and got on a record, 'cause we were in the country and didn't know anything about getting on records and had no idea that any of us would ever *be* on record. So that was something great. And he made money too. See, at that time we wasn't making much money—people would work for a dollar a day, dollar and a half a day, two and a half. That was the salary people was making. And musicians wasn't making anything—maybe two dollars to play for one night, like that, you know, and maybe a few tips. And then, see, the record company at that time they paid him two hundred dollars for a session, and I think the royalties were around two cents or four cents a record. And if the record sold pretty good, that was pretty good money for those days. The session fee later on when people were making money on records wasn't much more than that. That was real good session fee.

Whatever happened to your brother?

Well, after he made [records] for Paramount, you know, Paramount went out of business. And then he was out of the recording business for quite awhile until he got with RCA Victor. And after he made records with Victor, he went to Houston, Texas. He was living at Fort Worth at that time, but he went to Houston,

Texas, and played around a while, and he left there and went to Memphis, and he died in Memphis in the late thirties.

And was he making his living as a musician at that point?
Yeah.

Was what your brother Willard played reflective of what got played around the house? Or did he learn different stuff after he left?
Some of it was what he played around the house, but when he left he picked up that slide, playing that slide, bottleneck type. I don't know where he really got that from unless he saw some of the other guitar players doing it. And he said one time that when he heard that sound, that's what he liked—slide. Bottleneck type.

Did that give you the idea to make records?
Not so much when he made records it didn't put it in my mind to make records so much, because I didn't really play enough blues at that time. I could play guitar and sing a little bit, but it was mostly copying what other people were doing. And I didn't have no idea of making records. And what he did, I was just glad for him. What made me wanna make records was when I went to Dallas and saw Lonnie Johnson. And he was so popular at that time, and he was onstage at a vaudeville show and a crowd of people were carrying out so over him—just like they do at rock festivals now and other one-night stands where superstars playing. See, he was something like a superstar. And then when he come out on the stage, he would go over so big and the crowd would roar, and that excited me quite a bit. And I heard news that he was making big money, like thousands of dollars. His royalty checks sometime when he come in it would be around two thousand dollars. That was real exciting to know that a musician could ever make that kinda money, 'cause I never thought a musician made any money. I thought they would just play and have fun and make friends, you know. And that made me want to do something—make records, do like Lonnie Johnson. And then he would dress so—he'd come out on the stage with a suit of clothes on and play a few numbers and then go back out, come back out, and he'd have on a different suit of clothes. And I said the man changed suit of clothes twice on one set, you know! And I don't think I even had a suit of clothes at that time, because we were mostly in the country wearing what you call jeans, at that time called overalls. We didn't worry about suits of clothes. But that give me a real big mind and forced me to get into the music and travel and thinking I was gonna do what Lonnie Johnson did. But it took a mighty long time before I could even get on record or see anything like what he was doing.

So how did you finally make your first records?

Well, I had it in mind that I was gonna get on record, and I kept trying. I came to Paramount—I thought they were gonna put me on record like they done my brother, you know. And I auditioned in front of the guys in Dallas. You would audition in front of them, and they would send you up here in Chicago.

Do you remember who the guys were that you auditioned for?

They were the guys like the distributors, record distributors, they were distributing the records. And you would go to them and audition, and they would send you up here to the record company and put you on record. And they told me the songs I was singing was everything I had copied from other people— singing Blind Lemon songs and Lonnie Johnson songs and things like that. They said, "That's already on record, we already had that," you know, and they wouldn't put me on record. So I went back and tried to make up some songs of my own, but I didn't go to those same people. I went from Dallas, Texas, to Houston, Texas, thinking that maybe I can get on record down there in Houston, Texas, some way or another. But I didn't go, and I heard about OKeh Records—that was another record label. They were recording in San Antonio, Texas, and I hitchhiked to San Antonio to get down there. But they were finishing up their sessions when I got down there. They was through recording and leaving for, I believe, New Orleans. But I heard that they would be back in Dallas, Texas, in about a week, so I hitchhiked back to Dallas, Texas, to get on their label. And while I was auditioning for him, another man heard me play and said, "RCA Victor will be here in a few days, and you can get on record with me. I'm gonna be playing for a girl named Bessie Tucker." So I stayed around there with him awhile.

Was that K. D. Johnson, Mr. 49?

That was 49 that met me there in Dallas and told me I could get on record with him. And I left my address there with him and went to Oklahoma City. And sure enough, RCA Victor came and sent me a ticket from Oklahoma City, and I went back to Dallas and got on RCA records. That was 1929. I was eighteen years old then.

You weren't playing in your brother's style, were you?

No, not at all! Because I first started out playing piano, and that was really what I wanted to play, 'cause I heard pianos, you know. After I had learnt guitar, and we would play mostly the same tune all the time. We didn't learn many new tunes. In those days we would just play what the other guys was playing in that era, and that's all we knew. And we would just play that over and over on the guitar. And it just, to me what you call gorged out on it, tired of it, sick of it, you know? Piano was what I really wanted to play. I loved the piano—still like piano music! I wanted to be a piano player and I was learning pretty good. I believe that if I had auditioned at Paramount on the piano and had me a song—something of my own, or either copied from some of the guys that wasn't on record, copied some of the songs that hadn't been recorded and played piano—I believe I could've got on record right then with Paramount. And it would've paid me two hundred dollars, which would've been like ten thousand now.

Who were some of the guys you were listening to on piano that weren't on record? Do you remember any of the names?

When I first started playing piano it was just some of the guys around in that area that could play a few tunes. But I'd liked the sound of piano, 'cause it was doing so much more than what we were doing on guitar. We'd be strumming on guitar, maybe we'd play a little melody, but the piano was playing melody and carrying chords along *and* bass. And [I] liked that sound so well. They had electric piano was playing those piano rolls, like player pianos and electric piano playing rolls? That's what I heard and made me really like piano. I liked to hear that and that full sound, you know—bass, melody, chords, harmony. And they sounded so good, till that's what I wanted to play. If I could've got on the time I first tried, they was paying two hundred dollars a session, which was a lot of money. But at the time when RCA Victor came, that was two years later and we were going into a depression, and they didn't pay that much. I think they paid fifty dollars a session. I believe it was not over a hundred dollars.

Was that a disappointment?

Yeah, it was real disappointing to me. When I did make records, instead of getting two hundred dollars, I came up with just that fifty or whatever they paid me at that time. That seemed like nothing. Seemed like I hadn't done anything when I had in my mind, I thought, when I got on record all my worries would be over with and I would be a superstar with big money coming in and big income—where I wouldn't have to hitchhike up and down the road and continue playing gigs for little or nothing, you know. But it didn't do me any good to my idea, which it should've been different. But I hadn't had enough experience, you know, and no education enough to realize that *was* a foot in the door or step in the right direction. I wanted to be a big thing all at once. I was disappointed.

When the guy from Paramount said you sounded like everybody else and you tried to work some songs of your own, how did the songs come to you?

Well, I copied some [of] what I already heard. That's what I figured the main idea was—to get something that wasn't already on record. That's what came to me—just go get some songs that wasn't already on record. I had heard different guys in the country where we was singing songs that wasn't on record. And I would sing some of those. And then I made up a few of my own. Made "Blue Goose Blues"—that was an area there in Shreveport—I made it up myself. I think somebody gave a few verses to go in that song, 'cause I think I heard some guys singing some of the verses that I heard. The first part—like, *"I'm going down to old Blue Goose, I got two bits to lose."*—I had just thought about old Blue Goose there in Shreveport. And that tune, I think I musta heard Blind Lemon Jefferson playing that type of music, you know. Not Blind Lemon—*Blind Blake* was the one [who] played the type that I got the idea from. I put that verse to it, but I think the only thing I knew at that time was just one verse, the beginning of the song, which you should have at least five verses. And I just got those other verses, I think, from different sources, different people, 'cause I used to hear guys talk and say, *"I can take my partner and my partner's friend, pick more cotton than a gin can gin."* And I made a verse out of that and added it to my song. 'Cause everybody at that time in that part of the country was picking cotton, you know, and they would take it to the gin mill and gin it. And when they get a bale of cotton picked, it better be at least fifteen hundred pounds, and they take it to the gin. That was something like bragging, you know. If you can pick more cotton than a gin can gin, you're really doing something! That's where I got that verse. And then that last verse, I think, was *"When you go to Shreveport town, you find Blue Goose and it'll tear you down."* I heard somebody else say that, something similar to that, and just made a verse out of that.

Is Blue Goose part of Shreveport proper or a separate town?

That was a little old area over there. See, we used to have a union station where all the trains would come. It was near the union station in that little area over there called Blue Goose.

Let's go back to your session for Victor. Do you remember where it was held and how many sides you cut?

I cut four sides for Victor. One side was "Blue Goose Blues," and the other side was "No Good Woman Blues." Then I also played on two sides for Bessie Tucker. And the other songs were something I tried to make up, but they—I don't think they was even songs, you know, 'cause I really didn't know what I was doing.

One was "Heart Like a Rolling Stone," right?

I think *so!* It's listed in the book [Robert M. W. Dixon, John Godrich, and Howard W. Rye, *Blues Gospel Records, 1890–1943*], whatever it was, but I couldn't remember myself, because I didn't know what I was doing. I was trying to make something, 'cause the man had told me from Paramount that I'd have to go out and make some songs of my *own,* and I was trying to do that. I didn't know a thing about songwriting or nothing like that.

Was it just one day or a couple of days?

I think it was a couple days, 'cause I remember when I first went there, the guitar I had was so raggedy, and the guy Ralph Peer, the guy I was recording for, sent and got me a guitar. So it took a few days, maybe almost a week. I know it took more than one day, 'cause the first day I went there I didn't have a guitar, so I think he worked on something else, let somebody else record while he was getting me a guitar.

I know from the book that you did four songs yourself, and then on a couple different dates—in fact, in a couple different years—you were with Bessie Tucker.

No, that same session I worked with Bessie Tucker was the only time.

With K. D. Johnson?

Yeah.

And then you did records with another fellow. How did it happen that you recorded with Troy Fergusen?

I never did. I saw that write-up, but I never did work with him. I didn't even know him. I never met him.

What happened on the strength of your recordings? I know you had ambitions to be a big star, and what happened?

Well, I was so disappointed with the recordings with RCA Victor with such a small session fee that I was kinda discouraged. And when I was in Oklahoma City, at first I played with a group—they were playing popular music—and they asked me, "Did you wanna work?" And I was glad to work, because they paid me a good salary. But they were playing tunes that I couldn't play. I was trying to play, but all I knew was a few blues songs, and they were playing standard tunes and popular music that was coming out, new songs. And the reason I couldn't play 'em, I didn't know the chords, changes—I couldn't read music.

Was this on guitar?

On a guitar and I couldn't do that. I think it was about three young men, but they was playing horns and they said, "Let's tune up. Let's tune up." And we would tune up and I still couldn't play the changes, couldn't follow, and that would make the music sound bad. [They'd] say, "There's something wrong. We tuned up and there's still something wrong." They didn't know that I didn't know the chords. They said, "I guess we shoulda had a piano." They didn't have a piano; they was using me instead of a piano. Say, "Oh, I wish we had a piano." We played that whole dance that night and they paid us well. I think it was some oilmen giving some special party. I think they had an oil boom in Oklahoma City at the time. I went back to Fort Worth, Texas, and I knew then what was wrong: I didn't know my chords on a guitar; I couldn't read music. So I said, "I'm gonna learn to read music." And I went to a little music school in Fort Worth, Texas, and I told 'em I wanted to learn to read music, and they said, "We don't teach guitar." And I said, "I want to learn to read music—read music." They said, "We can teach you to read music, give you some piano lessons." And I said, "Well, give me some piano lessons." I wanted to learn to read music. And they give me some piano lessons and I learned to read music. And then I started playing different types of music. I said, "I'll never be caught in that shape again." That was a terrible, disgusting night that I had to play a whole session up there and didn't know what I was doing—trying to follow musicians playing popular music and I couldn't play it.

So I went ahead and learned to play popular music and different kinds of music and got with different groups. When they found out I could play guitar and could read music, different musicians was calling me. And I went on to playing different types of music and wasn't even playing blues, never played blues for years. I was playing different types of music. And then I couldn't make as much money playing blues as I could playing different kinds of music. That's what happened to me. You know, a lot of people at that time wanna get away from that sad, lonesome blues and miserable conditions and things like that, and seem like when I play blues some places they'd say, "Why don't you cut out that old, sad, down-home stuff . . . play some popular music, play something else." "Can't you play something else? Don't nobody wanna hear that." And that discouraged me, too, you know. What's the use of me playing something don't nobody wanna hear and I can't make me no money? When I can go out and play popular music and get on some of these live parties with some of the rich guys—play on the lake and places like that and make money. And I made my living playing music without playing the blues, 'cause I couldn't make a living playing the blues.

How long did that go on?

Went on till I went to California and started playing with Lloyd Glenn and them.

When did you go out there?

This was around '50—around '51—when I started back to playing blues. From '37 to '51 I didn't play any blues. I made my entire living playing popular music, country music, swing music—whatever you wanna call [it]. In other words, I was playing a variety and requests—whatever people asked for—that's what I played.

What brought you back to the blues?

Lloyd Glenn and them, there in Los Angeles, when I went to Los Angeles they was making records, and T-Bone Walker and guys like that. I met T-Bone Walker, and he was playing blues and going over pretty good. They got on record, made a name, got famous. Lowell Fulsom, Lloyd Glenn, Charles Brown—

What got you to go to California in the first place?

Well, I wanted to go to California 'cause I thought that was where the gold was. Everybody else was going there and that's where the movie stars was. And I heard people saying, "If you go to California, why, you can get rich." Everybody want to get rich, and I was a young man. I wanted to be rich just like everybody else, and I went to California and did good!

Were you staying in Louisiana or were you staying in Oklahoma—before you went to California?

I was in Texas. I spent most of my time in Fort Worth, Texas, but I was in several places in Texas: Odessa, West Texas, Galveston, Houston—

At any point were you married and had a family?

No.

During the time you were playing popular music, did you play strictly on guitar? Did you play on piano? Had you given up any ambitions of playing piano?

I gave up piano 'cause I didn't have a piano to practice on, and I was strictly on guitar.

When did you go with an electric guitar?

That was when I went to California—Los Angeles about '37—about '38 or '39, I think it was. It wasn't like the guitars that they make now; it was just a pickup. I think I ordered it from Montgomery Ward. And amplifier, I got a amplifier from Montgomery Ward. A pickup you would tape it onto your wooden guitar—acoustic box pickup electric like that.

What did you think of that sound?

I was glad to get it 'cause it brought the sound out, you know. I would always be drowned out on my acoustic box. It was good when you're playing with a small group or a small room, but when you get with a band, they couldn't hear me. When you get in a big crowd of people, you couldn't hear it. But when the electric came out, I was glad to get it 'cause you could hear it.

Was there anybody in particular that you saw play the electric guitar that made you want to get one?

No. It wasn't too many people playing electric at that time. Later on, Charlie Christian was playing with Benny Goodman—it kinda excited me a little bit, 'cause I never heard anything like that solo on an electric guitar with a band.

It seems to me you have a unique setting when you set your amp. Do you have a specific way that you set it?

No, there's no specific way. What that is, is the way I tried playing after I learned how to play music. I was so crazy about piano music and instruments like saxophones and clarinets. That's another thing that held me back quite a bit. See, I wanted to play piano so bad when I was young. I didn't even like guitar. When I did play guitar I would try and play like a piano, play the chords and the bass and the melody all at the same time. Well, I can do that on certain pieces, but you can't do that on all pieces and you can't do it on jazz tunes much—it just don't work. You can't solo and carry all that at the same time, not on a guitar. You have to play one at a time. If you're gonna play solo, play solo; you gonna play chords, play chords. Or you could mix it up. I do that now and it goes over big; it went over big in New Orleans. I play some solos and I strike some chords. That's the way my daddy played violin, 'cause you can't play all that on a violin. He would play way up on the high notes and then he'd come back to the low notes, but it would carry it in a rhythmic pattern and he would pat his feet like a drum. He would keep time patting his foot. But I didn't understand anything like that until later on after I studied jazz—that you got to have a beat. I used to play a lot of guitar without even patting my foot, and I didn't have a drum, you know. A lot of that what you hear me doing on a guitar was trying to make it go like a saxophone or a clarinet, but it never would—you can't make a saxophone out of a guitar. So I just come up with that sound, and that's where T-Bone got some of his ideas.

See, T-Bone got that from me, and I got it from trying to make it sound like a saxophone. (*sings a series of high-pitched phrases*) I was trying to go like a saxophone. You could get the patterns of what they were doing, but you couldn't hold that note like that horn. A horn can hold a note just as long as you got air to blow it—maybe two bars or one bar, sometimes four bars. You can't hold that on a guitar unless it's a synthesizer guitar now that they're making. More come like that now, but then you couldn't make a guitar sound like a saxophone, but I sure was trying—that's what I wanted to do. And then when I practiced with T-Bone Walker, we used to sit down and swap ideas and things like that, and he saw what I was trying to do and he took it and put it in his blues.

What year are we talking about?

Around 1939.

That's before he started making records?

Yeah, before he got on record me and him used to play together some, but not on record. I would go to his room and we would play something together, and then where I was rooming at, he would come by there some nights. Where I was rooming at was something like an after-hour house, you know. When the bars closed people could come to the house, play the jukebox in the house, play music, drink, and dance. Sometimes T-Bone would come by there, and when I was playing with another group at a little old bar down on Forty-second Street and Central, called Classic Bar, we played there for a while with the group, and T-Bone would come in and just sing. I used to see him go around singing without playing a guitar. And I think he went on the road with a band named Les Hite's, if I'm not mistaken. He mighta made a record with them—seems like he made a record with them: "*If you want my money, you can't run around. If you're gonna run around, stop and put my money down.*" I believe he made that record before he got on record playing electric guitar.

So you guys were playing acoustically at that point?

Uh-huh, both of us were playing acoustic. I remember the last time he came by the house, and he hollers, "I got me an electric guitar now, Jesse! I got an electric guitar now!" I say, "Yeah, you got an electric guitar?" and he says, "Yeah, I got an electric guitar!" After that I moved to Salinas, between Los Angeles and San Francisco. I went up there and went to playing in a nightclub. I worked there about five years, playing in that nightclub, playing mostly country music. And I turned on the radio one night and I heard T-Bone. He was playing downtown Los Angeles in a joint called Shep's Playhouse, and he was singing the blues and picking that electric guitar. And I could hear him making some of those runs that we had been trying to make go like a horn, and he was making those runs. And he was the only guy I heard could make those runs—at that time. And he was doing much more with them than I did. All I was doing was trying to make it sound like a horn; I just wanted my guitar to sound like a horn. And T-Bone took that sound and put it in the blues, play it in the blues with that sound, and the next person I heard playing the sound like that was B. B. King. He wasn't playing it exactly like him, but he sound more exciting to me than I did and than T-Bone did, because we had been used to doing that, you know. But B. B. sounded new and different, and he was making his strings ring—more than ours was. Now I hear everybody making the same runs that me and T-Bone was trying to figure out. We was trying to make it go like a saxophone, and these other guys are taking them and playing them and putting them in arrangements and stuff like that.

What was your reaction to hearing T-Bone actually on record?

Well, it was something that he took what we was doing and put it in the blues, and it sounded good and it was blues. And it made a hit and it made him famous, so he made a name for himself. And that gave me an idea, now, if I play the blues, put them runs in the blues, instead of just trying to make them go like a horn—play them! Put them in the blues!

Do you remember exactly how the record thing happened in California?

I saw T-Bone and them making records. And I know *how* to play the blues. I'd been playing them for years, but I never made a hit, so I went to Lloyd Glenn and them and told them I could play the blues. And I knew a little bit more about songwriting than I did at first, you know. And Lloyd Glenn and them told me, "Come on and make some records." So I did! But I didn't go on the road behind the records like a lot of guys did when they made a record date— put it on radio and then hit the road. That way a lot of them made a name, like that. By me knowing popular music and different guys that could play popular music, I didn't go on the road. I just stayed around and played around and made money, made my living. And I wasn't interested in going on the road, 'cause when I was out there on the road I didn't do any good, you know. It was tough and I didn't care to get back out there.

What label was that for, do you know?

Swingtime was Lloyd Glenn. He was the manager of that label, but the owner was named Jack Lauderdale.

Didn't you do a tune "Now Is the Time"?

That was the first record I made with Lloyd Glenn—"Now Is the Time for Love."

Did you slide on that at all?

No!

So just a sustain?

Well, a little sustain, but that was mostly Lloyd Glenn on the piano. He kinda drown me out on that. The piano was loud and drown my voice out and drown me out. That's another reason that one didn't sell.

Did that come out under your name or Lloyd's name?

Mine. The voice wasn't out front, so that was a mistake there, you see.

Where did you go from there? What were your next records?

When I recorded for Lloyd Glenn and I saw the records weren't doing any good—I don't think it took too long, maybe a year or two—and I had a label of my own. I had a label called Club label. And I put out some records on my own label. And there was a company there in Los Angeles called Central Sales—they were record distributors—and I went to ask them to distribute it for me. I think they did a few sales or something like that. Then they told me about Specialty

Records. They said, "You ought to get with them; you can't hardly distribute and run your own record company. This man's already established and he pays good!" Which he did! So from there I met Art Rupe, and he took over my Club label. I think he gave five hundred dollars, too, to take what I had—

What had you recorded? What titles?

Oh, some of that stuff that never did get out. "Same Old Stuff," have you heard that? I think that's what I put on my label, "Same Old Stuff." And, oh, just another blues—"*I asked my baby for some money, here's what they had to say, 'Take some, leave some for some old rainy day.'*" That was on there, and a few more, something that never did come out. (*sings*) "*I wonder why you said good-bye, and did you mean to make me cry?*" I didn't make too many, just that one.

How did you fare when Art Rupe took over?

When he took over I signed a contract to record for him, and that's when I made "Jack o' Diamonds," and "Your Ways and Action" on the other side. And what Art Rupe said, he said, "I'm gonna make a star out of you, Jess!" He wanted to give me three thousand dollars and let me get a brand-new Cadillac—a thousand dollars on the Cadillac, and a thousand dollars' worth of clothes, and a thousand dollars cash to travel with. And he put the record out and I go ahead on tour. I was working at that time for the navy, and I turned it down. But if I had known how to write songs and how to put those blue notes in the blues, I would've taken that and probably would've made just as big as anybody else. And the reason I didn't accept that [is] because I didn't know enough about the blues, and didn't know how to write songs, and didn't have confidence to even believe I would make a hit on the road, because I had been failing so much in the music business—in the blues especially. And that would have been an advancement, and I would have to pay him that money back, you know, and I would owe him that money—even if the record didn't sell. He wouldn't force me to pay that money back and he couldn't collect, but I would still owe it to him, and I wouldn't have anything for myself if I left my navy job and went on the road. And I didn't want to go on the road under those conditions.

After Art Rupe did you do records for other labels?

Yeah, for Modern label, the same one that Charles Brown and them was on.

The Bihari Brothers?

Yeah, Joe and Jules Bihari. Joe, I made a session for him—I even forgot the name of the record. I don't think I did but two songs for him. And he paid me one hundred dollars for that session. And *that* record didn't do anything to my idea. And after that I went to Houston, Texas, and made a session for a company they call Freedom, Freedom Records—"Let's Have Some Fun." That was one side of that—"*Forget about your worries. C'mon and let's have some fun.*" After that I didn't make any more records.

When you made your records—with the exception of the sides you made with Lloyd Glenn—what was the instrumentation? How many people were you using on your records?

For Art Rupe there were four of us—guitar, bass, piano, and drums. And then for Modern Records I just played by myself, like "D Double Do Love You." That was a little old label for John R. Fulbright and Walt Perkins. I think Art Rupe bought them out. They didn't do anything.

When you were out on the West Coast, was music your sole means of support or did you keep a day job?

Music was my main support, but when I went to Santa Barbara music fell off, you know. I played in a nightclub and they were paying me good, but it was kinda hard. You have to play so many different tunes; this guy wanna hear "Mack the Knife" and that guy wanna hear "Stardust," here's another guy wanna hear "St. Louis Blues." And all of that forced me to drink some, and people say, "C'mon have a drink!" Well, when they say give the musician a drink and the manager's standing right there and he's making money off of drinks, and if I turn a drink down, he figures, well, that's turning down money, you know. So I'd take a drink to hold my job and stuff like that, and I got sick of that. Some guys came in there and they was from Las Vegas. They say, "Come to Las Vegas!" and so I went to Las Vegas and I couldn't find the guys after I got there, you know. And I came back to Santa Barbara and I didn't have a job playing music, 'cause I left my job and the man hired somebody else. And that's when I went to work for the navy, in 1951.

I went to work for the navy—I hadn't been working much, no more than playing music—and that's when Art Rupe asked me to go on the road. And I told him I didn't want to go on the road, I just keep my regular job. But I didn't make any hits on those records, because I wasn't really playing the real lonesome blues. I knowed what the blues was, but I was playing mostly background music. When I would play blues, I would play background music and mostly copy what some other musicians done—that's the way I learnt how to play, see, copying what the other fellow did. I wasn't really doing anything of my own, and I wasn't making enough blues runs, do you know [what] I mean? That sound that sound[s] like a single string. I was playing more chords and background music, and that didn't sell on record too good to people that liked the blues.

T-Bone and them was doing it, but I didn't know the difference. I thought if you play the blues, just play the blues and sing them, you know. But you have to know something about the blues if you wanna sell it—like any other trade or other music. That's one reason I didn't sell, and my songs wasn't enough universal for the people to relate to them. I would just make up a song, sing it, and put it on a record.

Now, the record companies would accept it; you could go to a record company with a song and you be able to sing it and play it, they would accept it and put it on record, but the people, the public, wouldn't buy it if it wasn't really something they liked and they could relate to. And that music got to have some blue notes. See, I didn't make enough blue notes in my blues. I'd just make some pretty chords, blues chords, so you could back that blues up with blues chords. And that's what I was doing, but I wasn't making them blue notes. See, I learnt later, after I started studying jazz, if you're gonna play blues you have to play some blue notes. And the more lonesome and the more lowdown you get, the more blue notes you have to put in that if you want it to be real lonesome and real blue—put in those blue notes. Even if you have to repeat the same notes, you could repeat the same notes several times and that'd make it be more lonesome. I always called the blues—after I learned how to play them—I called that the crying type of music.

You know, music is a conversation, too—it's a language, I meant to say—it is a language, and when peoples want something, when grown-ups, people that can talk, they talk and ask for what they want. But, like, a baby can't talk—he'll cry for what he want. If you take his candy or take his toy, he'll cry and you know what he wants—he wants it back, 'cause he wants something. But a person that can talk, they can ask for it. So I figure other music, they understand the music— they play it and they understand the language. And the blues is a language, but it's a crying type of language or a begging type or in a rut—know you can't get out, but you wonder why you can't get out. That's the way you have to feel, as far as I'm concerned. That's the way I always looked at it. Always looked at the blues as you in a situation, in a condition, or attitude that you know you can do better than that, but still you can't do any better than that, that's just the way it is. You can do better, but you can't do better. And why can't you do better? How long is it gonna take me before I get out of this rut? Why do I have to be here? That's the way it is, and it can't speak the word—it just have to wonder or cry it out. So I say that's just like a baby crying out for what he wants. But, now, the blues music itself is just like any other music, but it just happen to be a type of music that can fit that type of song.

You say that you had to learn to play the blues. If we went through all your records, would we see the point where you actually learned to play the blues?

I ain't been too long learned how to play the blues in my own way or understanding I just had talent. I had musical talent and could play! But as far as me knowing what I was doing and could analyze it or know the uniqueness of it, I didn't know. All I did was I played, and like a lot of musicians that I know, that I worked with and talked to, they don't know.

So if we went and got all your records and lined them all up, you wouldn't say any of those were up to your blues standards?

No! I didn't a bit more know what I was doing than any other kid. And other musicians—I know some good musicians. I played with a piano player not too long ago, a blind man. You could go in another room and hit any note on the piano that you wanna hit, he could tell what note that you was hitting—his ear was just that good. And up and down the scale with his hands he could play anything that could be played on a piano, but as far as him knowing what the blues is and how to really play 'em, he didn't know. And people would tell you that's the best musician they ever heard in their life. And people used to tell me that—"You the best guitar player in the world. I don't see why you not on Broadway." Now, what would I do on Broadway if I didn't know what I was doing? But I really didn't know what the blues was and how to play 'em until just a few years ago.

Alberta **Hunter**

The classic blues singers were the women who pioneered blues recording starting with the very first blues record by Mamie Smith in 1920 and continuing on to 1930 when the Great Depression finally caught up with the recording industry. During this decade there were 260 different women who made blues records. Some, like Bessie Smith (160 records) and Ma Rainey (90-plus) recorded extensively while others made only a single record or a single side of a record. Not only did these women pioneer blues recording, getting into the recording studios at least four years before the first male blues singer, but they also served as the launching point for many of the early giants of jazz. In some of their earliest recordings, such notable jazzmen as Fletcher Henderson, Louis Armstrong, Don Redman, Fats Waller, and Coleman Hawkins could be heard accompanying classic blues singers.

Alberta Hunter, 1920s. Photo courtesy of Alberta Hunter.

Of the 260 women who made records during this decade, Alberta Hunter was the twelfth, making her first record in May 1921 for the first black-owned record label, Black Swan. Most of the big-name classic blues singers—and Alberta was among this elite group—were affiliated with a single record label. For instance, Bessie Smith and Clara Smith recorded exclusively for the Columbia label, and Ma Rainey and Ida Cox recorded exclusively for the Paramount label. Alberta, on the other hand, recorded for a dozen different labels in ten years. Alberta was one of two classic blues singers whose careers transcended the classic blues era. When that era came to an end, only Alberta Hunter and Ethel Waters continued in show business with any notable degree of success. Ethel did it by appearing in Broadway productions and recording popular tunes; Alberta traveled to Europe, becoming a popular cabaret singer in both London and Paris. She stayed in Europe until World War II broke out, then returned to the United States and immediately signed on with the USO. She spent the duration of the war touring and entertaining Allied troops in every theater of action, including Europe, Africa, and Asia. At the end of the war it was her intention to return to show business, but her mother fell ill, so Alberta retired from performing to tend to her mother. When her mother finally died, Alberta realized that she enjoyed nursing so much she became a licensed practical nurse. She pursued this career until the early 1970s, when she was forced into mandatory retirement at the age of seventy. But leave it to Alberta—she had lied about her age and actually was ten years older than listed. So at the age of eighty she returned to the only other business she knew—show business.

My best friends were planning a trip to New York City and asked if I would be interested in coming along. I was definitely interested—I had been corresponding with Ella Johnson, trying to land an interview with her. Ella was the younger sister of big band leader Buddy Johnson and was also his acclaimed vocalist, the voice on many of the band's greatest hits, including "Since I Fell for You," "That's the Stuff You Gotta Watch," and "Please, Mr. Johnson." I finalized the agreement for the interview with Ella and then started to sort through all the other names of people I might interview while in the city. The artist who fired my imagination was classic blues singer Alberta Hunter. Alberta had recently ended a twenty-year retirement from show business. On her return she initially worked at Barney Josephson's famed Café Society. From there she recorded a series of LPs with legendary producer John Hammond, settled in for a long run at the Cookery in Manhattan, made high-profile performances at a series of international music festivals, and appeared on all the television talk shows of the day—she was a media darling.

My first step was to contact Barney Josephson, who told me, "Leave her alone, she doesn't want to be bothered with you!" Next I decided to call Sony/CBS/Columbia Records to see if they could steer me in the proper direction. They suggested that I get in touch with John Hammond. He advised me to talk to her accompanist, Gerald Cook, and gave me Gerald's telephone number. I called Gerald and explained that I was going to be in town and would like to catch up with Alberta for an interview. He told me that Alberta was in the hospital, didn't know if she would be released by the date of the trip, or if she would be in any shape or mood to do an interview, but to contact him again when I got into town. My friends and I drove straight through from Chicago to New York, arriving around 4 P.M. on Friday afternoon. Within four hours I had the Ella Johnson interview in the can.

On to plan B and the possible interview with Alberta. I called Gerald, who said Alberta was going to be released on Sunday morning. He was to pick her up from the hospital early in the morning and would sound her out regarding the interview. If she agreed, he would pick me up and take me to her apartment. We spent Saturday exploring New York City, and on Sunday Gerald phoned to say that Alberta had agreed to do the interview. When Gerald picked me up, he laid out the ground rules and told me what I could expect, the main point being that the more knowledgeable I was, the better the interview was likely to be—*and not to expect more than twenty minutes under any circumstances.*

We arrived at Alberta's Harlem apartment, a high-rise senior complex with a beautiful view of the George Washington Bridge. She shared this apartment with a male friend, Harry, a former dancer. Gerald told me this apartment was one of three places Alberta owned. We entered the apartment and Gerald handled the introductions. When we were all seated in her front room, Gerald explained to her that I was there to do an interview, and all went fine until Alberta noticed the bag containing my tape recorder, tapes, and microphones. She asked me what they were, and when I explained, she flatly refused to be interviewed. Gerald, stifling a combination of anger and embarrassment, started to argue with her and she dug in. Gerald turned a deep crimson in exasperated silence as Alberta turned to me and began to explain that her lawyers had insisted that all interviews be arranged through their office and how she couldn't ignore their advice, capping it off with " *You* understand, dear!" I realized that the slightest argument from me would seal my fate, so I said a silent prayer and told her that I understood completely, that there was no problem, and that it was honor enough to meet her and to be received in her apartment—all of which was true *and* served to defuse the situation.

I continued by saying it was a real pleasure to be talking with her but that the real shame of the situation was that without the interview, listeners would never be able to learn the real story of many of her classic blues era contemporaries. I said she was probably the only person left alive at this point who could shed any light on the life and career of Katie Crippen (her eyes opened wide at the mention of the name), or Lulu Whidby, or Lavinia Turner (with each name her eyes opened ever wider). "Do you know Katie Crippen?" she asked. "Well, no—we have the records, we have the music, but we don't know anything about what they looked like or their lives and careers. I was hoping you might be able to fill in some of these blanks." She looked at me incredulously and told me I was mentioning names she hadn't heard spoken aloud in over forty years. Truly, I had struck a nerve. She turned to Gerald and said, "Gerald, get my lawyer on the phone. We must give this young man an interview!" Five minutes later, after a short phone call to the lawyer, Alberta patted a spot on the couch directly next to her and said, "Come over here next to me, young man, and let's talk!" Two hours later I ran out of questions for this ninety-year-old sparkplug.

The interview took place on January 30, 1984. Alberta died in October that year.

■ ▓ ▒

Well, I tell you, my mother sent me to the store to get a loaf of bread, and she give me twenty-five cents. And while I was at the store, a lady named Florida—we called her Miss Florida; her name was Floyd, Floyd Cummings. She married a man named Roy Edgerton. So as I came out of the store, having bought the bread, she said to me, "I'm going to Chicago tonight." And I said, "I wish I could go." She said, "Well, you may go if your mother says so." So I told her, well, I'd go and ask my mother. So I put the bread down on the sidewalk, ran up and hid between some houses, and I came back and told her my mother said it was all right. But I had not *seen* my mother. So as she started down the street, I went on down the street with her. As I said, I put the bread on the sidewalk. And when we got on the train, the man says, "*Alllll* out for the northbound trains." (*She almost sings when she says this.*)

I got on the train with my schoolteacher, Miss Florida Cummings. My mother had a friend who had a daughter in Chicago by the name of Ellen Winston. So when we got to Chicago, I got off the streetcar and left my schoolteacher, Miss Florida Cummings, and her husband, on the streetcar and got off *directly* in front of the door where my mother's friend's daughter lived: 2918 State Street. And the name of the building was the Burlington Building. I shall never forget it. I got off on this side of the street; I'm facing the building. And I walked to the building and there was a hall door. And I opened this hall door and went up these steps. There was a lady there washing. Her name was Miss Sarah Robbins. I got off and went on up these steps, and I asked Miss Sarah did she know a girl there by the name of Ellen Winston? She said, "No. There's nobody here by the name of Ellen Winston. Oh," she says, "wait a minute. There's a girl that live here by the name of *Helen* Winston. And this is her Sunday off. She works out in Hyde Park." So I said, "Well, will you let me stay here until she comes?"

Then the lady started questioning me. She wanted to know who I was and what I was doing there. So she let me stay. And when the girl came, it was my mother's friend's daughter, Ellen Winston, but she had become a big shot and changed her name to Helen. So when she saw me, she says, "What in the world are you doing here? What's Miss Laura going to think?" That [Miss Laura] was my mother. And I said, "Well, she thinks that I'm over to Irma's house." That was my little school chum. "She thinks I'm at Irma's house." So that's how my life began *in* Chicago. And I went to work. I was at this lady's boardinghouse, peeling potatoes. Because she said to the lady, said, "Can you give her a job?" She said, "Give her a job doing what? She's nothing but a child. What can she do?" "Well, just let her peel potatoes." And I got my job peeling potatoes in Chicago.

In Chicago we used to hear about the girls [who] could sing. Well, when I was a kid, I used to—well, you know, the kids sing up and down the street and like that. And I'd hear people say I could sing so I— Every night, while I was peeling potatoes there in the lady's house, everybody else'd be asleep. I would sneak out and go down where they said the girls was singing, getting that ten dollars a week singing. 'Cause I heard the lady telling my mother that the girls got ten dollars a week, you know. So I tried to sneak out when I was there to see if I could get some of that ten, you know. The first place I went was where the pimps and the prostitutes hung out. That was a place called Dago Frank's at Archer and State. It was a *blind* street, almost like Archer and State Street. So the girls—they was so nice, those prostitutes and pimps, nice to me—they say, "You be a good girl. You see the predicament we are in; don't *you* get into it." And they'd go out and buy little dresses and things for me and bring them in to me, dress me to keep me nice. And there was a fellow there named Bruce. Ha! Bruce was a piano player. (*laughs*) Now that I know show business—Bruce was lousier than I was. He was the worst piano player you ever heard in your life. And Roy, a fellow named Roy, was the manager of Dago Frank's. And so every time I'd go in there and sing, they'd put me out 'cause I was a child. Say, "You'll get my place closed. Get outta here." And they'd put me out. But I'd keep going. I never let them stop me. Every place they put me out, I'd go back again. So finally Roy, the manager of Dago Frank's, Bruce said to him, "Let her stay. You see she's nothing but a child. Give her a chance, Roy." He said no.

So one night the phone rang up at Miss Durham's, Sarah Durham's—this is the lady who lived at 3210 Dearborn Street in Chicago. And the phone rang, says, "Tell her to come down to Archer and State, down to Dago Frank's." And I go down there and Roy told me, "Come on in and sing." And I knew two new—two songs. I learned them off the player piano. 'Cause when I'd go to that Burlington Building, I'd stop in that hall and I heard that piano playing, and I'd hear the people singing the words to the songs, you know. And I'd listen to them and get them in my memory. And one of them was "All Night Long." That was one of the songs. The other was "Where the River Shannon Flows." I got them two songs. So when I went to Dago Frank's to get the job, I sang the two songs. So Roy says, "Come on in here and sing. You got a job." I stayed there a year and ten months. Prostitutes were nice to me. I stayed there. And after I started doing pretty good there, the girls would make all the fellows that came in to be with them, you know, make them give me money.

So the next place I worked was a place called Hugh Hoskins—H-u-g-h, Hugh, H-o-s-k-i-n-s, Hoskins. That was at Thirty-second and State. I worked there. Hugh Hoskins. And the girl— (*chuckles*) There was a pickpocket named Tack Annie, ugliest woman that God ever put breath in. Ooooh, if she heard me, she'd kill me. (*laughs*) Tack Annie. But she could walk up to a man and bite his diamond pin off and do anything like that. But she looked like a horse with a derby on! (*laughs*) She was the *ugliest* woman I ever— Oh, Tack Annie, don't you ever see me! She'd kill me dead. Oh. Tack Annie and— Now, they were the confidence women. They never had physical contact with a man. They would take his money, you know. But they never robbed them up there, what we'd call Harlem, never uptown. They'd go downtown and do the stealing and come on uptown. You know. (*laughs*) And Montgomery Mary—oh, was a beautiful, real black woman. *Beautiful.* She could steal a horse without you knowing. And never say a word. The horse'd be following her around, and she had stolen him from you and you wouldn't know it. (*laughs*) Oh, boy. And let me see, there was a fellow there named Lumsy. And he would pawn everything that he'd get his hands on. And his wife's name was Anna. And he went up and got the picture of Christ and brought it down, going to pawn it. Anna says, "Lumsy, you have brought *everything* in here, but you are not gonna pawn Jesus Christ!" (*laughs*) No! Anna wouldn't let Lumsy pawn Jesus'—Christ's picture. That's the truth. (*laughs*) But that's where the confidence men and the pickpocket women that hung out there at Hugh Hoskins. That was Thirty-second and State. That was a little place upstairs and downstairs. Miss Hoskins was a lovely woman, had a little boy.

And the next place I worked was the Panama [Café]. That was at Thirty-fifth and State. Owned by Izzy Shaw and Izzy Levine. I worked there for them. Downstairs they had five girls singing and a pianist. Upstairs five girls singing and a pianist. Upstairs was George Hall playing piano. It was Twinkle Davis, Goldie Crosby, Nellie Carr, Mamie Carter, and Alberta Hunter upstairs. Swingin.' Downstairs was Brick Top, Cora Greene, Mattie Hite, Nettie Compton, and Florence Mills. So now that was the five girls downstairs—I named them—and Glover Compton at the piano. They were the dicties [stuck-up or self-important people], you know. The dicties. That's where all the—they come in, it's supposed to be the class downstairs. The buzzards were upstairs. (*laughs*) Florence Mills, she was great. She was one of our greatest artists. Now, they would sing all the show tunes and all the—there was Brick down there, too. They didn't pay Brick no more mind than if she was that thing over that rug. They'd walk right on by Brick and Florence Mills and just come upstairs. 'Cause Nellie Carr was up there running and running into a split. Twinkle Davis was there 'cause she had the most beautiful limbs you've *ever* seen in your life. Marlene Dietrich had nothing on her. Mamie Carter couldn't sing a lick, but she could jive. And I was singing. I used to draw—funny, I was always a draw. Al Jolson and Sophie Tucker and all the big stars would come upstairs to hear me sing "Mammy's Little Coal Black Rose" and "The St. Louis Blues," come upstairs. So we outdrew them. So they found out about me. Then Mr. Bottoms, Bill Bottoms, he latterly became Joe Louis's dietitian. He heard about me and wanted me to come over to Dreamland, leave the Panama. So he offered me more money—$150 a week. You're breaking the bank, you know. Offered me $150; I'm going on leave—I'm leaving the social club, Brick Top and them.

So I went on over to Dreamland. As I told you, there was King Oliver, King Joe Oliver's band, with [Sidney] Bechet and Wellman Braud, the Dodds Brothers, the Miner Brothers, and May Alix. Well, May Alix, she wasn't in the band, no. She was a singer. But she could *sing* awhile. Let me finish telling you about Joe, though. Then we heard about this young boy down in New Orleans that could play trumpet. I said to Mr. Bottoms, "Why don't you go down to New Orleans and see him." So he either went to New Orleans or he *sent* somebody down there and they brought Louis [Armstrong] up. That's how Louis started to work in Chicago, with Joe Oliver's band.

You had a name that I want to know about—Cora Green. I have a record, Cora Green and Hamtree Harrington.

Yeah, comedy team. Comedy team. She was a *good*-looking woman, and he was—he was out in Hollywood there for a long time, doing comedy. Worked his eyes like this. (*rolls her eyes*) Yeah! You got them?

I've got one by them.

Yeah, all right.

When you went in and did this [recording], there weren't any microphones in those days, were there?

No.

Now, just for the benefit of the audience, tell us how it worked.

Well, there was, like, a hole in the wall, about big enough for a horn to get through. Like the bell of a horn, you know, the big part of a horn. All right. The big part of the horn would come here, where I am. The smaller part of the horn would go to that part. And there were the technicians on that side. They could see me and I could see them. You understand?

The end of that horn reached all the way into their studio?

Yes.

So that where they had the machine that was cutting the disc—

The big, thick wax. And this machine would be cutting the wax as you [were] singing. You understand? This happened in the studio where I made—

All the Paramount things.

Yes.

Since there was only one track— You know, nowadays, you've got this guy on one track, another guy on this track, and you can bring the levels up any way you want to. In the old days, you couldn't do that.

No.

How long did it take them to place you and the musicians? How many times would you have to try it in order to get that right balance?

Sometimes five and six, sometimes more than that. Now, there's a girl named Viola McCoy. She could record like mad. It looks like Viola and something happened. Viola and I, we could make a record—bang, no trouble. But sometimes they'd have to start—with some of the girls and boys—and they'd start and they couldn't finish. They'd have to stop and come back again.

So, many takes?

Yeah. And then they wouldn't have enough material to last, so they'd have to come back again.

Where would you be in relation to the instruments? Okay, here's the horn. And where are you and where are the instruments?

Instruments are behind me, back there. Here are the instruments back here. I'm here. And they would go over and—if it was too loud or whatever it was, they'd kinda try to turn it down, or move the instrumentalists or the musician over someplace else. You know what I mean?

So that it wouldn't come through so loud.

Yeah. 'Cause they couldn't regulate—I mean, couldn't fix their horns and things exactly like they'd want them. And some of them would sound so much like tin. They didn't have the good mellow sounds like they have now. And, you see, a lot of the fellows would just get in there and they didn't have arrangements, and they didn't—some of them, notes were kinda bad. (laughs) So they'd have to move them.

How close were you in relation to the horn? Were you right up in the horn, or did they have you stand back from the horn?

Well, they might want me to stand up to the horn sometimes, but I'd get away from the horn, 'cause the horn was too loud and it was blue. So I'd get away from the horn and get where *I* was comfortable. 'Cause if I was supposed to be the artist, give me a break! I'd take my own break, you know. Sometimes they'd be featuring the horn player. But I'd tell Alberta, "Alberta, get over there a little further; this guy's gonna take your place." 'Cause some of the musicians was selfish. They didn't care whether you came through or not, so long as they were performing. And that was your day, supposed to be your day, you know. But they'd take it from you if you didn't know how to—that's the reason I argue so. You see, that's the reason I know so much about business 'cause— (laughs) That's the first record I made, was "How Long, Sweet Daddy, How Long?" That was at Thirty-fifth and State Street, on Thirty-fifth and Seventh Avenue. You know one thing? Now, that's the one record I don't remember how I made connections on that one. I knew I went downstairs in Odessa's place and sang "Sweet Daddy, How Long" with Fletcher Henderson. That's all I remember.

What was Odessa?

She was a milliner—had a millinery store, a millinery shop. Her mother was Miss Sadie. Had the newspaper, the *Amsterdam News* first. The *Amsterdam News,* Gerald. Miss Sadie Warren. *W-a-r-r-e-n,* Miss Sadie Warren. And she owned the *Amsterdam News.* And she was gonna get married to a fellow named Davis, and they didn't want her to marry him. But she married him anyhow. That's how Davis got in on this *Amsterdam News* jive. Miss Sadie Warren owned the *Amsterdam News,* honey. I know; I remember. And Odessa was her daughter. And I made "How Long, Sweet Daddy, How Long?" Fletcher Henderson made that—played the record, just the piano. That's all. Fletcher Henderson just played the piano and there was something there. I don't know what took it—what it was that took it down. But it wasn't— Those horns and things were in the recording laboratory. They weren't there down in Miss Sadie Warren's. I went to the New York recording laboratories for Paramount.

Now, the person that, first person that spoke to me about going to New York to make a record was a fellow named N. A. Supper, S-u-p-p-e-r. A very fine young white fellow. There was a colored fellow with him they called Ink Williams. J. Mayo Williams. Robbed Jesus of his whiskers and everything. (*laughs*) That man was a thief from the day he was conceived. He robbed all of us. A crime. God's on his throne. He knows. God knows him. You reap what you sow. Ink Williams robbed me. Not only me, everybody. The people that didn't know how to have their songs copywritten [copyrighted], he took all their music. But God is still on his throne. Dear Lord, yes. 'Cause Ink Williams is *paying* for what he's done. He's paying. Ink Williams is paying for some of the things he's done. Oh, God, I'm sorry he had a stroke, but he had it. I didn't give it to him. But anyhow, you reap what you sow. Ink Williams, I'm talking to you. Yes, sir. All right. Now, Mr. Supper asked me to go to New York to make a record. [I didn't] know nothing about no records or arrangements and things, you know. No, you just go there and get by the piano and sing. Anyhow, I rehearsed the song. Went to New York. The first one I made was "Downhearted Blues." "Downhearted" was my first big record and "Chirpin'" was second. Then I made one called "Bleeding Hearted Blues" with Lovie Austin with a whole newspaper, whole page. But "Downhearted" was the first one. That's the one they robbed me of. Oh, God, help me. *Robbed* me, honey. Mr. Supper didn't. He was a good man. 'Cause Mr. Supper gave me $380, if I recalled, and I'm certain that's the amount; he gave me a check for $380. And from then—I don't know whether Ink was gonna beat him or do something about giving me all that money (*laughs*), but Mr. Supper gave me a check for $380. And from then on, I think when Ink got with him and started putting devilment in his head. But he was a good man.

When you played with Lovie, did you play with Tommy Ladnier?

Did I record with him? Once. He was a good little trumpet player, too. Good little trumpet player. Tommie Ladnier was a good little trumpet player. I think I made one record with him. One record.

Let me ask you something about recording. Most of your records—or a good many of them—were made for Paramount. Now, did they care if you stepped out and recorded for other companies?

Yeah! Sure they cared! Because that's the reason I put my sister's name on some of them. Yeah. Oh, sure. I recorded—I was recording for Paramount under contract. And another song—I mean, one of the songs I had to make—and I was afraid to use my own name. I've always had guts, you know, and sense, thank God. I was afraid to use my name, so I put my sister's name on it:

Josephine Beatty. Yeah! I've been slick, Gerald! Put Josephine's name on this record. Josephine Beatty. That was my half sister. Um-hm.

Those are the ones with Louis and Bechet?

Yep. Yeah.

Okay. Now, there were some other things. How did you get in touch with Victor? Did you step out on Paramount to record for Victor?

No, Victor—Victor, Victor, Paramount, Columbia—all of them were after me. I had—I got letters in the vault. You must look at those letters sometime, honey, and read them, where they was trying to get me away from Paramount. Say, "Paramount is a little—blah—if you want to be with the big one, then blah." All that kinda stuff. You know, jiving me. But anyhow, oh, I used to get offers all the time. Oh, my God.

So you went ahead and did those for Victor, but you did those under your own name, didn't you?

Yeah. Yeah, because you know what? I was slick enough to wait till the contracts left, you know, and then I'd get them on my own name. See, I tell you, I've been a businesswoman for years, haven't I?

How about—you did some things for Gennett, the Gennett label?

Yeah.

Were those under your name, too?

I believe, I believe they were. I believe the contracts had run out. Gennett, I made some for Gennett and some for some other company, didn't I?

Well, OKeh [Records].

Yeah, OKeh.

I've got one of those—"Empty Cellar" and "I Don't Want It All."

And those are my songs, incidentally.

Is that right?

That's right. You got some more contracts, kid! Yeah, oh, yes. And "Your Jelly Roll Might Be Good, but It Ain't Good as Mine"—I fix it so it was a baker shop. Yeah, ooh, you reminded me of a whole lot of material I got.

I see you recorded for Victor. You did those things with Fats Waller.

Yeah.

On the organ.

Yeah. "Beale Street Blues," and "Sugar," and which one was that— (*sings*) "*Come on home, come on home. Home ain't home without you alone.*" Gorgeous song. We must do that. Beautiful song. I don't know one note from the other, even today. One note from the other, I do not know. My pianist and my friend, my Gerald tells me I've got a marvelous *ear,* but otherwise I don't know music. Now, I at my house on Lane Avenue in Memphis, Tennessee, as a child, used to just go down to Miss Hattie's house and stay at her piano and just hit down on anything. If a note sound good, I'd keep that in my head, and after a while if I'd go the next day or next couple days, I hit another one that sound good, I'd get them two together. That's how "Downhearted Blues" was composed. At the Monogram Theater in Chicago there at Thirty-fifth and State, one day I was talking to Lovie or doing something. Lovie heard me hum that thing and she said, "Oh, that's a good song. That's a good song. We put that down." Now, Lovie put the music down that I hummed to her. They had it on the music that Lovie Austin wrote the music to "Downhearted Blues." Lovie Austin did *not* write the music; *I* am the composer of "Downhearted Blues"—words and music. Lovie Austin put the notes down on a piece of paper in order for it to go to the copyright department. Because I knew nothing about having to have a song copywritten [copyrighted], nothing about it.

Now, I will give her credit for this one thing—that's the reason I like to tell the truth. She was kind enough and honest enough to put my name as the writer of the words. That's what I tell you about honesty. She could've been nasty enough to have stolen the whole thing from me. Alberta Hunter is the composer—words and music—of "Downhearted Blues." So let that be known to the world. A song called "Down South Blues," I wrote the whole thing to that. And Ethel Waters and Fletcher Henderson and all of them, they had put their names—the publishers are slickers, you know. They put everybody's name—put Jesus and Moses and everybody's name on your songs that they had something to do with them in order for *them* to get some of the royalties. But each one of the people gave me letters. I've got them in my vault—Gerald, don't forget that—in my vault, saying that they had nothing to do with them. So when anything happens to me, there's black and white they had nothing to do with it.

You ran into Ink Williams. Did you ever have fun with that other slicker back there, Clarence Williams?

Well, I must tell you, Clarence and I got along pretty well. I think he cheated me a little bit, but I didn't mind, 'cause Clarence, he was all right. I liked Clarence a little bit. And he stole a little bit. People been stealing so much, you know. He did give me a chance; he let me live. He didn't kill me like Ink Williams.

You're the first person I know who's ever had anything nice to say about Clarence Williams.

Is that so? I liked Clarence. He was such a lousy musician. (*laughs*) And then his wife—his wife, you know, kinda made a way for all of us on radio.

Eva Taylor.

Eva Taylor. 'Cause she was the first, you know, to broadcast, Eva Taylor was. On a big station. So I liked her and I liked Clarence. He was lousy, but give 'im a break.

How about some other singers now, like we were talking about before? How about if I run off some names, and maybe you can tell me if you knew them and what they looked like or what you remember about them?

Tell me.

Let's start out with Katie Crippen.

Katy Crippen was a little light-colored kinda girl that I didn't know. I never met her to say "How do you do" to her.

You don't remember anyplace that she was playing? Did she play around here at all?

I don't remember.

Okay. And, let's see, what about Alice Leslie Carter?

Yeah. Big woman. Big black woman.

How about some names that you can call?

Well, you know, I didn't know Bessie Smith. You know, as I said, I wrote the song that made Bessie famous, "Downhearted Blues." But the only time I met Bessie Smith, I didn't say "Howdy do" to her. Like coming out of the Standard Theater in Philadelphia, she had been playing there and I was going in. Our paths crossed. That's the only time I had any—any chance to even say hello to her had I wanted to. But I never did. But I used to go to see her shows and go on out. I never went backstage or anything like that. 'Cause I always enjoyed her, 'cause she was one of the *biggest* blues. She had the biggest voice of any woman I ever heard in my life.

Discounting yourself, who else did you like to listen to sing?

Then?

Yeah.

Viola McCoy. A girl named Viola McCoy. Oh, I was crazy about that girl. Who else was it? Somebody else. I liked Rosa Henderson and Slim. And I was crazy about Momma Dinks. That's how Josephine Baker got her start. She, Josephine—Momma Dinks used to clown on the end of "Shuffle Along" all the time. And Josephine used to watch her. That's how Josephine learned how to do all that stuff she learned how to do. And then there was a girl named Maude DeForrest, had a wonderful voice. And they sent for her—she went to Europe and they sent her back, 'cause she got swell-headed right off the way.

She recorded for Black Swan.

Yeah.

Yeah. How about Mary Strain? You talked about Mary Strain. That's a name I've seen on records, but I haven't seen—

Well, I used to say hello to Mary. But that's all. I'd just pass her—"Hi"—one of those things.

How about Mamie Smith? Did you know Mamie?

Yes, I knew Mamie. I used to go to Mamie's to eat. Mamie could cook. I went to Mamie's, lived on 134th Street. She had a lovely little place, a nice little house. And I went to Mamie's. She was a good-looking woman. Good-looking. Had a trumpet player named Johnny Dunn. He set Europe on fire, you know. Yes, I knew Mamie. She dressed, too. She wore some clothes. Most all of us wore clothes at that time. That's the reason I look like a—what do you call it?—a bag woman all the time now. 'Cause most of us, we were dressing, and the rest of these chicks didn't know they made good dresses. So, but Mamie was always *very* sweet. A sweet person.

Now, Lucille Hegamin, were you close with her at all?

I knew Lucille *very* well. I knew Lucille very well. She was the first one to do "He May Be Your Man, but He Comes to See Me Sometime." Um-hm. Yeah, I knew Lucille. She was always a good singer, too, and quite popular. But she never got the recognition that she deserved. She was very popular, but still something happened, she didn't get the recognition she deserved. I don't think.

How about Lavinia Turner?

She was all right.

Did you know her or happen to see her?

No, I didn't know her. I saw her but I didn't know her. You know, I was so busy all the time myself, I didn't have much time. I've been so *lucky*. It looked like work, work, work all the time for me. I never had that chance. And then, I was the type—I've always been old-fashioned. I was never a social person. I never liked to socialize. I'm the one person—Gerald can tell you—he's sitting there now just surprised that I'm talking like I am, 'cause he knows I don't like to talk. I don't like to talk much, and I would just go on about my business. I'd do my work; go in. Never late. I was never late on a job. Do my work. Finish my job. Put my hat and coat on. "Good night, everybody." I left. I never drank, never smoked, never socialized. That was my life. And it's the same today as it was yesterday.

Oh, Harry ought to tell that. He knows it, 'cause he was the one in the wing watching for me, waiting for me to flop. (*laughs*) No. You see, the man needed somebody to close his show. He didn't have an artist to go on just before the closing of the show, so he had to have somebody. So Eddie Hunter told him, says, "I've got somebody. I know of a person's coming, be in in a few hours and I'll see if we can get her to come in and sing." So when I came down, he asked me would I sing. I said, "Yeah." I didn't know what was going to happen. So I said yes. Came from Chicago. Right in from the station, right to the theater, to the Apollo Theater, which was a legitimate and *the* musical comedy theater of the city at that time, of New York. Coming to Chicago, had my hat and my things. I laid my coat and things down on the chair in order to sing. Yeah. And I told the fellow, Will Vaudry, leader of the band, and Allie Ross and Will Tyler. Will Tyler, little old short guy. Violinist out of this world! And so was Allie Ross. And they had heard me tell Will Vaudry to play one introduction and no vamps. Instead, he start—played the introduction and started vamping back, and they started just playing the introduction like they had heard me tell him. So I walked out on the stage, and when the introduction started, I jumped in, 'cause my voice is bigger than his anyhow. I jumped in on that introduction and started to sing. And that Sophie Tucker, Blossom Seeley—oh, some of the great artists were in that audience. And I started to sing. Well, the kids had heard about this woman coming in sings so great. Gonna see what she's gonna do. So they had got in the wings to see what I was supposed to do, you know—what I was gonna do, rather. And when I started, the minute I hit the first note, the audience started raving and going on, you know. And they applauded so that I started off the stage. Said, "Go back, go back, you're stopping the show." And I thought I had cut a hog, you know. Had done the wrong thing. So they said, "Go back, go back, go back." And they pushed me back on the stage.

That's how I got my break in "How Come?" I think it was 1923—1923, and I think I have the date. I think I have a program—1923. And I came in, walked in, got myself a job, stopped the show, and went on about my business. (*laughs*) Honey, when you—Lord have mercy—put this somewhere. People play piano, play horn, get up and try to drown you out and steal the show from you. But, honey, when the time comes for to be accompanied, get *my* pianist, *my* accompanist. He is the world's greatest. When he touches that piano key, honey, it says, "Good morning." One of the greatest that ever lived. Anticipates your every thought. Knows what—he knows what you're gonna say before you say it. Don't stop. Let's talk some more. Ask me anything.

What do you think that the young can learn from the old here today?

First, they can learn to learn respect for themselves. Learn respect and by all means respect the other fellow's ideas and thoughts. Have a mind of your own. Don't let money get you off the track. And don't begrudge other people of their success. And don't sit around waiting for somebody else to do things for you. Do them yourself. And realize that there are things that are dangerous. And for the youngster, to remember their parents. I got to tell them this: Remember your parents. If you get away from home, if you need assistance, don't be ashamed to write and ask for assistance. You'd be surprised how quick a reply will come. Stick to your parents, because your parents are with you when the *world* is against you, children. Stick to your parents. And remember, time waits for no one. It passes you by. For no one. Do you hear what I'm saying? It rolls on forever like a cloud in the sky. Time. And if you want to make it in life, hold on to the hand of the almighty God. There is a God, you know. Other people are being taught there is no God. But there is a God. 'Cause I'm a living example of God's goodness—I'm a living example of it. And never become discouraged. There might be dark clouds, but in that dark cloud you'll see a silver lining if you look long enough and hard enough.

Grey **Ghost**

R. T. Williams, known to blues fans as the Grey Ghost, was among the last of the itinerant Texas blues pianists. For more than three decades these pianists hoboed from town to town, juke joint to barrelhouse in prewar Texas. They

Grey Ghost. Photo by Maryann Price.

seldom settled in any one place, hitchhiking and hopping trains to get from destination to destination. In the glory days of their genre there were scores—perhaps hundreds—of roaming pianists displaying every level of talent and technique. Ironically, with all the players traveling and performing, only a lucky few managed to make records: Rob Cooper, Andy Boy, Dusky Dailey, Black Boy Shine, Black Ivory King, Pinetop Burks, Son Becky, Big Boy Knox, Curtis Jones, and Whistling Alex Moore. The great majority never had the opportunity to record and left us with only a list of colorful names. The years after World War II were not kind to these pianists; the advent of the jukebox, the electric guitar, and changing tastes in music put an end to the popularity of the itinerant Texas blues pianists. Among the survivors of this genre were a hardscrabble group that included Mercy Dee Walton, Robert Shaw, Lavada Durst, Buster Pickens—and the Grey Ghost.

The Grey Ghost was another of the bluesmen I interviewed as he appeared at the University of Chicago Folk Festival. The Grey Ghost was accompanied on his trip to Chicago by his manager, Tary Owens. We made arrangements to do an interview with the pianist during his three-day stay in Chicago. One of my friends remembers the Grey Ghost as a complete misanthrope—reticent and disagreeable at all times. I, on the other hand, recall the Ghost and our interview with fond memories. I've always had an affection for cranky old men—perhaps one reason why I've gotten so many good interviews out of old-timers—and regard the saltiness as a part of the screening process these old folks use to keep strangers at arm's length, generally, before they warm up to them. Tary sat in on the interview and helped explain details that the Grey Ghost might overlook. The Grey Ghost never made any commercial recordings during his prime in the 1930s and '40s, but made a pair of fabulous recordings for the Library of Congress in 1942, which bear out his piano-playing abilities.

This interview was conducted on February 9, 1988. R. T. Williams—the Grey Ghost—died in Austin in 1996.

■ ■ ■

I was born in Bastrop, Texas, a little bitty place. You throw a rock over it with a slingshot. About 1903. December the seventh. They bombed Pearl Harbor on my birthday. When I used to throw off people—I'd put 'em on about it, say, "I'm mad they bombed Pearl Harbor. Why'd they pick out my birthday to do that?" But they didn't know I existed. They just bombed it on that day, though, December seventh.

What's your real name, and how did the "Grey Ghost" come about?

Roosevelt Thomas Williams. I don't use it; I sign all my usually signatures R. T. Williams. That's too much to put on a small envelope. All them words got a lot of letters on 'em. *Roosevelt Thomas* and the *Williams*. Small envelope, you don't write awful small, you run out of space. But Uncle Sam wants your whole name when you fool with him. Sometime you might get a letter with *Roosevelt T. Williams,* according to what it is. But he wants your *full* name.

Maybe you can explain to folks where the name the Grey Ghost came from.

Well, that come out of Smithville. Mr. Yagen Hill, them high-class people there, they give them big dances and I'd be in Amarillo or somewhere. Jack Craft, a friend of mine, he worked for 'em—chauffeured and cooked meals—and they'd get him to get in touch with me. Tell me they wanted to have a party or a big outfit up over the city hall, and the day, and if I could come. Asked me if I could come and I'd let him know. Then they'd get me word back the day they wanted me to play for their outfit. And I'd tell 'em I'd be there. So they'd go ahead and go to a lot of trouble spending and fixing for that certain day. And

I'd catch that Fort Worth and Denver [train] out of there and come on down to Fort Worth. Then I'd catch another train and go on into Waco. From there I'd catch that Comet that'd be in Houston every morning at seven o'clock, and leave there in the evening and arrive in Houston seven o'clock the next morning. Stop in Smithville. That was the roundhouse. Change engines and things. And I'd get off at Bastrop, where I was born and I had a few friends, off-branch kinfolk. And I'd hire somebody to take me to Smithville, just eighteen miles. And they'd be looking for me and everybody crazy. They went to all that trouble and the train done run, a couple of buses done run. Then I come walking up Main Street about seven thirty—gonna start at eight. They come talking about "Where'd you come from? We met the train; we met the bus. So-and-so, and so-and-so." I said, "Well, that's all right. I'm here. That's all that's necessary." And they went to saying I come up out the ground and all that junk, like a ghost. From that on, they carried it out.

I got my schooling in Taylor, Texas. And after my mother passed, I went to Waco and started working on a compress. I was practicing music then. That's where I got in the racket. In the fall in Waco, a friend of mine—we went to school in Taylor, Baby Van. Van had a piano and he was learning. So me and him being friends, I'd go out to his house—we didn't have a piano—and we'd practice out there, and both of us got started. Now, this Van, his cousin, he was a piano player, but he read and played classical music. They didn't even recognize him after me and Baby started trying to play, 'cause he didn't play the kinda stuff people wanted around there. That's the beginning of it.

Who were some of the people that you and Baby Van were listening to back in those days?

The man we was listening to didn't amount to much, Charlie Dillard. He was an elder man playing piano. But he couldn't play in but one key; that was B-flat. And we didn't try to follow him. George Mackey, he could play in a lot of keys, but he was a progressive man, too. So all we got is what we heard on records and things like that, picked it up. Always had a pretty good ear. I took music for a while, but that stuff run you crazy. Then you ain't got no oomp in it, so you gonna put some of your own hot licks in it when you learn it. And you ain't got nothing. You ain't got nowhere. And I could sing, and that's what helped me so much—that I could imitate anybody that sung, women or men. Can't do it now, but I could then. I listened to people like Earl Hines and Count Basie, them people, but they didn't even live in them parts. I just hear them through recordings, you know. Things like that. But I liked their style. And I picked it up. That is, not Count Basie—I didn't pick his style up. I didn't like it that much. Then after I hung around Houston, there's a few around there could play pretty good, and I took to some of those. And most of mine is my own thing, stuff what I created or fixed like I wanted to play it. So I don't know nobody; I just tried to play. Like some people tried to take pattern after, someone play like them. I didn't pick out nobody. I used Earl Hines's bass with my left hand. Those tenths and things, just playing his style. I didn't do Fats Domino and all that bunch. You have to play *all* of it if you're gonna make a living out of it. You can't just play one style—hillbilly or blues, or progressive or popular music—or you ain't gonna get far. I found that out a long time ago. You got to mix it up.

How would you find out where you could—where there were people playing piano, and how would you approach them about working there?

You mean about playing piano?

Yes.

I wouldn't. I'd fix it so they'd find out that I was a player. If they wanted to hear or they wanted to test me, well, it'd be up to them, then. It'd be up to them whether they wanted to hire me or whatnot. I never went there asking for no job. But I never had no trouble. Most people in them places; somehow I know would know me. Not all the towns, but they'd find out. "They tell me you so-and-so." I'd say, "Yeah, a little bit." That'd leak around, so I'd get more jobs sometimes than I could handle. Then, of course, I could sing and so many people played piano and can't even talk much less sing. There's a lot of ham-fat piano players up on the north end and around, so I didn't bother about 'em. They was doing all right till I come in and dug in. Then they'd be wanting to have them house-rent parties or whatever they had. Unless I was tied up, they didn't get no more jobs.

How about some of the piano players in Waco?

Naturally, you know every musician in town; if he can play anything, if he just play fair, you'll know about it. Now, me, and Son Alpert, and his brother—only he played clarinet and his brother played banjo—that bunch, we sort of pretty close, but there wasn't that many there. Son Alpert played clarinet and piano and had another boy, a man that they called Eddy something—I don't know; lived in the north end—he played. And they had the guy they called Honey Fishy. He played a different style from everybody. His style wasn't so nice. He played them old draggy low-down blues, and that's all he could play. But there wasn't no musicians there that I knowed of amounted to anything when I went there. They was using what they had. Then Alfred Porter, they charge fifteen cents, two bits at the door and all that junk.

How about Mercy Dee [Walton]? We always hear about Mercy Dee and we hear the records. Did you have much to do with him or hear much of him?

Oh, yeah. But we never run together or was too close, you know, or nothing. Just—I didn't know Lightnin' [Hopkins] till I stayed on Airline [Street] in Houston. He used to play at a café right across the street from where I lived. He'd be over there with his hair conked and his amplifier sitting up on another soda water case. Him sitting on a chair with one [case] in this chair. And that's where he played. That's where I met him. And I think he lived out in Acres Homes. I don't know—I didn't meet none of them guys. Then Gatemouth—I met Gatemouth and the one they call Widemouth Brown. But we didn't run together and socialize that much.

Tary—the musicians he did know were T. D. Bell and Erbie Bowser.

Well, they was from Rockdale and Austin City. That's where they was from. T. D.'s home is Rockdale, Texas. Bowser is Austinite. And them other fellas that passed—Boots Waldren, Baby Dotson, the one that had the piano down at his piano, Robert Shaw—well, that was about all of 'em that standed 'round there. I didn't recognize some of them, because they didn't come on strong enough. Baby Dotson never did come on. He could play a few blues and that's all. They wouldn't call him. Me and Boots run a roadhouse out there. He played pretty good, Boots Waldren. And Shaw always thought he played music—kind of a church-house bass with his left hand. And he played a few pieces. That piece I asked you about. And he—I said that's all he could play. I forget what they call it. But he wasn't hitting on [anything].—He'd get us out there, and them university boys and things would come out there to his house. And he'd invite us out and we'd do most of the playing. See? Me and Boots and that. He didn't have to try to play.

How about Joe Pullum?

Yeah, I know him. Not personal, but I know him, been around him several times. He's in Houston. I had a chance to meet him, but ain't too many people that I, in the piano field, that I had any much respect for, because they couldn't play what I could play. And I played for Mr. Dan that thirty months, Italian nightclub two years and a half in one spot. And we had that house packed every night. Didn't have no band; just had me and a drummer. One woman. But he'd have striptease, stuff like that. So on different nights, could hardly get in there. But Houston was so low-down. I just didn't like Houston. That's the reason I left. It wasn't a problem of money or a job.

When you say it was "low-down," can you be a little more specific?

Oh, so many things go on there that don't go nowhere else. Dirty things.

Like robbing you and house people running places, being in with the robber and play like they don't know the people and all that kinda junk. I didn't get robbed or nothing, because I knew I was hip to what they was doing. But if you come in and flash some money and went in that bathroom, you wouldn't come out with nothing. 'Cause he's gonna tell you if you come out in the next three to five minutes, he'd kill you. And he done gone out the front, and the man claim he just see him been dropping in there for a day or two. He don't know what his name is; he been hanging around. And he knows him well. All he want to know is what did he get from you, and you tell him that. That's what he want to know. So he gets fifty percent cut of it. That's why I said that. And that ain't just in one ward, Third Ward, or nothing. It's Fifth Ward, Fourth Ward. Most all over town about Thousand Acres Homes, something like that might be different. They swear that a woman come in that uniform room and get your twenty-dollar bill, gonna pay for your breakfast. You say, "Where is that lady with my change?" He say, "Which one was it?" You go to looking, and them women he got in there working ain't the one that he give the money to. He say, "I don't see her. These ain't none of her." He said, "These the oniest women work here. Man, you give your money to somebody on the way to work." That's what he gonna tell you. Then she don't come down all day. She come out at night. But he wouldn't know her if he saw her, 'cause she got all that flake white on her and a different wig, or a wig, period. I just didn't trust that place. People sitting on soda water cases with dark glasses on, looking over their glasses. I laid for 'em, though. Me and my friends would go down there and go somewhere. Didn't one of us go to the bathroom at the time. Both of us had a .38 automatic in our shirtsleeve, near the shirt blouse. He went in there, and somebody got up a little bit after he went in there, and I went right in behind him. He done me the same way. We never had no trouble.

I always wondered, as a piano player, do you get an uneasy feeling when you're in places like that? Turning your back on the crowd?

Unh-uh. Unless you are the type of guy ain't got sense enough to know how to carry yourself, you'd be wise to be kinda skeptical. But when I go to places like that, or anywhere, I keeps them women far away from me, because people are a little shy and jealous of musicians, anybody kinda professional, and they could hurt you thinking something that wasn't even so. So I don't bother them. I get in with the men before I think about a girl or a woman. Make friends with them and then they'll guard you. They say, "Yes, she's got a boyfriend, but he ain't much. If you want to talk to her, you go ahead and talk to her." That's the way they done me in Houston. I found out some of the baddest folks in that town—there's three of 'em. Down in the Third Ward. But everybody knew 'em all over town. And I wasn't scared to start with 'em, after I had them behind me. I didn't bother nobody's wife, but if a woman was a free —— (??) and I wanted to talk to her, I'd talk to her. Nah, that's a sorry place. I left there, going to Corpus. I had a job out on the highway playing music at a nightclub. My people talked me outta that when I got to Austin, about so many people left home, went down and got kilt. Get killed anywhere if you don't know how to carry yourself or treat people right.

What went on in Corpus Christi that was so worrisome?

Well, Corpus Christi was all right in its place, but, see, they got a lot of them sailors and seamen comes in on them ships, and they pretty rough. I remember several times I went there and somebody brought one of them—brought a man out the front door after him with a knife and all that junk. Corpus ain't such a good place. It's seaport-like town and get pretty rough there sometime when they come in there on them ships. I liked the town, but I didn't like the people there which you had to socialize with. They wouldn't do. When you know people like that, it makes you treacherous yourself, because you don't want to— I'd rather go to my daddy's funeral than go to mine.

And I never will forget out in Abilene. I stayed there quite awhile. A woman come to the church house on Sunday morning and killed a woman when she come to church. She told her twice to leave her husband alone. Had a witness to that. She's going to bully the woman, 'cause the woman was quiet and peaceful and she figured she wouldn't do nothing to her. Kilt her. She never did get in the church. And they didn't do nothing to her—give her a suspended sentence, 'cause she had a witness that she had warned her and told her, asked her to leave her husband alone. "We're trying to get along, trying to live happy." "You talk to him. Don't talk to me." That's what they say she told. I was in a place once where they had a gambling shack and a place where the piano was, where they'd dance, and drinking that grape juice, and pouring snuff in it, and all that. I don't know what they wasn't doing to get high. And they killed the man in the gambling shack. Brought him outside. Laid him down beside the house. And went on to talk about he's *way* overdue, and went on back in there with the gambling. I say, "Uh-huh."

The next morning I drawed some money to go buy me some underclothes, and I kept on with the underclothes till I wind up in Luling, Texas. Spent the night in Houston. Got me a room and slept. The next [day] I went on to Luling. Went down to Louisiana. It's sure a lot different life down there than it is here or anywhere else. People down there is nice people, and they're gonna to treat you nice, but you better keep your slate clean if you're going down there and mess with any of those people—women down there—'cause you come up graveyard dead. These Texas boys, they teach 'em some sense when they go down there! She's not gonna trifle fool around with you no kinda way. I know; I been around them and seen 'em and shake my head. You could come up there with a pickup truck of money and say, "Now, if you just talk right" or "Come in here and lay a little while, boy; you just help yourself to that money." She say, "No, I couldn't do dat. How would you like if I was your girlfriend, I fool with anudder man?" That's what's she gonna ask you. "How would you like it if," you know, she's your girlfriend and she would fool with anudder man—not another—anudder man. Well, you can't say you'd like it. You know you couldn't say it without you gonna tell the biggest lie of your life. And she ain't gonna trifle on you, and, brother, you better straighten up and fly right. Don't she wake up and she be sitting right straddle your stomach, your chest with an ice pick on it, —— (??) now crying a dog. She ain't crying for one thing. If she kill you, she won't have you no more, and that's what she's crying about.

One time I told George Francis, I said, "Man, you better straighten up." He wasn't doing nothing, but he was flirting and bull-corning, you know. And I was going with the woman's sister in the next room. And it seemed like I hear somebody crying. We got quiet, and she say, "I do." I say, "I think that's Sis." Then we got there and find a crack and looked around, and she sitting straddling that guy with a knife and a gun! Then we finally got in there, and she got close enough to talk to him, get her off of him without hurting him. And when I come, come south down to Smithville—Bastrop, LaGrange was really was where I was gonna come anyway—she and George followed me down there. He left her. He was a trumpet player. I hoot on him many a time. I say, "No, you sharp cat. You don't have to go." "I'm going down there with you. You say you going down there and get on with Sugarfoot Green's show." He had a show he showed at schoolhouses, you know. Nice, clean show. And he showed at all the high schools and things around these little towns. He followed me away from there. He's scared to death. So it's the way you carry yourself. You can go anywhere. I tell him in a minute, I say, "Y'all go back out here with you." They start up on a platform where the piano is—maybe it's two, three steps up. Ask me can I play certain things. I say, "I can hear you from down there." Some of 'em will tell you they ain't got no husband. When I say, "It ain't a matter of that; I can hear you from down there, whatever you wanna ask me." I never had no trouble.

You know, as a veteran train hopper—maybe for the folks listening—you could give us some advice on the old days. What were some of the rules that you made for yourself or that you found for yourself when you'd ride a train? What were some things that you should do and some things that you shouldn't do to keep you out of trouble?

Well, it wasn't no trouble to it. All you had to do is try to keep yourself clean. Putting on an overall suit over your suit and tie and whatnot, according to how far you're going, whether you're carrying any extra clothes or not. And get on the train and go to riding. Find you a place that's kinda comfortable out there, empty car or box car. If you couldn't do that, try to get in an empty gondola where you couldn't fall off or nothing. Them oil tanks is the worst place to try to ride and hug that iron around there to hold on, you know—too dangerous. I never thought nothing about it. We'd go out to Sears to see girls. Go and ride the freight out there. They stop and take water. All of 'em at Sears, Texas. Little old—wasn't nothing out there but a store. And we'd go out there, then when we get ready to go back, we'd wait till one of them freights come and stop there for water. And we'd get on it and go on back where we come. It's fun to us.

Well, you see in the movies, you know they always have the—I don't know, the mean brakeman trying to throw the riders off the train. You ever run into any kind of experiences like that?

Yeah. They try to—some of 'em would try to put you off. But most of 'em didn't bother, because they didn't know, figure you might grab 'em and push 'em under them wheels or something, you know. They'd go back to the caboose or go to the engine. If they could [send] word east to a few towns, they'd have the law to come in and shake the train down and all like that. But I never was arrested, never was bothered. And after my mother passed, I worried so much I like to have a nervous breakdown. And I'd get on them trains going somewhere; I had a terrible mind to just roam. But can't help how you feel. I figured after she'd passed, I'd lost everything. I wasn't going to be arrested, so I had a .38 automatic pistol with nine bullets in it. And I kept it on me, riding them trains. They just didn't bother me and I didn't bother them. But I'd made up within myself before I was going to be arrested. I'd rather go on down and get it over with it. But, now, that wasn't right. But you can get in that shape worrying. Some kids may not care; see, I cared about my folks. But I rode a train many a time with a pistol—wasn't going to be arrested.

Now, I been on three trains that wrecked, but I wasn't in the wreck. I got off just at the town behind and got on another place. And the same place I was, all of 'em went in the ditch. When it ain't for you—if the Lord with you, you ain't nothing gonna happen to you. I stopped in Temperance; Sonny Boy Pendergrass, he's an undertaker friend of mine in Smithville. Have a little fun; I'd go on to work. The next day, my sister had moved and I didn't know. I knowed the street where she said she stayed on, but I didn't know exactly the house. And I got off there so we could have a little fun, and the—there's three or four people that was on the same train, and they was all in that boxcar and I got off the train. Went on down there. I gets about halfway to work when they started around one of them curves and put sixteen oil cars in the ditch. Wasn't nobody survived. I'd a been in the mess. And they told me when they come up, "You sure would be glad you didn't stay on that train." I said, "What happened?" "Nothing. Just sixteen of 'em, all of them on there was dead, kilt."

I come out of Austin on the Missouri and Pacific—Iron —— (??) —and we come around that curve. We'd stop at that hurdle where that old car was jumping up and down and that's a way, you know. I said, "Let me get off of this thing before I nod or something and get shook off here and get killed." And I went on up there toward the engine; found a coal car and crawled over in it. And we got to tailing where we went around that stock pen, come around that curve coming into town, the edge of town. That old creek there—they call it Stan Creek—just across that. They had oil running down beside of this road like water where it busted them tanks when it went off. And I was on them tanks, oil tanks. So you see, if it ain't for you, you ain't gonna get it. I had three of those capers thataway. I didn't know why I didn't stay where I was or not. But that night I got off that train in Sears they took water. I said, "Let me find me a place up here." Told that boy that—we'd been to LaGrange down there, playing a little dance at the K. P. Hall. I said, "Before we fall off this thing and get kilt, sleep"—we ain't had proper sleep. And we walked around and find a boxcar open right next to the engine. We crawled in there and before we got in there good—man, we was nigh about sleep. Just tired. Went on down, and just as it turned that curve going into Elgin, the train brakes was grabbing and made a lot of racket. I said, "What is that?" Right when I heard the engineer say to the foreman, "What happened back there?" He got off and walked back there. And he say, "Ain't nothing but about eight or ten cars in the ditch back there." Oil tankers. We jumped straight up! And got off that car and walked on into Elgin. Then, of course, when they come through Elgin going north—we going to Taylor, we got on where they left. Or they went out there and got the cars that didn't wreck and brought 'em into town. Called the wreck at Smithville and they come out [and] took care of the rest of it. But—

That doesn't give you second thoughts when you see a train pile up like that? That didn't shake you up a little bit? Make you want to walk a little ways before you got back on?

Unh-uh. No, I tell you—I tell you my ideas about it. 'Course it may be, may say it's stupid; you may not. Doesn't matter. What's for you, [the] way you are gonna get it, you can't go 'round it. It ain't be a way if the Lord will for you to die by train or car, you're not gonna die. You gonna survive. But when you're bond is up, [you] can't go, "Now, I've caught trains and knowed about all of that after then," with that one thing in mind. If it's the way I got to go, I can't get around it. You can't dodge it. If it's for you, you gonna get it. And if it ain't for you—that's what I tell about man. Man can't do nothing but talk. If it ain't the Lord's will for him to do something to you, he can't do nothing.

I know a woman at work who got shot back of the head and come out here by her nose—the bullet did. And I was scared of that woman; I don't want her to get close to me, 'cause she's supposed to have been dead. And the guy that shot her in the hairdress place, he went on down the street and shot himself. The ambulance come by and got her and then picked him up. They oughta left him laying there. He was going with this woman and she had a husband. 'Course she was wrong to start with. But she told him that her husband was good to her and she decided she gonna try to treat him right. She told me he's nice to her and she going to quit messing around. That's what he shot her about. And he went into her hairdressing place, and she was in the chair. And the woman that had been working on her, she sort of backed off while they was talking. And he shot her back of the head, and it come out right by her nose. Right there. Now, how in the hell can you survive shot through the head? But every time I'd see her, I'd say, "She supposed to be dead." But she wasn't. He shot himself and fell down and then tried to get up. (*laughs*) That was out on Eleventh and Dutton Street, in Waco. I remember it just as well—

How about medicine shows? We haven't talked about that at all. Can you tell me any interesting experiences with the medicine shows? How'd you hook up with them, and what were they like?

Well, it's nothing to it. You're just a traveling outfit that goes everywhere and sells medicine. And you play the show. But, now, they got a few people like comedians that might sing and crack jokes. And by me being able to play in most keys, it wasn't no trouble for me. All I did is get the key they sang in and let 'em sing it. If they start to singing without music, I'd pick it up and follow 'em several times. Then I could go down with it.

The thing that's interesting about that today, those of us that are around have no idea what it was about. Can you describe a performance?

Well, they gotta show—some of 'em had as good a show you could hire. If you went to a tent and played a salary. And it's all free. Well, we had a platform. We put up a little stage, you know, and had a background canvas. You go up the steps and get on that stage and had it lit up with lights at the top. And we'd see the people standing down on the ground all around. You know, people want to stand out there and sit out there or nothing. Just dry. You play their overtures or something that might interest the people—not no blues or nothing, just some kinda song that was popular. And then when they get ready to put the show on, well, you disappear. And they make announcement about the show coming on. Then when they get ready, you open up the show with whatever song they gonna open it up with. They'd dance and do the show. Then after the show, they talk that medicine and then they sell a quite a bit of it. Because some of that medicine, they make it up with that oil of wintergreen stuff, and if you got a pain in your arm or somewhere and they rub it with that, that pain's gone. It won't cure it, but it'll stop it from hurting you. And one or two of them people testify to that in that crowd, and they can't get out there with it fast enough, people buying it. And when they start out there selling that medicine hollering, "Sold out, doctor," and "Go back and get some more," and all that, well, you just play overtures while that's going on.

How many people involved? In the shows that you worked in, how many people in all would be in a troupe?

Oh, I don't know. They didn't have no women on there. It was all men. They have—they all sell that medicine when the show wasn't going on. It was about six or seven of 'em.

How long would a show like that go on? I mean, what would be the length of a performance?

Oh, I guess thirty or forty minutes at the best.

How often would they do that? Would it be during the afternoon? The evening? Night?

At night. Sometimes they'd do it on Saturday evening, some late little town that they was at. They'd open up, but mostly at night, nighttime.

Would you do that just on the weekends, or would that happen during the weekdays, too?

Oh, every day in the week. In any town, every night they had shows going on. Them people in them little places ain't got nowhere to go. They'll go down there, and if they find out that medicine he's selling will help, or stop pain, or whatever ails you, and see them people buying it and somebody tells somebody about how good it was, Charlie, they'll buy that man out. Takelax and all that, people —— (??) coming that made that stuff. It was good.

How often could you play one town? Could you do one show in a town or two shows and then you'd have to move on? Or could you be there a couple of days? Or did it depend on the size of the town?

We'd be there a week sometimes, and we'd stay over in the second week. Didn't have no limitation. As long as the show was paying off, they're buying that medicine, you could stay there if you wanted. But if it wasn't too good, he'd make arrangements and we'd move on a Sunday to the next spot and put up our little outfit Monday night.

Would they have an advance man? Would a guy go into the next town that you thought you were going to go in and put up some posters or something like that? Or would you just hit town cold?

He'd drive over there. It wouldn't be too far. And get the spot where he going to put up the show at. See, they'd leave this town where we're at on Sunday. Not Saturday night. They wouldn't go— They'd go to bed and get up Sunday. Then move in there and they'd be ready by the night. Everybody go down and get 'em a room, a place to stay, or whatever they wanted. And Monday they'd put that thing up and have it ready way before night. That goes on. But you stayed sometime a week or two weeks in one place.

How about the law? You ever have any trouble with the law? Would they give the medicine shows any problem coming through?

The law?

Yes.

No. They don't want nothing but that little money they get for taxes, you know. Somebody rent it; you get a permit, pay a little money. They get a little money out of it; that's all they want at all. But they traveled quite a bit. They went to all states and things. That's just a hot time a year show. You couldn't use that up to late up in the fall; too cool and too chilly.

Can you tell us some of the nicknames you had other than Grey Ghost?

Well, it depended on where I was at. I's called Son Putney in Waco. That wasn't my name; that was my grandfather's name. And up in Oklahoma they called me Piano Son. I don't know, over there around Lutieville, they called me J. D. and one called me Shaw. I said, "I wasn't no Shaw; I was a Williams." But they give you all kinda nickname. But I don't pay that no mind. Son Kid, Son Putney, Piano Son. See, in Taylor that's what they called me. Son Kid. Everybody over there that live in Taylor now that knows me, that's what they call me. One of my grandfathers was named Kid Jones, and they said I was just like him or something, I don't know. Son Kid. You always tell where they was from, from what they call you. I could tell whether they was Oklahoma or Texas or what town by the name what they called, or what they knowed the nickname, what I mean.

How did you manage to be around Texas, be a well-respected player, and miss recording all those years? Didn't anybody ever want to record you?

Oh, they did. Some people come up there at the university, Mr. Owens know him, from down in Arizona, gots—had me record music for him. And he tell me about sending me, sign up and get some royalty. I told him, "Forget about it. Just whatever he do with it, that's all right." I didn't try to get nothing out of it. I was playing down there for skating rink. They's going round and round, skating. They had a piano over there. And I'd play every now and then. They come down there from the university. That's where they got hold to that Hitler down there, what I composed. But, oh man, that's way back there. You'd remember, I guess, when Hitler was in his prime—or heard about him if you wasn't here. Well, that was in them days that he was; the song was about him. Hitlerism. Mussolini. That was an Italian, I think. But I had all them involved in verses in that song I composed about Hitler. It rhymed good. They sent it to London and they played it over there. [I'm] sure, German people heard it. I don't know how they felt about Hitler. But I used to have 'em laughing outside. I ain't gonna play that piece. I ain't gonna have that man coming after me. But I wasn't scared of that. I was just putting 'em on.

I heard you say you played for a skating rink. Did you play any different there than you played other places? I mean, did you have to play special pieces? Or play them in a special way?

No. You wouldn't go to a skating rink and go to playing blues. You'd play some kinda tempered progressive music, something. Maybe "Twelfth Street Rag," or "Shine, Shine on Harvest Moon," or "Dinah." Things like that, you know. They's skating, but it's just to having music at the skating rink.

Would the skaters ever be after you to play special pieces for them?

Oh, you know that somebody always going ask you can you play so-and-so. But they stopped—all them skaters stopped when they come in and recorded that piece. They stand there listening.

I worked for a man from Kentucky, and he learned me how to make recipe how to make whiskey, three kinds. And the recipe to make pure grain alcohol outta Irish potatoes and sugar wood. Calls for some equipment for that alcohol. You got to have something like a cylinder where you can put the Irish potatoes and slice 'em, and layer your Irish potatoes and coat it with sugar, and then put another layer on it. Have it in a warm place where it can ferment. A hole in the bottom of that churn or whatever you got it in—that cylinder, like—then you put the weights on top of that cylinder to mash 'em down and let it ferment. When it come outta the bottom of that churn, it's pure grain alcohol. Irish potatoes and sugar—you wouldn't believe that. 'Course whiskey, you can set that with chocks [shocks], corn chocks and yeast cake make corn whiskey. You can make food whiskey outta prunes and peaches, apricots, stuff like that. Then you make rye whiskey and use rye instead of peaches or corn chocks. And you can't get a copper cooker—that's hardly, near about impossible—because they don't make 'em for them kinda bootleg outfit. But you can get an ordinary old zinc or tin five-gallon oil can, fix you a cork that'll go in there where you pull that oil out. Tight. And put you a copper pipe down in there, hollowed out, and seal it. And put that copper coil in some water. I think the water—it's better to put you about twenty-five-pound piece of ice in the tub and put the coil over in the tub. When that boil and that steam get that coil when it comes out the end of that pipe, nothing but whiskey.

What part does copper play in that?
Hmm?

It sounds like you've got to have some copper in there somewhere.
You got to have a copper coil, that's what you definitely got to have. Now, you can cook it in that tin oil can, five-gallon can, but it's got to have that copper coil, round and round it, put that in the water. Put you some ice in there so when it hit there it'll do okay. It comes outta there pure whiskey. And by me not drinking whiskey, I had a spoon that I put that in, touch, and take a match and light it, and if it burn blue, it's still strong enough. Don't bother it. Later on you can do that, and it go to fluttering like it want to go out. Then you pull it, put some more mash in the cooker, and start to cooking again. Yeah, I can make all that stuff. Well, I learned it from this man I chauffered for him. He's from down there in Kentucky. He runned a still down there once upon a time, and he give me all them recipes. Three or four kinda whiskey and grain alcohol. I never fooled with alcohol much, too much—expensive getting a cylinder like you had to have to put that stuff in, and sugar, Irish potatoes, and weight on it, and let it ferment—rot, in other words. And when it come outta there, it just knock your hat off your head. Oh, man, that's years ago. I was just a young man. I was grown. I was grown enough to be driving a car like around the house, but I was young. It's been a—let's say about sixty years. That was way back.

I read that at one point you settled down in Austin. What caused you to settle down?

My people and going to Corpus and they talk, talk, talk. They had me a job there with the school. One of my nieces' husband had been working in the school when they was, and they wanted to put me to work right away. And I was on my way to Corpus, take another piano-playing job. I'd been playing in Houston thirty months in one place. And they was mentioning people from home. We went down there and didn't get back. They got killed. They didn't want me to go. Say, "You can go to work here." That boy told me that married my niece, "Anytime you get ready, you just let me know and they'll put you to work." I said, "Well, I'll let you know." So they talked and talked and talked. Not that I was scared or anything, but one night one mind say, "Well, you don't know about that place down there out on the highway, you know, outta town. Might be a bad place. Go to work here and be 'round some of your folks and friends." So I hollered in, told him I'd go to work.

So that Monday they put me in Keene Junior High School. Stayed there. Then they put me over across the road in Martha Dawson on First Street. I stayed there a good little while and a storm break. Had to drive bus lot of time. Some bus driver didn't show up and the bus had to run. He'd have to get in it. He was the boss. He told me one day—he knew me pretty well after I was there awhile— "Hell, Roosevelt, I'm tired of driving the bus. I want you to come and take that bus-driving job." I say, "Mr. Dunbar, I can't leave here. I got to stay here. If you get some custodians out there and break them into the jobs, teach 'em about all the waterworks and the hoses and the mowers, what all that had to be done there." And he said, "Well, I'm gonna have to leave you there a week. That oughta give you plenty of time." I said, "Well, you got who you're gonna put out there; let 'em come out there and be broke in. Then I can help you out." He said he tired of driving the bus, you know, when he is. Wasn't nobody else and he's the boss, and the children had to get to school. I went to driving a bus, and that was the end of that school custodian work. I stayed there right at twenty years.

They give me the onliest run that nobody wouldn't keep long. They's quitting, threatening to quit all the time, going to the city park out there on that mountain. That curvy road. Them mesquite trees was the biggest trees they had out there. And if you come off that hill and them brakes failed on you, you're through if you don't know what to do. I told him, "Don't think I don't know how dangerous that is out there." I said, "But I figure I got enough skill in my driving to control it in case, you know, the brakes go out or something coming over the hill of the road." The road's crooked, going 'round the mountain. And so I stayed out there, and they all dropped their head and said, "We ain't think you're no fool." I said, "Yeah, you all thought I didn't know how dangerous it is. I know why you can't keep nobody out there. They work a little while and they either put an application for another job or quit." But, see, I figured this about it: I ain't gonna be coming up there running fast. And if the brakes go out, I just get over there against that mountain and just let it—put the pressure on it, and let it drag on that mountain till it come, it'll come to a stop. You hold that steering wheel tight enough. So I just draws on around there going 'round. 'Course you can't shift down. You can't shift into reverse if you're going forward. You'll just strip the transmission, that's all you do there. But if you have it in gear and it's rolling, like low gear, second gear, and you need to race that motor and let your clutch out, that would brake it. That'd slow it up; that'd stop it. So I stayed out there until I retired.

But I'm still holding on and I ain't give up yet, but time brings about a change. You ain't what you used to be, and don't let nobody tell you that you is, 'cause you ain't. And I just go 'round. I'm a piano man, on account of Mr. Owens. Ain't nobody else in the world I'd a come up here [for]. I know it's cold up here. I ain't been up here, but I read a lots. I hear about the weather—zero and all that junk, different places. You see, I been in and around, but I still have to do for myself. And I had pneumonia on both sides one time. Then I had it single. I had it double in Waco, and in Abilene I had it again. I left there and went to Amarillo and Pampa before I got well. I'm not the strongest person in the world, and I have to take care of myself. But I ain't give up yet.

Part Two **Postwar Glory**

John and Grace **Brim**

John and Grace Brim, a husband-and-wife team, were the king and queen of the Gary, Indiana, blues scene. John was renowned for a pair of sessions organized by blues harmonica virtuoso Little Walter. Walter arranged for these sessions to take place and accompanied with his own band. The tunes recorded at these sessions — "Ice Cream Man," "Rattlesnake," "Be Careful," and "You Got Me Where You Want Me" — rock and lope along as first-rank classics of postwar Chicago blues, fueled by Walter's high-octane harp and Fred Below's drums. These recordings are held in rightful regard by blues fans worldwide.

But it's the obscure earlier recordings John and Grace did for the Fortune, Random, and J.O.B. labels that truly define their identities as blues musicians. Grace Brim may be the only woman of the postwar era to sing pure, unadulterated down-home blues, untainted by pop influences, picking up

John Brim. Photo by Frank Zirbel.

where Memphis Minnie left off and Minnie's one true heir for the years after World War II. Fans lament her limited output — only six sides featuring her vocals.

Grace Brim. Photo by Illinois Slim.

Despite the celebrity blues status generated by his classic Chess label recordings, a truer profile of John Brim would see him weigh in as one of the rare "deep" bluesmen to record in Chicago in the years after the war. It was a short list: Muddy Waters, Floyd Jones, and perhaps Big Boy Spires. Deep blues is a genre devoid of most of the usual hooks that attract the casual blues enthusiast: it doesn't rock or swing, no string bending or guitar pyrotechniques. It's played at a dead-slow tempo and can—at points—sound atonal. Yet to those who understand the genre it packs an emotional charge and burns like a slo-mo lava flow. It took me years to appreciate this genre of blues and to comprehend its power and emotional impact. These are the kinds of recordings John Brim made in the earliest years of his career.

The relationship between John and Grace Brim was a curious thing to observe. I don't know to this day whether or not they were ever officially divorced. I guess the best way to describe their relationship was as a longtime couple who lived apart. Grace lived in the family home on Hanley Avenue in Gary, while John had his own apartment. Grace once told me that John had his own girlfriends and she kept her own boyfriends, but I don't know when they found the time to entertain outsiders. Anytime you wanted to contact John you called Grace, because that's where he always was—at the house on Hanley. Whatever differences had arisen between them over the years apparently didn't prevent them from hanging out together a majority of the time. And it was clear from his conversation that John considered Grace his wife, regardless.

John never did stop performing or trying to make it even though Grace had pretty much quit performing, but I do recall they showed up one weeknight where I was playing in Chicago, at Lily's on Lincoln. John came up and did a set, and Grace actually came up and sang a number—a real rarity. In the last years of her life Grace told me she promised her mother, on her deathbed, that she wouldn't sing anymore blues. As far as I know, she never did.

This interview was recorded in the Brims' living room on September 27, 1993. Grace Brim died on September 25, 1999. John Brim died four years later on October 6, 2003.

■ ■ ▓

Let's go back to the very beginning. Tell me when and where you were born.

JOHN: April 10, 1922—Hopkinsville, Kentucky. I don't know, Steve, I just liked the blues from a youngster on up. I always did want to meet a lot of guys I never dreamed when I was a teenager that I would meet, like Sonny Boy, Tampa, Big Bill Bronson [Broonzy], Big Maceo and Dr. Clayton—all those guys I would hear down home. Oh, I thought those were the greatest guys ever, you know! And the Seeburg [an early jukebox brand name]— Chet and I, we'd go out downtown. At that time—you know, seventeen, eighteen—you could get in anyplace. Anyway, they didn't bother you then much. So then we done quarrel with my girlfriend and everything; she liked Peetie Wheatstraw and I liked Big Bill. And then we'd kinda argue about who's the toughest, you know, and all that kinda stuff back in that time. I was an early teenager, and there was guy named Prentiss Clark could blow real good, and I just, you know, started blowing harp. "Train Puff," "Fox Chase," "Sittin' on Top of the World"—tunes like those. All them guys had this, whatchacallit—down-home style. Wasn't no style then, really, until Sonny Boy Williamson around '36, blowing the style he had, you know. Back in like the [old-]timey music—then later years he'd blow. He'd just blow and wanted to blow some. Didn't have a band, you know.

Was that the kind of stuff you were blowing when you played harmonica?

JOHN: Back in that time, yeah! And I got up around nineteen, I wanted to play guitar—saw a friend at home play guitar and showed me a few points. Then when my mother passed in '41, I came to Indianapolis. I had a grandfather living in Indianapolis, so I came up there to see if we could get better jobs, you know, better opportunities. So that's how I left home, figured I had a better chance.

Were you playing music for a living when you went to Indianapolis?

JOHN: No, I couldn't play guitar much. I got my first guitar in Indianapolis.

So you had a day job this whole time?

JOHN: Well, yeah, yeah. I worked in a cleaners, valet shop/dry cleaners. And I heard all about the other musicians and I wanted to meet some of 'em. And I followed guys like Pete Franklin, Scrapper Blackwell, Jesse Ellery, and followed 'round with them and we hung out together and learned some from them. Well, the first one I met was Peetie Wheatstraw—Harmon Ray is the second Peetie Wheatstraw, you know. He only made one record for RCA before I met 'im. Must have been in the late thirties for RCA, because I saw the record, you know. But I don't [know] whether he did anything else for 'em or not.

Was he billing himself as Peetie Wheatstraw or as Harmon Ray around town?

JOHN: He was known as Harmon Ray, but he sound so much like Peetie Wheatstraw—he sound just like him. So that's why a lot of 'em in Indianapolis named him Peetie Wheatstraw. And he took me around and we meet Jesse Ellery, was playing with Jack Dupree. 'Cause I been knowing Jack Dupree, too—since '41. And I tell people now I know Jack Dupree, but he may have done forgot me. 'Cause he used to play the midnight shows every week and Jesse Ellery'd play guitar—he was a very good guitar player. Jesse, where he come from, I really don't know, or if he was raised around Indianapolis. Jesse was a good guitar player, an all-way-round guitar player! He played jazz and the blues, and I think Jesse come up under Scrapper some, but veterans like him and Pete Franklin could play anything—"Body and Soul," "I Surrender Dear"—anything, not just blues, all the way 'round. Like Jesse, I think, got his style of playing in D, D-natural, and E from Scrapper. (*laughs*) But I don't know—I guess he was just a natural player, he was real good. And Scrapper used to be around with us. He used to go get Scrapper, or we'd go where he's at and we'd drink corn [liquor].

Do you know whatever happened to Jesse Ellery?

JOHN: I heard that Jesse had passed, 'cause I goes over there every so often. I was told, I think, that he had passed. All them I called their name is dead.

What had happened to Scrapper after Leroy died?

JOHN: I'm not sure just exactly what Scrapper did for his occupation. I know we'd go get him sometimes and he'd set up and hook up and play, him and Jesse. And they might go get Pete Franklin, and Pete Franklin was poison. (*laughs*) He wasn't but seventeen years old when I met 'im. And he was just—if you ask me—tougher than they was. (*laughs*) And they was tough! But Pete could do so many things!

Would you say that Pete Franklin had Scrapper's style, all the way?

JOHN: Yeah, he'd play his style—and Jesse Ellery's. Play his style and ideas that he put a little more in it than Scrapper did, you know. I think as time went by they'd add more to it, you know, to the soul sound. I switched to guitar. The first year I come I bought a guitar, but I couldn't do anything with it. And I followed these guys, and they showed me some points and helped me out some with the guitar. I know Pete used to tell me that I was gonna be faster than him one day, which I never believed it, you know. And I met his mother and she was nice to me, and I'd go to their house and met his sisters. I met Dorothy when she was about seventeen and Louise, too. And his father, he was a very nice man. They all just liked me and it was part of my home, like when I come here on Jackson. I call her Mrs. Franklin. Mrs. Franklin was a great blues lover. Something like the lady where I go here on Jackson—she play the blues all the time. Come over and sit down to talk, she put a blues record on. Mrs. Franklin was the same way. And she was a very nice lady. And they used to live on Twenty-ninth—*East* Twenty-ninth, years ago. Before she bought this home and she died where they're at now, the home they got. He died first, Mr. Franklin. And then she had sugar. It went to her leg and she finally died. She died in '53, I think it was, 'cause we had the cleaners over on Broadway.

Whatever happened to Guitar Pete?

JOHN: Oh, Pete been dead a long time. Pete drank quite a bit, but he was a heck of a guitar player. Boy! And Doug McGregor was really the one—and Homer Wilson—were the ones that helped me get myself together with the timing and everything. That was back in '44.

What kind of style was Homer playing?

JOHN: Homer was just a regular blues guitar player, you know. Him and Doug. And they played different songs, like whatever songs come out.

You wouldn't put them in a particular style of playing?

JOHN: No, not really, 'cause they would just do other people's songs: Sonny Boy Williams [Williamson]—Doug did "Sail On," and they named him Sail On around Kentucky and East Chicago Heights, where he lived at. And Homer, he played. You know the thing back in the thirties—[if] you played guitar, you'd have a string of people following you from here to the corner just playing guitar. Sometimes you'd go from one house to the other one—maybe seven, or eight, ten blocks—-and you'd have people following you having a few drinks, having a good time back in those days. So those are the guys that really helped me come along started trying to get together with the blues.

When I first seen Dr. Clayton in Indianapolis about '43, he come to the Log Cabin on the Avenue [Indiana Avenue, the main strip of the city's African American section]. He was booked there. Matter of fact, I met Doc outside the club and we talked a couple times. And lot of people say, "That's not Doc Clayton," 'cause he hit that bottle heavy. And they say anybody that be like him be drinking out there was not great. He was *famous,* you know. So when I come to Chicago a year or so later I met Doc again at Thirty-fifth and Rhodes. I don't [know] why I picked up on Doc when we got to Chicago, but anyway we got together, me and Sonny Boy Williams. That Dr. Clayton was a heck of a singer, man, and he was reversible, too. He could sing classics, rhythm and blues, and church songs, too—had a terrific voice. And I didn't get a chance to meet Bill Gaither but one time—I met him one time. I met him through "Peetie Wheatstraw" [Harmon Ray]. See, they knew one another 'cause he went to the army in World War II, and when he got out of the army I met him on the Avenue, and talked with him, he and Peetie. Peetie brought him by where I was at. And I talked with him, and I never did get to see him anymore. So I think he died a year or so after that.

Was he [Gaither] from Indianapolis? Was that where he was playing?

JOHN: Yeah, I guess he was there for many years before I came, you know. And he did a few things for—Decca, I think it was, after Leroy died. He just took over—[he was] called "Leroy's buddy."

What finally caused you to leave Indianapolis?

JOHN: Well, that's a long story, you know. I left Indianapolis, I come up here looking for a friend of mine. We had a run-in, and so she came up here in Chicago. And I had peoples here—I had two sisters here and an auntie at that time. And that's how they got me in Chicago!

Were they in Chicago proper, or were they in Gary?

JOHN: They were in Chicago.

So that's where you went before you came to Gary?

JOHN: Yeah! I was here from '45 to '52 before we moved to Gary. I was playing, messing around with a guy named Edward Hollis, blowing harmonica. He called hisself Sonny Boy. So my sister keep telling me, "Well, I told you, that guy's not Sonny Boy Williams." And she said, 'I'll tell you what I'll do. Sonny Boy'll be there on Thirty-fifth, between Prairie and Indiana. So when he come 'round again—I told 'im about you—just tell 'im you wanna meet 'im." So then one time she told [me], "Come on, go 'round his place, this club on Thirty-fifth. Sonny Boy's gonna be there." So I did. That's how I met John Lee Williamson [Sonny Boy Williamson I]. That was in about '46. I was playing with John Lee Williamson when Muddy Waters asked me, "Mister, would you mind me playing a piece on your guitar?" And Sonny Boy told me, "J-J-J-John, that's Muddy Waters." He had never made any record. And in 1946 at the Purple Cat—that's Madison Street.

What kind of a band did Sonny Boy keep when you saw him? How many pieces?

JOHN: Well, at that time he had a guy with him that did some recording, name Memphis Jimmy [Clark], played piano. Called him Memphis Jimmy, played piano for Sonny Boy. You know, on a lot of his recordings Eddie Boyd played piano for him, on some of his records there. Memphis Jimmy —— (??) light-skinned boy, he died—oh, I guess a good while after that. After a while Sonny Boy and I didn't play. I'll make it short. We had a gig that—I don't know, Sonny Boy, *he* wanna talk to some girl; *she* wanna talk to me. And Sonny Boy say, "I got the gig for us," 'cause we had played there—me and another fellow, Bill. And another guy, Johnny, had a club on West Madison—in the twenty hundred block. And this guy was a very nice guy, and he told me, "Yeah, John, you got Sonny Boy, come on!" I said, "Well, he's out in the car. He ain't feeling too good." (*laughs*) So he told us to come in for the week, you know. I got the gig and he [Sonny Boy] just kinda difficult about the girl. He told me that we weren't gonna play no more over there. The guy didn't want us to play no more. So me and Homer Wilson were living in the same place at that time. So we said we didn't believe that. We didn't have no car or nothing, and so we go along to the weekend. That was on a Friday night. So the next Saturday night, sure enough this time he had L. C. McKinley—he had L. C. McKinley playing the guitar. He still had the gig! (*laughs*) That's the truth—that's the God's truth. I wouldn't lie on it! (*laughs*)

How did you meet Tampa Red?

JOHN: Well, Tampa—only way I can tell you about Tampa, you go where he played at! And we'd talk, but we really didn't play anything together. Tampa and I, we didn't play anything together. But Big Maceo, he would take me by—they were good friends—around with he and Johnny, Johnny Jones, pale piano player. He had Big Maceo's style, you know. He was playing with Tampa at that time, before he got with Elmore James. And so we'd go by and holler at Tampa. I mean he was playing right there next door to where I live at—right there on Thirty-fifth, a little old club, he and L. C. McKinley. I'd go out, I'd go down there. But as far as playing, we never played together. We'd go out to his house. See, he was the headquarters. Just like you got your company, everybody come to your house to rehearsal for your recordings, that's what Tampa was. Thirty-fourth and State. So we'd go up there sometimes.

Would you rehearse or would you just watch the other folks play?

JOHN: Well, [Lester] Melrose was living—he was the white fellow that handled a lot of dudes to take to RCA back in that time. You know, Tampa Red, Memphis Minnie, Lonnie Johnson, and all them—they come through Melrose. And he handled all that part. And they come out on Bluebird, owned by RCA. So they'd go up to Tampa Red's, and he'd come by and listen to you. He's the one that would give you the okay.

Did you ever try to make records for him?

JOHN: I didn't really try to get with RCA at that time. I just think I wasn't ready, you know, or good enough to try anything, you know.

Wasn't the H & T, where Tampa used to play, located across the street from his house?

JOHN: Yeah, Tampa was on the opposite side of the street. The H & T was located on the west side of the street—just like this house is—in the thirty-four-hundred block, and Tampa was in the thirty-four-hundred block. His house was near the corner down the block, and the H & T's near Thirty-fifth.

How did you get the gig there?

JOHN: I don't know. Somebody told us—this colored guy named Red that managed the place for a white fella. Robert Nighthawk was playing there, I think, when he made "Anna Lee" and "Sweet Black Angel," and they left town. Robert Nighthawk, they say his wife play drums when he was playing at the H & T. And she played drums and Robert played guitar. And that's how come I think they wanted us, 'cause Grace blew the harp and I played guitar. So I went down and talked to 'em and we got the gig. I don't know, I think I only had two or three pieces at that time.

Who was in the band at that time?

JOHN: Me, Grace, and a piano player named Willie, Willie ["Longtime"] Smith. I don't know whatever happened to Willie Smith, 'cause we had got up in the bright lights then and all, and Willie [was] doing pretty good. Willie Smith copy Maceo's style.

What did Grace play at this point? Was she on drums or harmonica?

JOHN: Well, she was on harmonica first. And you know, I didn't know Grace could blow for a long time. There about '48 I came in from work and I hear somebody blowing harp. So I asked her, "Where's the fella at?" I said, "Where's the man at?" (*laughs*) She says, "No man." I said, "Well, who was blowing?" She says, "I was." I say, "You mean to tell me you can blow harp and blow in time like that?" She says, "I guess." So we got a guitar, got a harp, and worked out a little, you know. I didn't even know she blew it. So that's how she started working with me. Then she took drum lessons from Odie Payne and bought a nice set of drums—and started drumming.

About when did Grace start drumming?

JOHN: Hmm, she was playing drums about 1950, '51.

How did the two of you meet?

JOHN: Who, me and her? 1946?

GRACE: You and Homer Wilson were playing music—two guitars—and they were downstairs in the basement where I lived at. And I went down there and that's how we met.

JOHN: And that was back in, like, '46.

And how long did it take you, Grace, till you started playing harmonica, or come out with it in public?

GRACE: Not long, Steve. When I was a kid, you know how kids are. Well, my oldest sister's husband played harmonica. And you know how that is. You run around and you get it, and he'd tell me to blow it like this. My daddy blowed a little bit, too, you know. So one day he [John] came home, and I was at home and he heard me, and he came in the house and he says, "Where's the man?" I say, "What man?" (*laughs*) He said, "I heard a harmonica." I say, "Yeah, but that was me—it wasn't no man." So he goes, "Oh, I'm gonna put you to work!" And in about a couple a weeks, there we were!

JOHN: Yeah. I was telling 'em that you go on the matinee at 3609 Wentworth. You would go down and blow— Boy, people would come, just to come on a Sunday on a matinee, just to hear her blow the harp. 'Cause it was strange at that time—a lady blow the harp!

Were you blowing like anybody, Grace? Like Sonny Boy or Jazz Gillum?

GRACE: No-no-no-no-no—nobody but my sister's husband. That's the way he blew. I learned how to do that like he did. Just his style and I picked it up. It was my style.

JOHN: Grace, what time you started drums? '50? '51?

GRACE: I started drums in '51, 'cause after Boonie was born—'50, '51.

JOHN: 'Cause Odie Payne come to the house.

GRACE: Was Boonie born in '50 or '51—'51! I bought 'em [drums] before he was born and started playing after he was born.

Why did you make the move to Gary?

GRACE: All my family was here.

JOHN: All her peoples live here. Her close people—brother, sister, mother, father.

During this whole time when you were playing music did you have a day job?

JOHN: We had our own business, and I worked practically all the time. We had our own record shop and cleaners.

GRACE: Then we came over here and opened one up.

JOHN: Then we had a machine and we moved. We had a place where we could have living quarters in the back. We had the same—similar in Chicago. So we moved over here.

GRACE: Father & Son Cleaners.

JOHN: Father & Son Cleaners.

You had a record shop and cleaners together?

JOHN: Uh-huh.

You sold the latest records?

GRACE: Oh, yeah!

JOHN: I know when Elmore made "Dust My Broom"; I know when Howlin' Wolf made "Moanin' at Midnight." I know the year. I know all of 'em.

GRACE: I remember when Ray Charles wouldn't even sell. We couldn't sell Ray Charles records. And what was that record he came out with?

JOHN: When we were on Vincennes [Street] we couldn't sell Ray Charles records. He was with Swingtime Records out in California. But when we moved over here he made "It Shoulda Been Me with That Real Fine Chick"—"*eatin' ice cream and cake.*" That started selling for Atlantic, I think. Then he come out with another one a year or so later, I think—"I Got a Woman Way Across Town." And he ain't looked back!

GRACE: He really went then!

Did owning a record shop and hearing records help you at all as musicians?

GRACE: No. As far as I could see, it didn't help.

JOHN: We just sold the records for the money, and we were already in the racket with the cleaners. You know, we was into playing.

Was there a separate blues scene in Gary?

JOHN: Yeah—oh, yeah. We had clubs like the Pulaski Bar, over here on Nineteenth and Virginia. And Muddy, Walter, and me, and Jimmy Reed, we played over there on and off for five or six years, didn't we?

GRACE: And the one over on Fifteenth and Adams. What was the name of that one?

JOHN: Buddy Guy played over there a pretty good while—three or four years. And the new club.

GRACE: Also on Thirteenth and Adams. We played over there quite awhile.

JOHN: I'm trying to think of the name of the club over on Fifteenth and Adams, Grace. And there'd be a lot of roadhouses right back here. Know where I met you at, used to be four or five roadhouses right there. We'd get through playing at one o'clock in the morning then go to a roadhouse and play—sometime till four or five in the morning. Oh, Gary used to jump. This used to be a money town.

The two of you are the best-known blues people from Gary. Did Gary have its own blues people in addition to the folks we know from Chicago?

JOHN: *We* were well known. They had a lot of musicians, good musicians playing blues, jazz, and semiclassics, like Charles Fergusen—Little Jazz we call him. Morris Lane, Chu Crump. We had quite a few musicians here in Gary [who] go way back.

What were Jimmy Reed's and Eddie Taylor's connection to Gary? Did they ever live in Gary?

GRACE: Jimmy Reed stayed here for a while, but they lived in Chicago. Jimmy lived with us.

JOHN: Jimmy and his family stayed with us awhile. He stayed with us when he made his big hit "You Don't Have to Go," '55.

GRACE: He was working in the steel mill when we first met him.

JOHN: It's funny how we met Jimmy Reed, Grace and I.

GRACE: Maceo was sick and we didn't have nobody to play with us. The lady told us that she knew where a harmonica player was. And so she told me where he lived, and I went across the street to Jimmy's house. That's how we met him.

JOHN: Was that Club Alibi?

GRACE: Yeah, that was the name of it!

JOHN: Right at Ninetieth and Mackinaw. And Jimmy stayed across the street back down there. Say, "I know a boy John that might could play with y'all." He come in and set up, and I let him play sometime. I believe it was in the forties, wasn't it? About '49?

GRACE: Yeah. Somewhere along in there.

JOHN: So I say, "Can he play all right?" She said, "I don't know if he could play with y'all or not, but I'll send and get 'im." And I said, "All right."

GRACE: I went and got him.

JOHN: Did you go get him?

GRACE: I walked in the door and told him who I was, and he said, "Okay, Cousin Peaches, I'll go with you." That's what he called me. He called me that all the time.

JOHN: He come over and said, "I don't know if I can play with y'all, but I'll try if you want me." I said, "Sure!"

GRACE: He had a real nice wife, too.

JOHN: So Jimmy and we played that night, but that was the end of the gig and we didn't see Jimmy anymore for a couple of years or so. And we heard a record out, you know, that Vee-Jay made put out on Jimmy. And Grace and I say, "That sounds like the fella played with us that time." So then advertise on radio here, you know, they played East Chicago Heights, Black & Tan, a club over there. So we gets in the car and go over there. There's Jimmy Reed! And Blind John Davis, I think—you know, the piano player?—and Jimmy Reed, and I don't know who else played drums with 'em. Then we had got back with one another, you know, from then on.

Did Kansas City Red spend time in Gary?

JOHN: Red would be over here. Red would be everywhere—

GRACE: But he lived in Chicago, though.

JOHN: Me and Earl Hooker— How I met Kansas City Red back in the fifties, we had the cleaning shop—you remember, Grace? Earl Hooker brought him by, 'cause we kinda raised Earl Hooker in a way, me and her. So they hooked up together and played together a lot. Earl Hooker brought him back from Kansas City or wherever. I been knowing Red a long time. Well, see, at that time— It got to be '50 or '51 that we started playing more [or] less professional-like—maybe a little before that I was, and then me and my wife. So Earl and all us were friends, and L. C. McKinley. So Earl would come over to our house all the time, stay, work out with us, and eat with us. His mother liked me and Grace. He'd just be by my house, over all of the time.

GRACE: And he had his own little group he played with. He had his own little group and he'd go down the street. One had a washboard, one had a tub—they'd play on the streets out there. They had a band wasn't nothing but kids.

JOHN: About twelve or thirteen years old then. 'Cause we been knowing Earl Hooker since he was about—fifteen, sixteen, Grace?

GRACE: Yeah, he was about that age. Used to come over to the house all the time when we first met him. But he was a good guitar player. He had three or four young guys and they'd be sitting out there with him.

JOHN: And he could play country and western, man!

GRACE: Oh, he could play anything. Cuss you out on his guitar—he could do all of that. I've never heard anybody say the things on a guitar that he could say on his guitar. Sit his guitar down, walk over there, and walk back, and his guitar would still be saying what he put on it to say. He'd say, "Forget you," and that guitar would still be saying, "Forget you—forget you—forget you!" And he'd been gone and come back, and that guitar was still saying, "Forget you." I never saw that before!

JOHN: People say that some people get it and make it and get off pretty easy. Well, it's been a long struggle with a lot of us—Little Walter, Muddy Waters. And they didn't get where they got just a jump. It was a lot of work—and work for nothing almost a lot of times. We have played with two or three guys a night, because it was in our blood to play. And to play for the crowd, it makes you feel better. Just like now—if you playing out in a club or something, you feel better. And just sitting around doing this, you sit around play your drums, you want somebody to hear you play that drum. If I'm playing guitar and somebody hear it, somebody else gonna like it, too! But it wasn't no money in it for us, for a long time. All us used to be together over at 3609 Wentworth—Son Joe, Memphis Minnie, Willie Mabon, and Eddie Boyd. See, they have a matinee, every day about this time. And Muddy and them was playing out there, Little Walter and them. And Muddy had first made "Catfish Swimmin' in a Deep Blue Sea" ["Catfish Blues"]. Then they was plugging it so good, you know, kinda brought Muddy on up. And all us would meet there on Sunday for the matinee.

Did you have anything to do with Jewtown? Did you play Maxwell Street at all?

JOHN: Yeah! Earl Hooker and them—I'd go out with 'em. We'd go out there on a Sunday, you know, and we'd play all around the front that end. They play around the back there now. There'd be three or four different bands.

GRACE: They would save places on the street to play—

JOHN: Right on the street—no, we'd play on the street. We'd earn nice bread out there, man. They'd begin throwing that money. That was about '46, '47, '48—before we ever made records.

Did either of the two of you ever make a dub, a noncommercial recording, just to hear how you sounded?

GRACE: No, I never did.

JOHN: Well, I have did a dub. That's before me and Grace started. I made a little dub, you know, to hear ourselves. It wasn't with no company or nothing.

You didn't take the dub to any company to try and promote yourself?

JOHN: I think I did take a dub to Sunbeam, 'cause they operate the little cleaners on Chicago and Thirty-fifth. They had a label going that had this lady, Little Miss Cornshucks, she sing something like Dinah Washington. But she did one thing for them on the Sunbeam label. That was the name of the cleaning shop they had there on Thirty-fifth. Their brother was an arranger and everything, but they didn't keep it long. Marl Young—that was Harry's baby brother—he did a lot of arrangements and he was in college. He had a brother Harry, had a brother Richard, he had a brother Vess. Yeah, there was about four or five of them boys.

And so you brought a dub to the Young brothers?

JOHN: Yeah, but they didn't do nothing for me, but Marl was handling that part. They had a heck of a cleaning business going on. They had a shop, man. They didn't have a cleaning plant. They had a shop and they bought a cleaning factory from their shop, bought a record label—till they got swindled outta a lot of artists. People dubbin' on 'em or something—I don't know.

What was the dub you took to them?

JOHN: By that time I was doing something on the style of Bill Gaither. I done forgot what the tune was.

You were on guitar?

JOHN: Yeah. I told you that Big Maceo and Tampa was hooked up together for years, you know. So Maceo come around the H & T, where me and Grace was playing. That was about '47, somewhere in there. And Big Maceo heard Grace blow the harp. So then he told us about this guy in Detroit wanna do something—said he'd get us on doing some records, and we was interested in that, you know. Cutting some songs, you know, and give us a little up-front money. And we made records with Big Maceo. He took me and my wife to Detroit [in] 1950. She did that "Strange Man/Mean Man [Blues]," and I did a couple of tunes for Fortune. Far as I know, he never did get to release them. So then Maceo started playing with me and my wife. You know, he couldn't do too much with that other hand, but he was hell with that left hand, but he had that stroke of his—but he was pretty good.

So he was playing a one-handed piano at that point?

JOHN: Yeah.

Was he playing one-handed piano on the records themselves?

JOHN: You know the record we made, "Strange Man"? That['s] him playing piano on it. Well, he was about the baddest piano player around—at that time.

And what about "Mean Man"?

JOHN: Yeah. Grace sang that. It was on the other side of "Strange Man." "Mean Man" was on the flip side.

For Fortune Records—you and Grace made recordings for Fortune. Maceo also recorded some sides. Were you on guitar accompanying on his sides?

JOHN: Um-hm. I'm on guitar, bass, and piano.

James Watkins is listed on this session. Who was that?

JOHN: James Watkins must have been the bass player.

How did you make connections with Joe Brown and J.O.B.?

JOHN: He was a little company trying to get up. We met Joe Brown through J. B. Lenoir, which was a good friend of ours. We did his clothes, and before we got famous we was all friends anyway. I met J. B. the first week he got here, 'cause Doug was living in a place where J. B. was living there on State Street. And he told me he could play some guitar and sing his voice like a lady. So Doug was telling me about him—say, "I'm gonna bring him over!" so me and Grace could meet him. That was before we got the cleaners. Remember, Grace?

We was on Brown when Doug brought J. B. Lenoir. Do you remember we were in Leonard's [Leonard Chess's] office when J. B. first came here. When he first came here, before he got with Williams.

GRACE: Yeah, when he first came to Chicago.

JOHN: Yeah. Before he got with Leonard we both knew J. B. Lenoir. He was with J.O.B. before he got with Leonard. Yeah, he was with J.O.B. all the time. And when he did things with Leonard, he was still publishing with J.O.B. But anyway we did some with J.O.B. Try to get up, get his company going, you know. Joe Brown, me and Sunnyland [Slim] and a few of us.

How did you end up with Sunnyland and Moody [Jones]?

JOHN: Moody ain't never been on the session. Moody was never on a session with me. But me and Sunnyland and—I think, Grace, you playing drums on it—on that "Trouble in the Morning," weren't you? "Trouble in the Morning"—I forget what the flip side was. Sunnyland was on "Humming Blues," and he was on "Trouble in the Morning," too. Sunnyland's on most of the stuff I made for J.O.B. "Young and Wild"—J.O.B. Records.

Where would you cut for him? Where was the studio?

JOHN: It was down in town—down in the Loop!

So he used a regular recording studio?

JOHN: Yeah. It was a big studio, wasn't it, Grace?

GRACE: It was over there on Wacker Drive, wasn't it? Somewhere downtown. I think it was Wacker Drive.

JOHN: I got a record and I forgot about it. Pete Franklin and I played on a Leroy Carr and Scrapper Blackwell style. And it been so long that I didn't know that was me playing the guitar. And I told my wife, I said, "You know who that is? That's me and Pete." We'd be in the studio, 'cause I got Pete to play on some stuff with us. "Moonlight Blues." Pete Franklin was playing guitar on that. We got Cotton on the tenor sax. We got Alfred [Elkins] that played bass. Alfred that played bass, we all used to call him Second Muddy Waters, he favored him so. He play bass. I ain't saw him in so long. Grace, don't you remember? You ought to remember him. You sung in some places, too, that used to play with somebody. And he favored Muddy Waters so much. He played bass? He played that session with us and he played bass, and Ernest Cotton blowing tenor sax, Sunnyland on piano. I think I was just singing and let Pete play guitar. I don't remember if I played guitar, too.

How long did you cut records for Joe Brown? How did the thing with Joe Brown end? What finally put an end to it?

JOHN: What put an end to it, Steve, by being in records and being in and knowing it for a good while—that he didn't have the national 'bution [distribution] that Chess and Atlantic had during that time. He didn't have the national 'bution.

Who had the Random record label?

JOHN: That was a Jewish fella had a big distributor on Fifty-fifth here in Chicago. Roosevelt Sykes was a good friend of mine, too. And his wife worked there where you go down and buy records—you know, go to different distributors. And Passhay [Monroe Passius], he had a little label called Random. And me and Roosevelt Sykes did—I did one record, I forgot. You got the name of it there?

"Dark Clouds"?

JOHN: Yeah!

"Lonesome Man [Blues]"?

JOHN: "Lonesome Man"! That's right—you remember, Grace? We recorded that for Passhay on the Random record label he had. His name was Passhay. I don't know the rest of his name, but he was a big distributor on East Fifty-fifth.

How did that connection take place?

JOHN: I approached Passhay about it. I had some good stuff, you know. As a matter of fact, I did some for J.O.B. Records, called "Trouble in the Morning," and got airplay from Randy's Records in Tennessee, you know. Randy's Records—you know John R? They played it some, and Passhay told me he would do this on me—with me and Roosevelt Sykes on the piano.

So the J.O.B. session came before the Random session? You already had a record in hand?

JOHN: Yeah. My next step was to go with the Parrot Record Company—one of the big step[s], which was Al Benson. Me and Albert King, Albert played some with me over in Gary before he got going, too. So we went to Al, told 'im he's B. B's brother and so forth. I knew Al before he started the record company. But Albert went there and was gonna cut a record for Al Benson. And he wanted me to play second guitar for him. And he told Al, he said, "If John don't play, I don't wanna cut it!" And I said, "I also got a number, Al." He said, "We're gonna do this on Albert, and you come back next week." This was in '54, and me and Grace and Eddie Taylor and Jimmy Reed, we all played together most times. And he offered me to do an audition. So Al walked in—we'd already set up and run it down. He heard one verse and he said, "That's enough! I wanna get a dub on this!" He said, "John, I wanna play this about eight days." He played it about four days and he had to pull it off the air. They went to calling for it. It's called "Tough Times."

How did you wind up taking Jimmy Reed and Eddie Taylor in there? They were on that record, right?

JOHN: Yeah, and on "Gary Stomp"! Eddie Taylor, Jimmy Reed, myself, and Grace.

GRACE: Jimmy Reed. Was he playing with us at the time you made that record? I think he was playing with us, wasn't he? Off and on? And Eddie Taylor was playing with Jimmy.

How come you two were never on the Vee-Jay label?

JOHN: Oh, it's a long story, Steve, about that Vee-Jay connection. I knew Vivian well, me and Grace both. She had a record shop over here, and she was a big disc jockey over here. I was supposed to do "Tough Times" with her. As I said, it's a long story about that. I was gonna go with her on that, but something happened and we didn't get together. And I'll tell ya about it sometime. . . . Well, what happened, Steve—I'll make it short—I went to Detroit, as I told you. Big Maceo took us there and so forth and so forth. And after Leonard Chess heard this, he wanted that number to do it again. Because [he ran] a little small company which he could get away with it. And the man brought me the number, and I brought it to Al Benson's nephew—a record distributor for him, this fellow in Detroit, the fellow we made the record for—Fortune Records in Detroit. And the record that Al Benson made, Sam Evans plugged the record and plugged the record, so it was doing good. So Chess wanted it. I said, "Okay, but why you got to have Muddy and Little Walter and them to play behind it?" I said, "We doing all right, and we playing behind me and Big Maceo and so forth." So there was the difference, right there. He said, "Well, I'll do something on you the next day," which was a lie. So I told 'im, "No, I won't do it like that." He got mad and stayed on me a long time.

GRACE: See, he didn't want me to play with Muddy Waters but just that one time.

JOHN: Well, if she and Muddy Waters and them gonna do a tour together, I wasn't gonna have any wife, see, and I knew this. I knew this was so. That was the whole idea of that.

GRACE: Oh, please—please—please—

JOHN: And he kept that against me a long time. I'd go over there to buy records and he'd [come] hard at me. He told Little Walter, "I'll call John sometime." Walter said, "Hell, no! You're gonna call him tonight!" Walter had told Grace to tell me to be at the studio. I told Walter I don't wanna do nothing with him.

'Cause it's a funny thing, Steve. He record that session; he paid me session money. He put them records on the shelf, you know. "Rattlesnake"—that was recorded in '53. "Ice Cream Man," "I Got a Lifetime," and another one—I forgot right now just what it is—"Just a Dream." And they put them records on the shelf. He was still angry. You know he was dead before he knew that "Ice Cream Man" with Van Halen sold over eight million copies. I mean, he never knew.

But they never came out until after Leonard's death?

JOHN: They leased those things out because Phil [Chess, Leonard's brother and business partner] closed the company up. But it sat on the shelf for over twenty-something years.

The sessions you did with Walter list the Aces. Were they in the studio on these sessions?

JOHN: Yeah. For "Ice Cream Man" and "Rattlesnake"—all four of 'em—"I Got a Lifetime Here."

Did you rehearse these tunes ahead of time?

JOHN: Unh-uh. You know, Walter and the Aces, they was heavy anyway, fall right in. Just run it down maybe once. (*laughs*) All four of them tunes. Little Walter was in command then, see. He had made "Juke" and "Can't Hold Out Much Longer." You know, Walter used to be around Leonard and them, sit around the studio. And it was a little while before he let Walter blow on Muddy Waters's records. Then when he made this "Juke," he could tell Leonard what he wanna tell 'im. That's how I got the recording. Then he let them sit on it. So now I go [in] '54 and I sign with Chess. I go to Al Benson and make "Tough Times." It took a big seller, so he didn't give me my royalties, I went back to Chess. Chess know I would sell then, and I made this "Go Away" and "That Ain't Right." After Walter got through doing his session, I'd do my session.

Do you recall what Walter cut?

JOHN: No, I can remember what me and him did one Saturday when we did "My Babe." Phil come out of the office and did that. We did "My Babe" and, I think, "Off the Wall." And I did "You Got Me Where You Want Me"—and "Be Careful." Chess gave us one record apiece.

And Walter cut the same day you cut on that second session as well?

JOHN: Yeah, Little Walter's band backing me. Little Walter backing most of the stuff I did on Chess.

GRACE: Was that [Fred] Below on drums?

JOHN: Below on all of it on drums, yeah.

GRACE: And the Myers[es], Dave and Louis on there?

JOHN: In '53. But they left. Little Walter had got rid of them, you remember?

We had Robert Jr. and this boy that died just not long ago—Luther Tucker. He just died not long ago. And Little Walter spoke some good words to Leonard for me. Me and Al didn't get together on the royalties. (*laughs*) I was already with Leonard. I had cut some stuff, like "Ice Cream Man" stuff. It stayed on the shelf for twenty years before they released it, see, 'cause Leonard was away from me 'cause I didn't let my wife do the stuff with Muddy Waters. But he told me a long time after that, that he really got angry with me, 'cause I didn't let him. Well, I had my wife for my band, not for Muddy Waters's band. (*laughs*) And he didn't release the stuff. Muddy had him to cut it in '53. So then when I made "Tough Times" in '54 with Al Benson, he saw I would sell. And Leonard was the kinda man, he didn't like to gamble. He wanted artists after he know they would sell. So I get my release from Al Benson, I go back to Chess in '55. So I made a record that's not on that *Whose Muddy Shoes*—it got into *Cash Box* and *Downbeat* for ten plays—called "Go Away."

Your band on that record featured the Dalton Brothers. How did you pick up the Dalton Brothers, and who were they?

JOHN: They were in our band. They were two brothers. That band we had in Gary. I picked them up over here.

GRACE: W. C. Dalton and James Dalton.

JOHN: They was on "Go Away" and "That Ain't Right."

Who played what?

JOHN: James played the harmonica.

GRACE: W. C. played guitar.

JOHN: He played second guitar for me.

How long was that band together? Was that a working band you had here in Gary?

JOHN: Yeah, they worked with me. I don't know—a couple of years, wasn't it, Grace?

GRACE: Yeah, a couple years. Wherever we played they was with us.

JOHN: I was with the Chess—that was in the fifties. I didn't do anymore recording, 'cause I left Chess. He had so many artists, so I left Chess. I was supposed to go to Vee-Jay—well, I told you it was a long story about that. And then I just held up a while, you know, before I did anything else. Quite a few little companies wanted me, which I wasn't interested in.

Was there ever a point when you said "I'm not going to do music anymore" and let it go?

GRACE: Not him. No! No! No! No!

JOHN: (*laughs*) No, Steve, I never did that. But I'll tell you one thing—as a professional blues artist, I don't do anything for little or nothing anymore. It's got to be worthwhile.

GRACE: I said that [no more music], but John never say he ain't gonna do no more music!

JOHN: She quit awhile, but, you know, they wanted me over in Europe last year and the price wasn't right, so I didn't go.

But you're also the guy who won't fly, aren't you?

JOHN: Well, if the price get up good enough, I may take that chance. They say what's gonna happen, gonna happen, but, you know, the way I feel about it—if I'm afraid of something, you can't change my feeling. Money's gonna be here when I'm gone, you're gone, and everybody else. It ain't no good to you gone. (*laughs*) So you feel it's gonna happen the same way in a car or something, but you feel better driving that car, right? I have a pretty bad accident, I may make it. But you get me up there flying in that airplane, *it ain't gonna stay up there!* And if it falls, it's gonna destroy everybody. In a car you have a bad accident and still may not be killed—that's the way I look at it.

GRACE: If I had the money, I'm going on up there.

JOHN: Oh, you know, she ride a motorsickle or anything. She got a lot of nerve. She go fishing, she not scared of snakes. I'll be running from snakes, she be laughing at me. She gotta lot of nerve, but there's certain things I'm kinda afeared being around or with, you know. She like airplanes—*she like it!* I say, "I'll wait till you come back."

Jody **Williams**

As a teenager in the 1950s Jody Williams was a highly regarded guitar player. During his time on the Chicago blues scene he made a series of classic recordings under his own name, played and recorded with Howlin' Wolf, and is heard on records by a variety of artists in postwar Chicago.

Jody Williams is a unique individual in the world of blues. In the early 1960s, when blues was eclipsed as a commercially viable music by rock 'n' roll and soul music, Jody, alone it seems, saw the handwriting on the wall. He put the guitar in its case, hid it under the bed, and prepared for a new career. While most of the legendary names of postwar Chicago blues starved in the urban backwaters, Jody sent himself to school, became an electronics engineer, and retired twenty-six years later from Xerox. After his retirement in the late 1990s, he reemerged with his classic postwar guitar style intact, unpolluted by the passing decades and the various types of pop music.

Those of us who ventured onto the Chicago blues scene in the 1970s were privileged to know and interact with many of the biggest names in Chicago blues, including Sunnyland Slim, Big

Jody Williams, 2002. Photo by Kurt Swanson.

Walter Horton, Floyd Jones, Eddie Taylor, Billy Boy Arnold, John Brim, and many others. But Jody was among a small cadre of highly regarded players whose names and records we knew but whom we never had the opportunity to meet or see perform: Reggie Boyd, Lefty Bates, Lee Cooper—and Jody Williams. Among our circle of friends, only Randy Weinstein, a student at the University of Chicago, had ever met Jody. In the early 1980s Randy took the initiative by simply calling Jody at home. They did an interview that was used as the basis for a Jody Williams profile for a local Hyde Park newspaper. The rest of us had to wait until the late 1990s to make Jody's acquaintance.

Jody Williams's reappearance was big news. In a music genre where each passing year is noted by the number of casualties drawn from a dwindling pool of vintage blues people, the reappearance of one of the music's true guitar slingers was a reason for celebration, and I was in a position to appreciate it firsthand. Jody chose one of the bands I was in, Chicago-Bound, to hone his chops. This wasn't just a nod to the blues tradition of sitting in for a number or two. Jody would show up at least once or twice a month and play for an hour—or ninety minutes. I also had the good fortune to work a couple of the bigger gigs he scored early in his comeback. First we worked the University of Chicago Folk Festival, and then Jody hired me to play at the 2001 Chicago Blues Festival—on the main stage. In the course of all this shared bandstand time I asked Jody if he'd do an interview with me for the radio program.

We met at Jody's place in Hyde Park, which was like entering Geppetto's workshop. There must have been a hundred or more electronic devices—I think most of them were clocks. All of them lit up, buzzed, chirped—and all of them, it seemed, at the same time. In listening to recordings of the interview, during pauses in the conversation you can hear the amazing ambience of a low-level electronic cacophony in the background. Jody's was the longest single-session interview I've ever done. I believe that I came away from this interview with three hours of tape. Jody seemed to take great joy in his comeback and related the tales of his early days with that same joy and enthusiasm.

This interview was conducted on October 12, 2000.

■ ■ ■

I was born in Mobile, Alabama, in 1935.

And when did you come to Chicago?

When I was about five years old. Between five and six, around there somewhere.

Did your entire family come here?

My mother, my brother, and my sister. My father died. So it was the four of us. Well, music wasn't in my family, but I did play the harmonica. But not blues. I wasn't introduced to any blues. I played stuff like the Harmonicats. "Peg o' My Heart" and all that kind of stuff. "September Song" and all that. That's what I played. I even played the harmonica on stage shows at school. And I liked it. As a matter of fact, I'd been on radio shows down at the Merchandise Mart on NBC, playing my harmonica. Well, I was—as I say, I played the harmonica and that was my thing. And that's what I enjoyed doing. And I was also drawing and painting at the time. So it was a toss-up of me playing harmonica professionally or being a commercial artist.

Well, when I met Bo Diddley—see, we did a show together. Let's see, the previous week, I'd just done a show over on the West Side. It was either the Broadway or the Joy Theater. It was over on Roosevelt and Ashland. There was two theaters over there. Well, the following week, I did an amateur show over at the Willard Theater. The Willard Theater was on Fifty-first and Calumet at the time. And that's where I met Bo Diddley. With him playing the guitar and Roosevelt playing that washtub bass. I liked that sound. That's the first time I'd heard a guitar played and paid any attention to it. And I liked that. So we got backstage, me and my harmonica and him on the guitar and that washtub, and we—had a nice little group going there. But I liked the sound of that guitar. So I asked him, I said, if I was to get me one could he give me some pointers on how to play it. He said sure. And the next week, I spotted a guitar in a pawn shop over on Forty-seventh and Wabash—between Wabash and State, rather. And I told my mother about it. The price was—it was a Silvertone, electric Silvertone—$32.50. I told my mother about it; she got it for me.

So the next week after that, I was out there on the corner with Bo Diddley. He showed me how to run that little bass line, and that's all I did. Dum-dum-dum-dum. Dum-dum-dum-dum. That was it! Throwed the hat down there on the ground and out there on the corners. Sometimes—there was an old guy—as a matter of fact, there's his picture right there. Casey Jones. You ever see him? Well, he'd be around over on the Maxwell Street area. We played over there. He'd be all around the West Side and the South Side. That's the only man I know that trained a chicken. He had the chicken jumping through the hoop, drinking out of a cup, and everything. That's Casey Jones; he's dead now. But I think he lived to be about 102 years old. Sometimes he'd be playing on one corner and we'd be playing on the other corner—two guitars and a washtub, with the hat down on the ground. We did pretty good. We did pretty good.

Like down on Forty-third Street, we would play—well, there was a lot of traffic on Indiana on account of the cabs and stuff. But we would play that corner there on Forty-third and Prairie and all up and down Forty-third Street and Forty-seventh, Fifty-first, over on the West Side. But we was all over the West Side and the South Side, playing the corners.

What kind of material was Bo playing at that time?

Stuff like Bo Diddley. That's it. That's all he did. Sometimes we played house parties. As a matter of fact, you see some of those things up there in some of the taverns up and down on Forty-seventh Street. And now the Indiana Theater was right there at—it was on Forty-third Street between Indiana and Prairie. So we ended up playing there. I remember the old Rhumboogie [Club]. Are you familiar with old Rhumboogie? They used to be down on Garfield Boulevard, just east of the train station, east of the el station there. I think that originally was owned by the boxer Joe Louis. Well, they had a—I remember, I think, Von Freeman, or was it George—the guitar player? The guitar player George Freeman. They were playing down there and there was also a modeling show. They had models down there at night. And George Freeman and his band would play. And Bo Diddley and I, we were the extra added attractions. So when they would go on intermission, we would play. They had more clubs than you had musicians to play in them. So that's how we did it. That's how we did it. Two guitars and a washtub. That's how we started.

When I started, I wanted to learn to play a lot of the blues. But I wasn't learning anything out there on the corners. I got to the point where I was just about starving for information and knowledge about playing that guitar. Well, Bo Diddley taught me about all he could, running that little bass line and a few chords—a couple of chords, rather. I took some lessons from a music teacher—a couple of music teachers. They weren't teaching me what I wanted to know. I didn't want to know how to play scales; I wanted to know how to play some music and some blues!

Then Henry Gray, Morris Pejoe, and Frank Kirkland, we were playing at a club. It wasn't a club; it was a tavern down here on the corner of Thirty-eighth and State Street. The Tic Toc Inn. Bandstand way up—almost up in the ceiling. As a matter of fact, the drummer, Frankie, almost fell off of there one night. Got drunk. But they even had the piano up there. Henry Gray played the piano. And about the middle of the night—I wasn't doing a lot of singing then. I'm playing a lot of background, and I'd wait until everybody get drunk—about three quarters of the night gone—and I'd ease up to the mic there and sing a song, and then I ease on back into the background. (*chuckles*) Had to build up your courage for that kind of stuff, you know. I wasn't ready for it yet. But little by little I started learning more and more of the things I wanted to play. Not scales—I mean, it's all in the music. But I wanted to hurry up and play something, learn how to play it. And little by little I got it. As a matter of fact, I went to a club where Muddy Waters was playing, down on—it was a hotel down on the corner of Fortieth and Michigan. I went in there and talked to him and Jimmy Rogers. I started hanging out with those guys. And I started picking up more.

Now, to show you about coincidence, Henry Strong and Otis Spann, they played with Muddy. But we all worked together before they played with Muddy. As a matter of fact, we had a flat together. Down on Thirty-eighth and Wabash. Henry had came here from down South. I forgot where Spann came from, but somehow we got together and we started playing together, the three of us. And even Little Walter's uncle, he even played with us. As a matter of fact, he stayed there with us some time. Louis. They looked like brothers. I don't know where he is now, but he was down in Louisiana. And, see, I think he went with Muddy first, before Spann did. Then after Henry got with Muddy, then Spann went with Muddy Waters. But we were still living together. So they had just got back in town and Muddy had been out on the road. And Henry went out to the store to get some bread or something that we had run short of. Well, meantime, while he was gone, about ten minutes after he left there was a knock at the door. So Louis or somebody went to the door, asked who was it. The guy said, "FBI!" (*chuckles*) Then he asked, "Does Henry Strong live here?" He said, "Yeah, he live here, but he's not here right now." So he was getting ready to close the door, and the FBI man put his foot in the door. Showed his FBI identification and everything. He said, "We'll come in and wait." There was two of them. "We'll come in and wait."

So in the meantime, Louis, he's up in the window combing his hair, trying to fix his hair. And he looked downstairs, here come Henry coming down the street with a bag of groceries. So he come upstairs. The FBI men, one of them's sitting down; one's standing. So when Henry stuck his keys in the door, everybody tensed up. So when Henry opened the door and come in with the grocery bag, the FBI man, he stood up. He said, "You Henry Strong?" Henry said, "Yeah, I'm Henry Strong." He kept walking, you know. He acted like the FBI man wasn't even there. So he says—he put the bag down on the dresser. And he usually put his change in the drawer, you know. So he pulled the drawer out. The FBI man did like that, like he thought he was going for a gun, you know. So Henry hadn't noticed what he was doing, because he kind of had his back to him. So he went back in the kitchen, getting things together. The FBI man had been looking for him since he left down South. They sent him induction papers to go into the army. And he didn't show up. Well, he didn't show up—they'd been tracking him. Everywhere Muddy went, when the band left, the FBI showed up. They'd been tracking him about six months. He didn't know, because he wasn't down there when the papers came. So what they did, they took him over to the—where the post office is over here, around Forty-first and Halsted. They examined him then. And they said—they brought him back to the house. They said he'll find out if they would accept him in a week or ten days. About three days later, he got a notice he had a bad heart. They rejected him. Then he went back out on the road with Muddy. And it wasn't too long after that—

About what year was that?

Let's see. He had a '54 Dodge. It must have been around '54. Around in there somewhere—'53, '54. And remember—the reason I remember is because he had this car and he wasn't paying the notes on it, right? So they was trying to repossess the car. But he had it hid. (*laughs*) And so one night when he'd come in, you know, there was a mechanic's shop. He put it in the mechanic's shop and lock it up. Well, one night he didn't have enough space in there, because he had cars that he was working on, so he left it outside. So that's where the repossession man found it. So it must have been about three o'clock in the morning, you hear a horn blowing downstairs. We were up on the third floor. You hear a horn blowing. So we finally got up and went to the window. It was the repossession man, had it on a tow truck, and he blew the horn and waved to him. (*laughs*) To let him know he had the car, you know. Then waved to him. That was the last time he saw that car. We had some times back during those days.

We were living in the building. Leonard Chess's father owned this. It was a big court-way building right on the corner of Forty-sixth and Greenwood. And everybody thought Jake was the janitor down there. Even though he cleaned up, but Jake was the one that owned the building. That was the father of Leonard and Phil Chess. So McKie Fitzhugh, the disc jockey, he lived in that building. Some of Muddy's musicians. Wolf's musicians. Danny Overbea. A few other people. Musicians.

And they were scheduled—Muddy Waters was scheduled to go out of town. They were going on a tour, do some one-nighters. Well, they had played out at the 708 Club this particular night. Well, Henry had a jealous woman. Juanita was real jealous. You know, when you're in show business, there are a lot of people—men and women—they want to buy you a drink or something like that. Send you a beer and all that. Well, that's what happened to him. Some woman sent him a beer and he dedicated a song to her. Well, I guess Juanita didn't like that.

And remember, it was in 1954. The reason I remember that is that Muddy Waters had a gray and red Oldsmobile Holiday Coupe. I remember that. So when he come from the club, he was upstairs—supposed to go upstairs and get his stuff together. And as he's up there getting his stuff together, this is when Juanita approached him about this woman. And he's trying to pay attention to what he's doing so he can get out of there. So she stabbed him. And the way the building was arranged—the back door all the way to the end of the hall—that wasn't the stairs; it was a little balcony there. And we're up on the third floor. He had ran— when she stabbed him, he'd ran past the back door. The back door was almost in the middle of the hall where you go down the stairs. Well, when she stabbed him, he ran past the door and found he couldn't get out on the balcony. He had to come back past her. She stabbed him again. Blood was all up and down the hall. So I go in my room and locked the door. She wasn't getting to me! So Henry ran down the stairs. So Muddy come upstairs to see what's going on. So he came in the door, asking what was going on. She started at him with the knife. So he ran back downstairs. Meantime, I slammed my door and locked it.

So in the meantime, Henry, they got him in the car and they took him to the hospital. He died on the table. He died that night. Muddy had to get rid of the car, because blood was everywhere. So they caught her a couple of weeks—well, she turned herself in a couple of weeks later. Out of curiosity, I went to the trial. I don't know how true it is, but they said a couple of her uncles in New York paid off the judge and lawyers, something like that, about ten thousand dollars. Ten thousand dollars was a lot of money in those days. So she claimed self-defense and she walked. I was there in the courtroom. As a matter of fact, that book The Chicago Blues Scene [Mike Rowe, Chicago Blues: The City and the Music], I've got a couple of copies of that, and it's even got his death certificate in there. The story of it in there. See him and Muddy playing.

How long were you actually in Muddy's band?
I wasn't in his band.

You were not in his band?
I was in Wolf's band. We just played together off and on. I wasn't in his band. I was in Wolf's band.

Earl [Philips] told me that somehow you and he hooked up. And that you were hanging around Muddy Waters and that Muddy actually sent you over to Wolf. He said that he had a new musician in town and he wanted to help him out. And so he sent you and Earl.
He may have, because I remember going down to the recording studio and—I think that's where I met Wolf at. Down at Chess Recording Studios.

(*Left to right*) Howlin' Wolf, Jody Williams, Hubert Sumlin, Earl Philips (*back*), 1954. Photo courtesy of Earl Philips.

He had just got here from the South. He had a big brown DeSoto, one of those suburban jobs with the jump seat in there, I think it was, like the cabs used. That's what he drove here in. So that's how we got hooked up. That's how we got hooked up. But I was the first one to play with the band here in Chicago. The very first one.

Who was in the band at that time?

Nobody. We started from scratch. Right here in Chicago, we started from scratch.

Do you remember how the band came together? Who did you recruit? How did you find them?

Well, I don't remember how Earl got in the picture, but after being around here for a while, he sent back down South and got Hubert [Sumlin]. Hubert came up, and Hubert and I played up there together. I played most of the lead and he played background. Then we had the piano player. You can see him there in that picture there. (*points to a picture on the wall*) Hosea Lee Kennard. That was his name. He sang, too, and played piano. But Nat Cole was his man. That's what he wanted to sing. As a matter of fact, he would nickname him

Yak, because he talked so much. (*laughs*) He called him Yak. But last I heard, I thought he went to New York. He could be dead after all these years.

With Wolf's band would you use a bass man, or would it just be two guitars?

Just two guitars. Hubert and I. That's all—from the time I started and ended with Wolf, that's all that was in the band at the time.

When did you start with Wolf?

It was in '54, because that's when he got here, that's when he came. Probably the early part of '54. The early part. And I stayed with him a couple of years. And we played over at Sylvio's. We played at Sylvio's; we played at 708 Club; we played at [Club] Zanzibar. Us and Muddy Waters, we played basically the same places a lot of the time, on just different nights. We played over on the West Side. I think at the Happy Home Lounge. Walton's Corner. There was a number of places we played. But the only ones—when I was in the band, the only ones that was in the band was the guys you see on that picture right there. Well, see, Philips not on there, you can't see him. But there's Hubert, myself, Wolf, and Hosea right sitting at the piano behind us. We would play at least five or six nights a week, if not more. Just in a different place every night.

Did you fellows have uniforms?

No, no.

How about Wolf's shows? What kind of venues would he play when you went on the road with Wolf?

You know, during that time, we didn't go on the road. We played right here in Chicago. Played all around the South Side and the West Side. But mainly places like the Zanzibar; all the clubs we played right here in Chicago.

Ask me about Wolf. The unusual thing about Wolf is his voice. I've heard one other person with a voice like that. That's Wolfman Jack. And he talked the way Wolf sounded. But that was Wolf's natural voice, the way he sang and talked. He talked like that all the time. If I tried to sing like he did, I'd be hoarse and my throat would be sore. He said, "*How many more years do I have to let you dog me around?*" (*singing in Wolf's voice*) That was his natural voice. If I sang it, I'd be coughing and carrying on. But you cannot sing like that without hurting yourself. But that was Wolf's natural voice. He was good at what he did. His voice was unusual. That's the thing that made him.

How long would you play a tune on the bandstand before you'd take it into the studio? Or would you? Would you learn a tune in the studio and record it there? Would you have it in hand on the bandstand before you took it in?

I don't know, because first Wolf's got to learn the song. He's got to learn the lyrics. Because if Willie Dixon would write something, the sort of songs that

Willie wrote, you're not going through all that stuff right in the studio. That would take some time. So he would have to learn it beforehand, before he got in the studio. But sometimes we would get in the studio, then maybe Hubert and I would decide how we're going to do the background and stuff like that. Like something like "Forty-four Blues"—I think we come up with that in the studio. (*sings*) *Da, da, da, da.* That thing we did in the studio. And the way Big Willie Dixon would write some of that stuff, you've got to know some of that stuff ahead of time. He'd give it to you ahead of time, and he'd hum it to you and tell you how it's supposed to be played.

Also, the stories about Wolf manhandling members of the band. Can you put that straight, or what you saw of it?

I didn't see any manhandling. But, now, I heard Hubert was getting man-handled every now and then. And Willie Johnson, they'd actually fight. (*chuckles*) But, see, I wasn't in the band then. I left. I left. We were playing Sylvio's and I quit the band that Sunday night. That Wednesday, I opened up at the Premier Lounge in Nashville with Memphis Slim. I had people standing in line waiting on me.

What year did you leave Wolf?

It had to be somewhere around '55, around '55, because I was on that tour there in '55 and also in '56. That's two separate tours we had.

Let's talk, then, about your records. Let's just go right through the list of records that you made and how they happened. Who was your first record for? Under your name.

Al Benson. Al Benson, he was one of the big disc jockeys in Chicago. That was on the Blue Lake label. And if I'm not mistaken, I think Big Willie Dixon wrote that. "Looking for My Baby" and—what was the other side? I'd know it if I hear[d] it, but I can't think of it right now. Oh, "Easy Lovin.'" I think that's what's on the other side of "Looking for My Baby." But "Looking for My Baby" is the side which— Back in those days, a lot of times disc jockeys would only play one record, one side. That's why when I wrote the song for Billy Stewart, he wanted to know what we were going to use for a B side. A lot of times you'd have a hit on both sides. Because a lot of times, Mark would say we're going to play the A side. That's the side that got played most of the time. Once in a while somebody would turn some over. "Hey, we got a hit here, too." That's the way it was doing.

So you did this—what is this, 1953, '54?

Around there somewhere.

Is this before you were with Wolf?

I think so. I think so.

Who were the side men on that? Who was the band?

Harold Ashby on the tenor [sax]. Lafayette Leake was on the piano, I think. Big Willie Dixon on bass. And the drums—I'm trying to think, who that first record—it might have been Earl Philips.

Okay.

It might have been Earl.

Did anything happen with the record that you did for Al Benson?

Not that much, because it's a small label. See, when you're dealing with small labels out there, you've got a problem with distribution, see, and that's something I didn't think about at the time. I'd just say, "Hey, I want to make the records." They thought enough of me to record me, and I just wanted to make a record.

You see that picture right there? You see what it say on the background there? Muddy Waters, Howlin' Wolf and the Aces—that's the Four Aces. Little Walter was playing with Muddy Waters up until "Juke" came out. When he recorded "Juke," he left from down in New Orleans. And Dave and Louis Myers, Fred Below, and Junior Wells, they had this little group called the Four Aces. And I mean they all played the same type of blues and stuff, you know. So Walter wanted his own band. So what he did, Little Walter and Junior Wells, they switched places, that's all. So Junior went to play with Muddy Waters. Little Walter took over the Four Aces. That's how they made it. So you had Dave and Louis Myers playing guitar.

As far as musician, Walter was about the best out there. He could play the harmonica like a saxophone. And I mean, he enjoyed—he was a hard-blowing player, too. As a matter of fact, he played the chromatic. He was about one of the first I'd seen to play blues like that on a chromatic. So he mastered all that stuff before a lot of these other guys did. These guys come along and they followed in Little Walter's footsteps, trying to play what he played years ago. He was good. People like Sonny Boy Williamson, those guys are good. But they had a different style. If you hear Sonny Boy and you hear Little Walter, you hear the styling is different like night and day. Different like night and day—like Henry Strong. If anybody want to copy anybody, they'd copy after Walter. And a lot of these harmonica players you hear out here playing harmonica nowadays on these records, they're playing Walter. He was like a pioneer.

I heard often that Henry Strong was as good [as] or better than Walter.

Oh, he was good. He was good. He was good.

Was it in Walter's style?

Um-hm. Yeah. If you listen to some of those records, you'll hear it. Everybody's playing Walter.

How many—Henry Strong's only on what? A couple of sides? I mean, there's only a couple of recordings that exist with him on them, aren't there?

He was killed before he could make any more, I guess. But he was good. He was good.

So you would say that he was as good as Walter? In your opinion.

You know, there are some musicians that—guitars is a good example. There are some musicians that play to entertain the public. Then there are some musicians that other musicians enjoy listening to. A good example—Earl Hooker. He was what I would consider a musician's musician. He played for other musicians. His style and techniques and stuff like that. Even though we played together a lot of times—with Junior Wells, stuff like that—I enjoyed listening to him play, even though I was right there with him.

The same thing with Little Walter. If you want to hear somebody play harmonica really good, you listen to Walter. And it seemed like that's what a lot of musicians would do. And they'd learn from him and they'd go play on their own. That's the way I saw it. Now, Walter was a damn good musician. He had other faults, but when it come to playing that harmonica—he had temperament, a short temperament and all that kind of stuff—but he was a hell of a musician, damn good musician when it come to the harmonica. People like him—Sonny Boy—that got the harmonica players into the union, because there's a lot of money out there being made and the union wasn't getting anything off of it. Until they started putting them into the union. Then they can get a little bit of it.

Let's talk about, for instance, Big Walter.

Walter Horton.

Walter Horton. Any comparison between the two of them?

Between Shakey and Walter?

Yeah.

I still think Little Walter—his style and technique—was a little better. More original. Because he played right along with the saxophone players. I've seen him do it. Now, that's not taking anything from Walter Horton! Because Shakey was good at what he did. They were good. And I worked with all of them. Shakey Head Walter, they called him. Then there was another harmonica player, Shakey Jake. Do you know Shakey Jake?

Shakey Jake Harris?

You know how he got his name? Shooting craps. (*chuckles*) People who knew him wouldn't shoot craps with him, see. But Shakey Head Walter, he got his name on account of his head shaking like that. But Shakey Jake, he got his name from shooting craps. See, everybody—if they got a little title like that, they got them somewhere. But I've listened to Walter. I played with Walter. I played with Sonny Boy. Then I don't remember exactly when Louis started playing harmonica, but he played harmonica, too. Because a lot of time he'd put the guitar down. Somebody else would play it and he'd play the harmonica.

Were any of the musicians bad? I mean, were any of them rough fellows?

Little Walter was rough. He'd fight in a minute. (*chuckles*) Yeah, he'd fight in a minute. But that was just his temperament. I remember he was going home from a gig one night on the West Side. And some—there was a car blocking the street or something. And he wanted to get them to move and they wouldn't move. And he jumped out of the car with his—grabbed his tire iron. And he approached them with a tire iron. They took it away from him and left him for dead out there.

For about three weeks he played—his head was all bandaged up. But he wasn't supposed to be blowing harmonica on account of—he'd blow so hard, veins were popping all out of the side of his head and everything. The doctor told him not to play. But Walter just had to play his harmonica. And one night he's down there at the Hollywood Rendezvous. I think his head was all bandaged up then. But not as much. And there was this woman, Billie, that was one of his girlfriends, I think. I don't know what he had done to her, but Walter was a Cadillac man, see. So he had this black fishtail Cadillac. I think it was a '49 or '50 Cadillac—Fleetwood—parked right across the street from the club. There was a vacant lot there where the funeral parlor was. So Billie, she had grabbed a house brick, one of those great big bricks. She just started throwing them to see which one she could throw the farthest. And she wind up and threw the brick across the street, trying to hit his car, and missed it. So she was looking for another brick. So somebody told Walter. Say, "Man, you better get out here. Bitch out here trying to tear up your car." He loved that Cadillac. He loved his Cadillacs.

So he run out there; he dropped the harmonica [and] everything and run out there. His head all bandaged up. Just in time to see her winding up. (*chuckles*) And he hollered. She threw it anyway and took off down the alley. (*laughs*) He run to the trunk of the car. He didn't chase her. He went to the trunk of his car. He had a little pistol in there, I guess. I don't remember if he shot it or not. I don't know what happened after that, but I think they finally kissed and made up. But, oh, he was crazy about those Cadillacs. Sometimes he would make a record or something, and he'd go down to the record company and tell Leonard he needs a down payment on a Cadillac. And Leonard would give him some money to keep him quiet, to get rid of him. As long as he got that—I don't know if he got any more out of him, but he got a down payment on a Cadillac where he got him another car. So I guess as long as the record company was keeping him with down payments like that, they were satisfied.

My thing—I didn't drink anything. I can see Elmore James and Sonny Boy Williamson and Johnny—the piano player, Johnny Jones. They drank Old Foster. Old Taylor. Old Grand Daddy. All those "Old" folks they drank. That's some strong bourbon. And if you listen to Elmore talk and sing, that stuff was killing his voice! That gravel voice. Sonny Boy Williamson, he's a good example. Now, I saw this. Sonny Boy—I'm sitting down front stage, in front of the stage in the Regal Theater. Sonny Boy is on the show at the Regal Theater. And have you ever seen anybody do the camel walk? Well, you have to see it done. Well, anyway, Sonny Boy, he's playing some —— (??), going back and forth across the stage doing the camel walk and a half a pint of Old Grand Daddy or something sticking out of his back pocket! (*laughs*) And he don't even know it. He's doing a camel walk across the stage. Stage is packed. The place is packed. And he's got a half pint of whiskey sticking up out of his back pocket. But that's the way those people were. You ever hear—I think he played saxophone—King Kolax?

Sure.

We were doing stage shows on the North Side somewhere. And in between shows out there onstage, he got a bottle and he tried to pass it to me. I said, "I don't drink. What you got?" He got a bottle of wine. (*laughs*) That was his drink—wine. Same thing. Now, take a musician like James Moody. That was his drink. They drank wine. They was wine drinkers. Because when I was down in the studio when Bo Diddley come in and tell me about giving Mick and Sylvia [Mickey Baker and Sylvia Vanderpool] singing "Love Is Strange," James Moody just went out to get some wine. Just went out to get some wine then. But, hey, that was their thing.

See, there was something—I didn't drink anything. I just wanted to play my guitar. I've been drunk maybe a couple of times in my life. Yeah. I was drunk. Once I was drunk about two days, two or three days. Me and Bo Diddley was playing somewhere. I'm sitting down. Sitting down, playing my guitar. And these women, they kept sending me liquor. Giving me shots like—I'm downing them just like that. I don't know any better. They send me a little shot; I down it. I don't remember how long this has been going on. But I think I was still in school at the time. And I was—I was a member of the South Side Boys Club. I was halfway going with one of Jesse Owens's daughters, because he was the manager of the South Side. You know, the Olympic champ? Well, he was managing the South Side Boys Club at the time. And I lived right there on the corner of Thirty-ninth and Michigan in the building right around the corner. So I'm sitting there, playing my guitar and downing these shots. All the while, I'm sitting down. The liquor hadn't affected me. Come time for us to go, and I tried to stand up. Somebody had to grab my guitar to keep me from dropping it. I was drunk for three days! They got me home. I sneaked in the house. My momma didn't know I was drunk. Sneaked in the house and I tried to sleep it off. The next day, the bed, the whole room was spinning! They say you put your hand on the floor to stop the room for spinning. Yeah, it stopped it for a little while, and then it would go on back and do its thing again. So I don't know how long that went on. I went back to sleep. So I got up. I was feeling pretty good. Drank some water. Got drunk again. Just drinking water! Got drunk again. Went down to the South Side Boys Club and drank some water or something down there. I staggered home. I haven't done that since. Haven't done that since. But I'm just not a drinker. I may take a little taste once in a while, just sociable. But, you know, there are some people out here, they only drink on two occasions: they're either by themselves or with somebody else. Sonny Boy and Elmore James, those guys drank like that, see. But I couldn't handle that liquor like that.

Well, you must have been the only sober one in Wolf's band, huh?

Yeah. The one night at the Zanzibar. Did you ever go to the Zanzibar? Did you see how that place is arranged? You see how this rug is here? Well, the Zanzibar, it had a long oval bar in the place just like that. One end of the place to the other. Women's washroom on one side; the men's washroom on the other side. The stage right here. And I'm standing there right by the women's washroom, because every night they were lined up there, jumping around. I'd tease them. You got something on your mind, baby? All that kind of stuff. Just playing with them. One night we was playing. Wolf's standing up. We was doing a shuffle. We was going to it. All going to it. All of a sudden the tempo starts slowing down. Wolf started stumbling. His feet try to keep going, tempo would start going slower and slower. Then all of a sudden the sound changed. He looked back there. Earl Philips, drunk as he can be. He'd fallen off the drums, going on down. On the bandstand, going on down, beating on the bass drum. (*laughs*) And Wolf standing still, says, "What's the matter with him?" Say, "He's drunk! Look at him." (*laughs*) He just fell out, just kicked. That's Earl Philips did that. (*laughs*) Drunk as he could be! I've seen all kinds of things.

Were you on his record? Earl only had one. It was on Vee-Jay, called "Oop-De-Oop."

That's probably me on there. Yeah, that's probably me on there if he made it. Yeah. But I remember that just as plain—Wolf stomping his feet trying to keep the tempo. Beating on the cymbal and all of a sudden going on down, hitting on the bass drum with a stick. (*laughs*) Yeah, that happened, right at the Zanzibar.

Hey, tell me how you and Bo actually came to a parting of the ways.

You know, a lot of times, a lot of entertainers, singers, and musicians, you come up with something new. You may play it a few times out in the public to see how the people go for it, you know—how they like it. They'll let you know if you want to make some change either one way or the other. Well, we had a valet, Billy Stewart. And Billy Stewart, I think he was out of Washington, D.C. He had a pretty nice voice for singing. And I recognized talent when I saw it. And I'm saying to myself, "This youngster's got some talent. He can sing. He can play the piano like Fats Domino." He resembles Fats Domino. So sometime we'd call him up and let him do a couple of tunes with us, you know, when we're playing some of the clubs and stuff like that. Well, when we got back to Chicago, I wrote something for him.

So I was pretty tight with Leonard and Phil Chess at the time, because I did a lot of studio work for him and Mercury, places like that, you know. So they took my word for a lot of things, you know. So I took him in the studio and I introduced him. I said, "Leonard, this is our valet. I want you to meet him. This is Billy Stewart." So I say, "When you look at him, who does he remind you of?" Leonard reared back and looked at him. Said, "He looks like Fats Domino!" I told him, "Not only does he look like Fats, he can also play the piano and sing like Fats Domino." So I told him, "I wrote a song for him that I would like for you to hear." So I got my guitar and amplifier out of the truck. Billy sat at the piano. And we did "Billy's Blues." And Leonard Chess liked it right away. He was ready to record him then. He said, "Well, what are we going to use for a B side?" I never wrote a B side. I only wrote that one. So I thought about it and I said, "Why don't we make this part one and two?" Do an instrumental and a vocal. That's the way the record was released.

All the guitar work I did on this, when Bo Diddley and I were together traveling around the country, we'd play the song. We played this song in the Apollo Theater also. People went for it. I know we had a nice hit there. This guitar, the type of guitar work I did in it was the same type that I did in "Billy's Blues"—that twang, you know. Let's see, one where I did maybe four notes and I either added or subtracted a note from it, just a little different technique. But basically it was the same technique and everything. So I put that together for Bo Diddley. And we got to the Howard Theater. Mickey and Sylvia was on the show. I'd never met them before. But I heard later that Mickey Baker, he was a hell of a guitarist. He did a lot of session work for Atlantic—stuff like that, you know. So we were there for a week. And we had done "Love Is Strange," and someone told me one day—because Sylvia, she wanted—Mickey wasn't teaching anything. So she wanted me to teach her a few things about the guitar. So I agreed to it.

But we never got together on anything. Somebody told me, say, "You shouldn't be playing certain songs, because certain songs you're playing, new stuff, certain people are taking a liking to it. They're paying a lot of attention to it." Well, I didn't pay too much attention to that, because that was the first time somebody'd told me that. So we're playing "Love Is Strange," and I happen to look around. There's Mickey Baker right at the end of the curtain. Behind the curtain, right at the end of it. Just taking in all he can. So I told Bo, I said, "We better stop playing the song here, because too many people are taking an interest to it and we haven't recorded it yet." Well, we did our little tour thing around the country, and when I got back to Chicago I told him I wanted to stay in town for a while. Well, I was down to the studio. As a matter of fact, I was just listening to some—me and James Moody—we were listening to some albums that Ahmad Jamal had just made. And Bo Diddley came in and he pulled me over to the side, and he said he had let Mick and Sylvia have that song and for me not to say anything to Chess—"And don't say anything to Leonard Chess"—and I'll get my writer's royalties.

Well, as long as I'm getting my writer's royalties, I wasn't going to say anything. See, usually if you're under contract with one record company, they've got top priority for whatever you do. Well, I didn't say anything. About a week passed. I was down in the studio and I heard "Love Is Strange" played on the radio. Because in the studio, these record companies have got the radios on all the time, because they're paying these disc jockeys to play these tunes and they want to make sure they're being played. I heard "Love Is Strange," and I don't remember if it was Leonard or Phil, they say, "That's a pretty nice song. It sounds familiar. That's going to be a hit, sounds like." Well, I didn't say anything. When he talked about it sound familiar, what they're listening to is my style of playing, my guitar playing. But I didn't say anything. Another week or so passed. The song's getting higher on the charts. And down at D.C. they're talking about the record. That particular record when it comes up. Wished they had had something like that, you know, because it's going to be a hit. It's getting hotter and hotter on the charts. Well, I don't know how they found out, but a few weeks later they found out that I wrote the song. Bo Diddley is the one that gave it to Mickey and Sylvia. He told me they gave him two thousand dollars. I didn't get anything. I just kept my mouth shut. So when Leonard and Phil Chess found out that I wrote the song, right away they drew up a contract and predated it. And I signed it. So then they set up the lawsuit to try to get in on the money.

Well, I don't know how much time passed. But anyway, I got my induction papers to go into the army at the time. Because I was on the road and I came back to the city just for that. Well, the first time I went down there, they let me slide. I forgot what I told them. I told them everything. Because I wasn't interested in the army. I was interested in playing my guitar. But when they inducted me, I went down there. Everybody went down there that day. They shipped them to Fort Leonard Wood, Missouri. So since I was out of the country, they held up the trial until I came back from Germany.

So when I came back from Germany, I went down to the record company so they'd know I was back in the country. And they set the wheels rolling to have this trial going against RCA Victor about "Love Is Strange." Well, they put me on a plane and sent me to New York. Benny Goodman's brother, Gene Goodman, he met me and took care of me and put me up in a hotel in New York. He took me down to BMI, since I was a BMI writer. They had a whole lot of money down there, but nobody could touch it. It was tied up until the trial was over. Until they found out who won at trial. Then that's who would get the money.

So we went into the courtroom. When I went into the courtroom, I think Sylvia might have been sitting over there. I couldn't say anything to anybody. She spoke to me. I nodded to her. She push me on back behind the judge's chamber, in a room back there. I couldn't hear anything. I'm back there an hour, hour and a half, a couple of hours. I can't hear. I don't know what's going on out there. I can't hear anything. So somebody finally comes back there to get me to take me into the courtroom to do my testimony. But what surprised me when I got into the courtroom, the place was full. And the jury, the jury was sitting in there. Got music detectives in there. Got stereo equipment set up in the courtroom there. I wasn't expecting all this. So I got up there. They played my music—"Love Is Strange," "Billy's Blues," all that—so they could see where the song came from, the playing techniques, the style, and stuff like that. So I did my little testimony. That's about all I heard was my testimony. Right back in that back room I went. I don't still know what's going on. So when they finally come back there and got me, the trial's over. I said, "Well, what happened?" Nobody knows yet. The judge has got to make up a decision on it. Well, the next day he put me on a plane and sent me back here to Chicago.

A week, around there somewhere, I heard that we lost the case of "Love Is Strange." We lost the case. Then sometime later I heard that Chess and RCA

Victor froze out everybody else and split the money. That's what I heard. And on the record, to keep Chess from finding out that I wrote the song, they put Bo Diddley's wife on there. Well, now, her and I went to grammar school together for a while. Ethel Smith, yeah, I think that's probably what you see on the record. But they still found out about it. But, now, just by chance, Bo Diddley been telling about some lie about me giving the song to Sylvia because I'm trying to hit on her and all that. There was nothing like that. I mean she was a pretty foxy chick, all right, but it probably would have been only a matter of time before I did hit on her! But I didn't. I didn't. The song didn't come into question. I never discussed the song with her, with her or Mickey Baker. Because I never said hardly anything to Mickey Baker. But I talked to her a little bit. Nothing about the song or nothing like that. No music at all.

So about a month or so ago, I got on the BMI Web page, and I started going through some stuff just out of curiosity. And I was looking up the millionaires, the songs that played with big hits, stuff like that. There's "'Love Is Strange.' Writer: Mickey Baker, Ellas McDaniel, Bo Diddley, and Sylvia Robertson." Well, we're talking a lot of money. Because last year sometime I heard Mickey Baker being interviewed on one of the National Public Radio stations, talking about all the boatload of money he made and he's living off of it now. I think he's living in Paris, France, somewhere. And he's still making money off of that. So you know how mad that makes me feel! I'm out here working every day. Billy Boy was telling me—see, Billy played out there on the corners with us for a while, too—and he'd tell me that he's supposed to play an engagement with Bo this last month, I think it was. So when he came down to the club that night, when I got a play down there with Russ —— (??), he told me he played the gig with Bo at some festival, engagement or something. So I told him, I say, "I haven't had a word to say to him in forty years. And it's going to stay like that, because I found out that he put the three of them down as the writer. They stole that from me." And, you know, I can be sitting up looking at TV, some movie, or something, and I hear "Love Is Strange" on the sound track. That just infuriates me. Just infuriates me. So he was in on it, it looked like. So I can't deal with people like that.

Did you ever run across Two Gun Pete?

Um-hm. I played at his place one night. Yeah, Henry Gray, piano player. Myself and Morris Pejoe, and maybe Frank. Because I asked him, "Where are we going to play?" He said, "We're going to go play for Mr. Washington." I thought about Mr. Washington. I didn't know—that name didn't sound familiar to me. But when I got into the club, or that tavern, or whatever it was over there, I'm looking at this guy. I said this guy looks mighty familiar to me. And I'm still in my teens, you know, I'm young. And I'm up on what's going on in the streets, you know. So I asked him again, "Who are we supposed to be playing for?" He said, "Mr. Washington." I said, "Do you see him in here?" He said, "Yeah, there he is, over there." I said, "Do you know who that is?" He said, "Mr. Washington." I said, "But do you actually know who he is?" I said, "That's Two-Gun Pete." At the same time, Pete was hitting on his old lady. I said, "Do you see what he's doing? He don't give a damn about you!" So I just sat there and played my guitar and watching him, because I knew he would kill somebody. This man, I don't know how many people he shot out here on the South Side. But I was glad when that gig ended. And I haven't been back in that place since.

Was that over on Oakwood?

Yeah, Oakwood. It's just east of Cottage. It's just east of Drexel. Right at Drexel and Oakwood Boulevard, there was a club around the corner there where Junior Wells and them used to play a long time. But Two-Gun Pete's place was farther up, closer to the lake. It was called the Hilltop. You go up a little hill there and it was right at the top of the hill. That's why it was called the Hilltop. And that's the first and last time I've been in that place. First and last time. I don't know how many men, how many youngsters out here he killed. But I know he killed a few. And he was quick with his guns. Now, I had never seen him in uniform or anything. But they said during that time he was the only one that carried a pair—a matched pair of .357 Magnums. And that's what he used out there on the streets, shooting through car doors and stuff at people. He probably had a weapon on him that night. But I've never seen him in uniform. That's the first and last time I saw him. Me being a teenager at the time, naturally I'd heard of him, because he shot teenagers! He shot all up and down Fifty-eighth Street. Because Fifty-eighth Street—from Calumet over to Indiana, I think it was—that little strip there was just as active as down on Forty-seventh Street. Very active. And he shot and killed people all down through there. But there was a couple more. Because I was living down—when I was in school—down on Thirty-ninth and Prairie when I went to Wendell Phillips [Academy High School]. And there was a couple of cops coming around there. Guys, youngsters out there on the corner, and one would get out of the car. And he'd say, "Everybody, go somewhere!" And the corner would get clear just like that. So that's the reputation he had.

So I didn't get involved in that kind of stuff. All I wanted to do was just play my music, play my guitar and learn more and advance myself. That was me. I played one time! Once I found out where I was, I wasn't going back. I wasn't going back. Because the man was too quick to shoot. And he was hitting on—whose woman—that was Henry's girlfriend that he was hitting on. And Henry didn't open his mouth. (*laughs*) I think I told him, I said, "Henry, do you see what he's doing, hitting on your old lady like that?" I said, "What are you going to do? Are you going to say something?" "Just keep on playing. (*laughs*) Just keep on playing." And that's what I did until the gig was over. Then I got my guitar and finally got out of there. I haven't been back up in there since.

After you did the records for Al Benson, what were your next recordings?
"Lucky Lou" was done for Chess.

Now, who was the band there, do you remember?
On "Lucky Lou"? That's Harold Ashby playing tenor [sax] on there. Big Willie Dixon on bass. And Lafayette Leake on the keyboard organ. It might have been Below—I'm trying to think who was on the drums after "Lucky Lou." I think it might have been Earl Philips. It might have been Earl.

Somebody told me that you also spent a good deal of time with Otis Rush. Is that true?
It wasn't a good deal of time, but we—we went out on the road together, me and Otis and Big Willie Dixon.

About what time would that be? When Otis was hot with the Cobra sides? [Otis Rushs's most highly regarded recordings were done for the Cobra label between 1956 and 1958]
Probably so, yeah. And to listen to him tell you, he'd say we starved to death out there almost. (*chuckles*) Almost got put in jail out there in Florida for just being there! We were playing one-nighters. We were based out of Tampa. Based out of Tampa. It was Otis Rush, myself, Tim Overton playing the tenor. As a matter of fact, he used to play with Memphis Slim. Tim Overton. Big Willie Dixon. I forgot who was on drums, exactly how many pieces we had.

But we were based out of Tampa. And we'd go out and play one of the surrounding towns at a dance that night or something, then come back to Tampa. Go out the next night, play someplace else, come back to Tampa. Tallahassee or someplace. I never will forget that place. When we finished playing the dance, we didn't have enough gas to get back to Tampa. Otis Rush had his Cadillac. He was driving his Cadillac, the Coupe de Ville Cadillac. Big Willie Dixon was driving that red and white Chevy station wagon. And I think Tim was riding with him and the drummer. I was in the car with Otis. Well, we were driving around looking for a gas station so we could get some gas so we could get back to Tampa, you know. So we pulled up. There was two cars like this (*gesturing*) in the street, talking to each other. Come to find out, they were police cars and policemen in this little small town. So we pulled up there and—I don't know—I think Dixon, Willie Dixon talked to them. Or it was Otis? He asked where can we find some gas, a gas station open so we can get enough gas to get back to Tampa. And they was talking and talking. So I'm sitting in the car. And so Otis came back—Otis went up there and talking to them, him and Dixon both. So Otis came back and got in the car. So when he got back in the car, this police car—one pulled up alongside him and said, "Y'all boys, follow me." So Dixon was behind us, or we were behind him. A police car in front and one in the back. So we make some turns, going into turns. So I told Otis, I said, "Damn, it looks like they're leading us to the jail!" He said, "That's just where they're leading us!" It was to jail. I said, "In jail for what? We ain't done nothing." He say he talked to the cop, he said, about the gas. He said, "Didn't you all niggers just play that dance down at that such-and-such a hall?" He said, "Yeah." He said, "Where are you boys from?" "Chicago." "We can take these niggers to jail." (*laughs*) So we're following the police car; right there in the jail is the courthouse there.

So I forgot what the pretext was supposed to have been. Working in Florida, gainfully employed without a—some kind of permit or—Florida state license, that's what it was at. So we're at the police station; Big Willie Dixon said, "They got the sheriff up out of bed. He's down here with a nightshirt on. Barefooted, nightshirt on." Man here, man with a nightshirt on and khakis. Barefooted with his feet up on the table. The guy that was leading us around down there, directed us to the place, is supposed to be the manager. He was from down there. That's how he knew where the places were, you know. So he was in the jail there with us. So the sheriff is sitting there, he said, "Now, y'all boys supposed to have so-and-so, state license plates, or Florida state license plates. You're gainfully employed down here and it's a law against—" So the guy that was from down there, he said, "Wait a minute! Sheriff, what about them big movie stars that's down there in Miami, down there on the beach?" He said, "Shut up, boy! I'm the law here!" And he said, "Now, what I say goes here!" He said, "Now, these boys from Chicago, they don't know any better. But, nigger, you live here; you know better!" That's what the sheriff told him! And he said, "Well, it's going to be fifty dollars for each car or you boys are going to have to spend the night in jail."

So, now, I had some money. I learned a long time ago, don't go out there on that road without enough money to get back home. You're not going to get stranded. So I had—I don't know if I had fifty or a hundred dollars, something in my pocket, in my wallet hid. My momma's baby was not going to get stranded out there on the road. We hadn't got paid. Big Willie Dixon didn't have any money. So they're fingerprinting him before they put him in the cell. And commented about his hands. So he said he had been working with concrete or something. So they locked him up in the jail. I think Otis might have paid fifty dollars. He had fifty dollars. So I'm thinking—because this is back in the time when they had chain gangs, road gangs, and all that kind of stuff—and I'm saying to myself—I'm still in my teens thinking about all this stuff, you know, and I'm seeing this, and I'm thinking to myself, "Say, now, I don't want daylight to come on Dixon down here in this southern jail, because they're going to have him out there on the road, beat him and everything else, you know." So I went back there. I told the sheriff, I said, "Sheriff, can I talk to him before you lock him up?" So he took me back there in the cell and I talked to him. So I told Dixon, I said, "Look it. I've got some money." I said, "Now, I will pay whatever they're asking, the fifty dollars, whatever it is." See, that's supposed to be like a bond or something or other until the court date. Then you go to court and then maybe get your fifty dollars back. Maybe. So I told him, "I've got some money." I said, "I'll let you have it, because if they lock you up in this jail overnight, ain't no telling what's going to happen by morning." So I gave him the money so he could get out of jail.

In the meantime, we're standing there talking. Tim Overton, he was alcoholic. He's full of his whiskey. He said, "I'm going to hit this mother." (*laughs*) I said, "Tim, you do that and they're going to kill us all down here." He's full of his liquor. He's ready to fight, you know. I said, "Just be calm, man. Just be calm until we get out of this." So they held Tim back. (*laughs*) So when we finally got out of there and went back to—as a matter of fact, they took us to the gas station, called for somebody to open it up. Got him out of bed to come out and fill up these cars, get these niggers out of here. (*laughs*) There was some sailor in the jail, too, when I went there to talk to Dixon to get him out of there. Now, he's in the service, uniform. He just happened to be at the dance. He hadn't done anything—drunk, that's about it. They locked him up. I haven't been in that town since. Haven't been in that town since, down in Florida. Otis probably hasn't been back either. (*chuckles*) So we played those few dates down there; I haven't been back since. But I've seen some bad experiences out there on that road.

Back during those days, I did a lot of studio work for Chess, Vee-Jay, Mercury. Back in those days, when a black artist would have a hit tune, a white artist would cover it. This is how I got to record with Buddy Moore's big orchestra. They covered "Rib Joint," which was made by a black artist.

This is Sam Price, right?
I don't remember the name.

I think so. I think Sam Price did the original.

But Buddy Moore—the guitar was featured, was the featured instrument. And he didn't—he had about a seventeen-, eighteen-piece orchestra, but no guitar. So they got me through Chess. And, let's see, "What Kind of Gal Is That?" I did that for Chess.

Now, here we are, we're playing at the Apollo Theater in New York City. We were staying at the Hotel Theresa. This is where Castro was staying. They was killing chickens in the room, you know. So we had a suite there at the hotel. So we're playing at the Apollo, and I think it was Clifton James. Somebody must have got to him, someone with a confidence game or something. He said they had a bag of money. Some kind of way. And down one of them streets, some-body wanted to beat up on one of the guys, so he threw the money. It's in a bag. He threw the money in one of these garbage cans and took off. So he said the money's in one of those garbage cans around there somewhere, so all we've got to do is find it. He said it's quite a bit. He said, about five, eight hundred dollars or around there somewhere. So I said, "Well, I'll go down there with you." So it's him and I and somebody else. I forgot who. It might have been Jerome. So I get to the street, all these houses look alike! Garbage cans sitting out front, right with the house there. And there's some—it's right there in one of those English basements, you know. Garbage can right there. So we're going out there looking in garbage cans. (*chuckles*) Big stars at the Apollo Theater going out looking in the garbage cans. Nobody—nobody was out there, you know. So we were ramming through the garbage cans. We get to one basement, English basement, and go there in the can. A dog—a great big dog run to the window and barked. Woooo! Well, somebody yelled, "Get out of those garbage cans!" So we took off, you know. We're going down looking in the other garbage cans. We didn't find anything. Said, "Maybe we missed some." James says, "It's in one of these cans somewhere. I saw the guy throw it in there." Now, I wasn't thinking then about a con game, you know.

So we go back down there, all three of us. I think it was James and myself and Jerome. We look in these garbage cans. So we get to this—this English basement where this garbage—where this dog was, you know. Got in the can there and the dog come barking at the window again. And I heard some guy say, "God damn it, didn't I tell you to get out of them garbage cans?" And I was leaving out of the gateway, heading out, and the last thing I heard was "sic 'em!" (*laughs*) I run off and back to the hotel. I don't know where I left them at. But when I heard "sic 'em," I was gone! Up in the room there, shut the door, (*panting*), I was trying to get my breath. (*laughs*) Aw, —— (??) thinking about stuff like that, and it tickled the hell out of me.

Another time, we was in Kansas City. We was there with Johnny Guitar Watson. You know, in that song "Going to Kansas City," "*going to be standing on the corner at Twelfth Street and Vine*"? Well, there used to be a nightclub right there on that corner. Well, we played—us and Johnny Guitar Watson, we did a week together down there. So there was this woman. Huge like Etta James. She said she told him that she was Guitar Slim's sister or somebody. So one night a big girl, she picked him up. There was like a—the stage was kind of roped off, you know. She picked him up and she carried him across it, you know. So she took him home with her that night, after we left the club. So we had a suite there at the hotel. So we—we ain't been to bed. We was up playing cards or something, you know. All of a sudden, James busted the door down. Slam the door, with his clothes in his hand! (*laughs*) Said, "What's the matter with you?" He said, "I just barely got away!" She didn't tell him she had an old man. And good thing they was on the first floor, because he said he had to go out the window. Run all the way to the hotel, clothes in his hand! I think that might have been our last night there, too. We had some times out there on that road, man.

The years you're talking about, from the time I was in my teens playing with all these people, I learned a lot. I met a hell of a lot of people. And like I say, to this day, at the time when I was playing with these people and looking at some of these in the movies and stuff like that, I didn't realize the greatness of a lot of these people until later years. Muddy and Jimmy on guitar. Little Walter playing the harmonica, and Elgin [Evans] on the drums. Then he started— after Little Walter went with the Four Aces, I'm trying to think—oh, Junior Wells went—see, Junior was still with him then. But they called on Junior to go into the army. I think that may have been when Henry started playing with him. Around that time somewhere. Well, Junior left here for about six weeks, training or something or other. He run off; he went AWOL. (*chuckles*) But they knew where to find him. The FBI just came and wait on him. They knew where his hangouts were and everything. He was a musician. He wanted to play his music. That's all he wanted to do. He said, "To hell with the army!" That wasn't his thing. So what they would do—because I was down there when they come in sometimes—if he wasn't playing, they'd just sit there and wait on him. The FBI—two FBI men. It was always in pairs. So one night Junior was on stage. This was about the second time he'd run off; he went AWOL. And he was up on stage playing his harmonica at the time. Two FBI men come in—I watched them! Two FBI men came in and stood by the door there. When they got Junior's attention, they—(*gestures*) like that for him to come on down. (*chuckles*) They let him finish the set. Then they took him on.

Would these FBI guys—would they all be white?
Yeah.

So they were sort of sticking out.
Yeah. Like a coal in a snowbank. Everybody knew them. You know, it was hard then for the police—and somebody like that to try to blend in. They couldn't blend in. They couldn't blend in. You could tell them every time when they would come in. Now, there was whites that came into the 708 Club and some of these others clubs around here. Yeah. Because I played [Club] DeLisa—you got a lot of white come in there. But I was with another orchestra when I played down there. But white was all over the place. They loved the blues, too.

The FBI and Secret Services, there was just something about them that shouts out, "Hey, I'm the FBI!" Just the way they carry themselves. Junior Wells is a good example. Leonard Chess, what he did—now, I know this for a fact. Junior come in there one day—because I was in the studio quite a bit. Junior come in there one day and he had a song. Chess liked the song, but he didn't tell Junior that. He just wouldn't record Junior. So when Junior left out of the studio and went outside, Leonard Chess told me, he said, if I can get Junior Wells to give me that song, he would let me record it. I forgot what the song was. But that's what he told me. If I could get Junior to give me that song, he would let me record. So I went outside and talked to Junior. And I told him what Chess said. If he'd let me have that song, I could record it, you know. I said, "What do you want for it?" "Give me twelve dollars." (*laughs*) I gave him twelve—I don't know if I had it in my pocket then. Twelve dollars, that was a lot of money. But he said "Give me twelve dollars and it's yours." I gave him twelve dollars. And I got the song. I don't remember which song it was. I don't know if I recorded it right then, but I gave him twelve dollars and got the song. Yeah, twelve dollars.

Sometimes it surprised me, the people that I worked with in my young years. I was in my teens when I met a lot of these people! The first day I met B. B. King— that was in '54—I didn't know who he was! The way I met him, we were in the studio—[me and] Wolf. We was doing—I forgot what tune we were recording at the time. But I could play B. B. King style, 'cause Hosea, he sang B. B. King and I played it. And at that time there wasn't too many guitar players around Chicago that could play B. B. King style, but I could. I could play B. B. King; I could play Johnny Moore, because I worked with those guys. Charles Brown. I picked up a lot of stuff from Johnny Moore when I was out there playing with him. So we were sitting there and the Chess says, "We're going to take a break here. We're going to play the stuff back. See how it sound and see what need to be changed." Well, in the meantime, while we were playing—before he said that, when we were playing, this guy comes in the door, in the studio. I didn't know who he was. He was just standing over there, watching me! I'm saying to myself, "This dude's trying to steal some of my stuff!" Watching my hands. So I turned where he couldn't see my fingers, you know. (*chuckles*) So I turned. I'll be all on this—I'm squeezing. I'm all up into it!

So when Leonard Chess said we're going to play this stuff back, everybody take a break, you know. See how this stuff sounds; see what changes got to be made. So I'm sitting there talking to Hubert or Earl Philips or somebody. And Wolf called me. He said, "Jody, come over here. I want you to meet a friend of mine." So I go over there. And he said, "I want you to meet a friend of mine. This is B. B. King." Oh, man, when he said that, I felt like going through the floor. I'm playing all his stuff, man. And turning, don't let him see what I'm doing. And it's his stuff! (*laughs*) So we hit it off—we hit it off right away. I guess he say, well, if somebody can play his stuff that good, you got to respect him. And that's the same day we made "Five Spot" and did the recordings. "It Must Have Been the Devil" with Otis Spann playing the piano. Because Spann was playing on Wolf records. So we did "It Must Have Been the Devil" and "Five Spot" with me and B. B. King playing guitar.

I did a lot of studio work for these companies. You've got a lot of guitar players around here, but everybody wasn't playing what I was playing. And I played behind doo-wop groups and a little of everybody.

Can you tell me, how did you—how'd you start doing studio for Vee-Jay? How did that happen?

Vee-Jay was right across the street. That's who Billy recorded for. And also Jimmy Reed. The guy who was doing the work over there—Calvin, I think Calvin used to sing with one of the doo-wop groups. That was on the label. Vee-Jay—Vivian Carter, I think she was a deejay over—somewhere over in Gary somewhere. She's all mixed up in there. Calvin, I think that was her brother. And they're recording— That office was right across the street from Leonard Chess when it was out there on Forth-eighth—in the forty-seven-hundred block there on Cottage Grove. He was right across the street. And a lot of those musicians, we played together. And we all knew each other. So if somebody needed somebody to play for a session or whatever, a certain number of us were available. Since Chess wouldn't record Billy, he recorded for Vee-Jay. As a matter of fact, his first song he wrote—I mean, the first song he *recorded*—I wrote. I think it was "I Was Fooled." So I just went right across the street.

Some of the enjoyment that I got out of being in show business— When I was a little kid going to the theater, looking at movies and all these people in movies, and going to the Regal Theater down there and seeing some of these entertainers on stage, never did I ever dream that I would be on the same stage with some of these people. People like Louis Jordan. I worked with him for two weeks. My band had just closed up at a club up north on Belmont. And he was playing at Robert's Show Lounge. We were getting our instruments together, and the organ player, Baby Face Willette, told me Louis Jordan need a guitar player for a couple weeks, what was I doing. I said we were just closing up and my other gig with my band was supposed to start in another couple weeks. I had to wait till the band close out there before I went in. So I would be free to play with Louis Jordan. So I went down there. I got a kick out of that! He'd say, "We're gonna play so-and-so and so-and-so. Play whatever you wanna." I grew up listening to all that stuff. "Saturday Night Fish Fry"—hey, that's when they had all the fish fries going! He was playing all that stuff then. You go to the Regal or some of these theaters, you see a movie and a trailer and selected short subjects in between there and you saw bands like Louis Jordan, Count Basie, and Duke Ellington, and all those people playing. Nicholas Brothers dancing and all that kind of stuff—that's what you saw. And you hear his records all over the South Side. Everywhere, Louis Jordan and the Tympany Five, all those records. And Charles Brown and the Three Blazes. I grew up with all those people. I really got a thrill out of playing with them. I'd have played for nothing! (*laughs*) I enjoyed it—I really did! Robert's Show Lounge was here in Chicago. I think there's a bowling alley there now around Sixty-sixth and King Drive. That's where it was—right across the street from his motel. I got a kick out of playing with those people. I really did!

I played behind Percy Mayfield in the Club DeLisa a couple of times. When I went to the DeLisa I didn't have my own band. I was with a saxophone player— damned good—Lorenzo Smith Orchestra; I was playing with them at the time. We had a Hammond B3 organ. We had a nice group. I was with a lot of people out there. I worked with T-Bone. T-Bone and I, we did some shows together. I'd never met him before and he'd never heard me play. We were playing a matinee over on the West Side. He rattled off something there. So I played the same thing he played. He looked, then he played something else. I played the same thing. So we just go back and forth there, enjoying ourselves. So he went up behind his head, like he always do, you know. So I went up behind my head! (*laughs*) We were enjoying that, and then he started doing his famous split. So I told him, "You got it!" (*laughs*) I had a lot of fun with those people!

L. C. McKinley?

Now, there's a name I'd forgotten about. He did a lot of T-Bone stuff. That's all he did, strictly T-Bone. He's kinda hard to get along with. He loved [him] self so much, ladies man. He was just hard to get along with. But he played T-Bone. He even held his guitar like T-Bone did.

There used to be a club down on Sixty-third Street called the Crown Propeller. Jackie Brenston—and he was playing with Billy Gayles and another saxophone player. They'd been down around St. Louis out on the road there. Well, Jackie Brenston lived here. He had a wife and kids over on Langley or St. Lawrence or somewhere over there. Well, anyway, he'd been out of town. He'd been gone about six months. We were down there to see Bill Doggett.

The band hadn't started yet, but Billy Gayles and Jackie Brenston came in. We all work together, you know. But what Jackie Brenston didn't know, his old lady had the police on him. He left town, no money or nothing. It was like he deserted the family. They came down there getting ready to take him to jail. (*laughs*) They had to raise some money right there! This is what they did back in those days! They had to raise some money to send to his wife *right then!* 'Cause they were gonna take his butt to jail!

Now, when me and Bo Diddley went to the Howard Theater in Washington, D.C., I saw the same thing happen with a doo-wop group. They had been there before, and one of the singers had got some young girl pregnant there, you know. So I just happen to be passing by. There was this policewoman and this big detective. They were looking for so-and-so and so-and-so. So they got him. Say, "You got so-and-so pregnant when you was here last time, and you haven't supported with anything. You got to come up with some money or you're going to jail." So they had him—they put the handcuffs on him. So somebody else in the group came by to see what's going on. He said, "Wait, wait, wait, wait, wait! Can I talk to him?" She said, "You better talk fast, 'cause the boy ain't gonna be here long." (*laughs*)

I just got fed up with it. I couldn't take it no more. I got to thinking and was talking to my wife. And I was really dissatisfied with the way things were going in music—people stealing my stuff. I wasn't making any money. Nobody was making any money but the record companies! I got to thinking. I said, "What could I do, or what would I do if I hurt my hand so I couldn't play my guitar, or lost my voice where I couldn't sing. What would I do?" It dawned on me then that I had never been trained to do anything else but play music. That's all I wanted to do, and that's all I'd been trained to do—play music, entertain. So I got to thinking about what could I learn in order to sustain myself and my family. And I thought, electronics. Guys coming up with all these computers and everything, somebody's got to fix them. So I got into electronics school. I graduated from Quinn Electronics Institute. As a matter of fact, when I started making preparations my band was still playing. Come intermission time, I'm either up on the stage or down in the booth, reading electronics books. And I did that until I felt I was sufficiently independent to get me another job in electronics. That's what I did. I graduated from Quinn Electronics Institute. I got a diploma in AM/FM radio, black-and-white/color television, air conditioning and refrigeration. For two years I was an electronic technician for Embassy Radio, serving stereo systems and stuff like that.

But I come to a standstill after I'd been there for a while. I wasn't making the kind of money I thought I should have been making. So quietly I went to another school under the G. I. Bill, at night—a school named Business Method Institute, where I learned how to wire up all the control panels of all the IBM office equipment at the time. I learned how to keypunch and I learned how to program the IBM 360 computer. I went to one company—NCR, I think. Well, all their computers was in Dayton, Ohio. But I didn't want to leave Chicago. I didn't want to relocate, so I just let that job slide.

My wife was working in insurance at the time, and she was telling me about the Xerox engineer that came in there, working on equipment. She said it looks like it's pretty interesting, you know. Maybe that's something I should look into. And sure enough, on my day off I went down there to check out the Xerox Corporation. Took all the electronics test[s] and everything for evaluation. So they sent the tests to Rochester, New York, to be evaluated by the psychiatrist and everybody there. And they called me one day and told me to report to the office out in Hinsdale. So I was [a] Xerox technical engineer specializing in color for twenty-six years, until I took early retirement in March 1994. Then I run my own business in Nashville for a year—in a shopping mall. Then I come back to Chicago and I got the engineering job that I'm in now, working with cash machines in banks and different places. That's what I do now, until I retire from this job. And if I can get a foothold with my guitar again, then I'll retire from this job.

Were you close or were you friends with Robert Jr.?

Oh, yeah! People used to say he was my father! (*laughs*) Yeah, a lot of people used to think he was my father because of the physical resemblance. We hit it off real nice. Matter of fact, a couple of years ago (*in a questioning tone*) Dick Shurman called me on the phone and we got to talking about what's going on out there [on the blues scene]. You know, I don't go around these joints, 'cause a lot of youngsters coming up now, they may have heard of me, but they don't know me by sight. But a lot of old-timers, some of them still out there. They haven't all died off yet. If I go out there and just listen to some music and try to enjoy myself, somebody's going to recognize me and throw a guitar in my hand. But I'm not ready for that, 'cause I haven't been playing my instrument, and I say I'm not going to get on anybody's stage and sound like a rank amateur. The way I want to be remembered is the way I left. I consider myself to hold my own with those guitar players out there. And that's the way I want to be remembered. I don't want to go out there sounding like an amateur.

I said about the only person I'd like to go out and see is Robert Jr. Lockwood. And just by chance, that next Saturday he was going to be down at Legends. So Dick asked me if I'd like to go and see him. I said yeah, but I didn't want anybody to know who I was. He asked if I would go if he gave me a couple of tickets for my daughter and I. Sure, I'll go, but I don't want anybody to know who I am. He said there'll be a couple of tickets there on the door. Just go there and identify myself to the doorman. So, sure enough, my daughter and I went down there that Saturday night. Big crowd outside the door. So I pushed her through the crowd and we got to the door there. And I kind of softly told the guy at the door there who I was. He let the chain down 'cause Dick was coming in. And everybody look— "Who is that?" I'm in there then. (*laughs*) So we sat in the VIP section.

I figured I'm gonna ease in there without anybody seeing me. Sure enough, here come some musicians I hadn't seen in years. When I went out to see him [Robert Jr.] that night and almost about a year later I got home and I got a long distance call from California. It was this agency that books him—American Legends Music. It was Michael James. He was telling me that. Robert Jr. was going to be here to celebrate his eighty-fifth birthday, down at the Hot House. He wanted me to come down. So I went down there, my daughter and I. That's the night Robert Jr. was presented with a brand-new five-thousand-dollar guitar. I mentioned the guitar and Michael told me, "You play your cards right, you might get one, too." (*laughs*)

So some time passed. I got a call from California, and he was telling about a concert with a lot of his artists and asked me if I'd like to play. No, no, I don't want to play. Billy Boy and a bunch of other people down there. So I thought about it, you know. I discussed it with my wife about me playing my guitar. She had talked with somebody else about it, and they said that playing might make me a much better person, 'cause she knew that I missed playing my guitar, you know. A lot of time people would ask me "Don't you miss it?" Yeah, I miss it sometime. I really do miss it sometime, but I got a lot of bad memories about the money and the music. You got a lot of artists from the fifties still trying to get with these record companies. So I thought about it. About a week or so later I sent him an e-mail and told him I really would like to play a few numbers. And that's how I started to get back into it. I went down there, I played about three or four numbers—got a couple standing ovations. It surprised me that people even remembered who Jody Williams was. I talked to some guy in Australia—he had the first record I ever made. I signed a bunch of autographs. I wasn't as far gone as I thought. As a matter of fact, when I went down to New Orleans for that engagement, the doctor who was throwing that thing had the first record I ever made—and "Lucky Lou"! So I autographed both of them. Both sides.

Rev. Johnny **Williams**

Since the very inception of blues music there has been deep conflict between the world of blues and the black church. Regardless of denomination, African American religion has little if any tolerance for blues and the people who play blues. It's regarded as the devil's music and a practice in defiance of God. African American clergy in particular are adamant in this position. The chasm is deep and wide and it's real.

This is ironic because most blues players start their lives and their musical journey in the church and later cross into the world of blues. They don't regard this career as a choice in defiance of God, but rather what God chose for them to do. Yet many blues players have been conflicted by their decision to play blues away from the world of the church, and many return to the church at the end of their lives. Son House was probably the most renowned example of this dilemma, but throughout the history of blues a certain percentage of bluesmen and blueswomen have experienced this same conflict.

Rev. Johnny Williams. Photo courtesy of Mike Rowe/ Blues Unlimited.

One of the unexpected residual effects of this ongoing conflict is that it is difficult to find black clergy who are willing to officiate at the funeral services of bluesmen and blueswomen. The Rev. Johnny Williams was one of the few black clergy in Chicago who would preside over the funeral services of blues artists. Over the years and the continuing series of funeral services in Chicago's blues community, we all became familiar with his easygoing manner and tolerant ways. Johnny Williams had an abiding sympathy for blues musicians and the world of blues, because he himself spent decades in Chicago as a bluesman, known as Uncle Johnny Williams. He played and recorded during the 1950s but was actually a generation older than the well-known names of postwar Chicago blues. He had fond recollections of the musicians who played Maxwell Street in the years before World War II — before Muddy, Wolf, Walter, and Elmore.

I was introduced to the Rev. Johnny Williams after services for the late Smokey Smothers. I had worked in Smokey's band for six years, and Williams had taught Smokey how to play. With that in common, conversation was easy. He agreed to be interviewed and I dropped by his apartment a few days later. He lived in a small but modern apartment at 5600 West Gladys — just east of the Chicago city limit — and about a mile and a half from where I lived. Both he and Floyd Jones lived within hiking distance. When he spoke, Williams talked with energy and enthusiasm. He was articulate but with phrases and turns of language that would immediately identify him as being from an earlier era. He talked of his days as a bluesman and spoke dramatically of his call back to God and the church.

At the time of our interview, Johnny Williams was eighty-seven years old and was planning the celebration of his one-hundredth birthday. In fact, the subject of his celebration crept into nearly every conversation I ever had with him and every interview I've ever read with him. I don't think I've ever met anyone looking forward so much to their one-hundredth birthday. Sadly, he came up six months short, passing away of natural causes on March 6, 2006. This interview took place on September 15, 1993.

■ ▪ ▫

Take me back to the very beginning. When were you born and where?

Nineteen-oh-six. Alexandria, Louisiana, but I mostly called Texas home. And from there to Mississippi when I was very small—somewhere around ten or eleven—and from Mississippi to Chicago.

How did you get from Louisiana to Texas?

Our parents. Our parents moved. See, I have a bunch of half brothers. My mother died when I was only eight years old. And these boys here—they're my half brothers. And that's how I got from Texas to Mississippi—Belzoni, Mississippi. I was raised up there. I grew to a man there—Belzoni, Mississippi.

How I come to play a guitar, I had an uncle, Unca Antnee [Uncle Anthony], which also was Johnny Young's uncle. See, Johnny Young and I was first cousins. Ant was also his uncle, and he played way back with a guy they called Charlie Patton. That was back around '27. And from that I said I wanted to be like him. So I took it up as a kid. Well, when I was up around ten years old, I could play a guitar. But I couldn't play it at home—the religious family didn't allow it, see. Whenever I got out and someone had one, I'd learn to play it.

So after I got out on my own, well, then I began to play. Charlie Patton, he ranged from Cleveland to Shaw, Mississippi. That was his range—from Cleveland to Shaw, Mississippi. Now, Charlie Patton was a one-key man. Everything that Charlie Patton made he made in Spanish—he played in Spanish. That's a step higher than cross-noted like Hound Dog Taylor played. And everything he made, he made in Spanish, but he could get more outta Spanish than any man I seed [saw] in my life—outta that one key. And everything that he made, I could play it. That's why I played in Spanish, everything that he made. He didn't make a record that I couldn't play.

Did you learn from the records or by watching him?

I learned from the records. And I went to a couple of places where he played at—a couple of times. But I knew Spanish before I met him. I knew you could tune your guitar in Spanish. And I had one or two pieces that I played in Spanish, but after he come on the scene in '27—and really the guy went over big—everything he made, I could play it!

Can you describe Charlie Patton? What did he look like?

He was a mulatta colored guy, curly hair; he was short but not too small. Oh, I would hit the road sometime, go out. I met Robert Johnson way back there. I know you heard of him. I met him on the road in Arkansas. I used to just take the guitar and get on the road. So I met him in Hughes, Arkansas. He was on his way there to Marianna, and so he was playing someplace there, in Marianna. And that's how I met him, you know, just that one time.

Had he made records already?

Yeah, he had done put out the "Terreplant [Terraplane] Blues." He was a slide man. That's what put him over, the "Terreplant Blues."

Would you say he had a big reputation at that time?

Yeah, he was a well-known man all-out through Arkansas. I don't know about the other countries. I never did see him in Mississippi anyhow. But I did meet him that one time. I never did meet him anymore. That was in 1936. And for the time I was around him, he seemed to be a very nice person. He used to have one guy followed him had a jug. (*laughs*) He played the guitar; the other guy blowed the jug. Yeah, some guy used to follow 'im like that. But anyway I met him for that one time and I never did meet him anymore.

Me and another fellow was playing together by the name of Tom Toy—we was playing together. Now, Charlie Patton he was recording—that made him a popular man. We wasn't recording nothing. We was just guitar playing for country dances. They have these country dances every Saturday night. They had a country dance somewhere, Tom Toy and I would play there. Now, he was a good musician. When I turned pro I did my best to find him, but I couldn't find him. I don't know what happened to him, but that guy could play a lot of guitar, Tom Toy. Then I met some boys named Tom and Andrew. They never did come to be famous, but they was about the greatest guys I ever been around that didn't do nothing for themselves. And that's who started me outta Spanish and playing with a 440 pitch [440 Hz, standard tuning]—to jump in any key, you know, take it and go regardless of what key it was. They'd take any key and go in it and play in it.

Where were those fellows located?

They was from Indianola. They came from around where B. B. King came from. Well, them boys was along with me—a little older, I think—all of 'em is dead now. And there was two other guys—Pet and Can [Maylon and Richard Harney]. I know you heard of 'em if you never seed 'em. One played the guitar and the other played accordion.

Was one of those guys Hacksaw Harney? He was part of Pet and Can?

Yeah. Yeah, he was part of Pet and Can.

I understand he was one of the best guitar players around.

No, I wouldn't say that. I wouldn't say he was the best. Those two boys, Tom and Andrew, they was—for that time—about the best that I seen. Those boys were great, but they never—nobody ever picked 'em up. There's musicians that walk around here in the alley, when the blues was really ringing here in Chicago. They walk around here in the alley and they could play more guitar than some of the guys that was recording, but nobody don't pick 'em up. If nobody don't pick you up, you never get anywhere.

How did you happen to come to Chicago?

The first time I was ever here was 1924—that was my first time here. I had a uncle here. They wrote me and told me that he got burnt real bad. I came up here to see him, and I stayed up here about two weeks. Then I went back

South. And when I came back the second time, in 1938, I came to stay. I been here ever since, and that's about fifty-five years.

In 1924 you would have been about eighteen years old. What was your impression of the city?

I didn't like it. No, I didn't like it. I just rather to be in the South than to be here. I could have stayed then, but I didn't like it.

What were the differences that you found?

Well, I was under the impression that you were liable to get stuck up or get killed. You know how it is with a country boy, you know. He's not used to the city. They talked about how bad it was around Thirty-first Street, and when I came here that's the first place I landed. And that's where I lived 354 East Twenty-sixth Street—right around Thirty-first Street. That's why I didn't stay the first time I was here. And in other words, I had just married and she didn't want to come up here, and that told me not to even come up here.

I goes all the way back with Big Bill [Broonzy], Tampa Red, Big Maceo—I goes all the way back. We were all good friends. And Sunnyland Slim—oh, my God—I been knowing him for years. If that guy ain't ninety-something, he ain't nary a day.(*laughs*) Because he's older than I am. And I'm eighty-seven. He's a good *bit* older than I am. All us used to play on the streets in Jewtown, every last one of us. That's where we was picked up from. Off of the streets of Jewtown, every Sunday, you know. We'd have guitars and horns from one end of the street to the other. So that's where a lots of us were picked up. Really I would go down there, but I wasn't playing nothing. I'd come down there and listen, you know. Sit and listen. John Henry—I don't know if you ever met him.

Would that be John Henry Barbee?

Yeah—yeah, yeah.

What would you say his style was like?

Well, John Henry was pretty good, but he was a D man. He was a one-key man. Practically everything he played, he played in D. That's what he played—

Did he make any records that you know of?

Not that I know of—I never heard of any. He could have. Now, I worked with him in '58. We played at a place two or three nights. I never did just have a job *with* him. But he was a D man. He played in D.

Who else did you see down in Jewtown? How about Daddy Stovepipe?

Oh, yeah! Don't say nothing about Stovepipe! (*laughs*) Yes, yes! That Stovepipe was something else! You know, he used to follow minstrel shows way back? Oh, yeah—Stovepipe. I knowed Stovepipe well.

What instrument did Stovepipe play?

Stovepipe, he just would drum on a guitar, chord on a guitar. But he wasn't really a guitar player. He could make chords on a guitar. But Stovepipe, he mostly would sing and dance. That was the biggest thing he would do.

Would you call what he did blues? Or was it minstrel songs?

No, it was blues. One-Leg Sam, I know you didn't meet him. No, because he was dead. Now, that guy was a musician. He was a good musician. He was a background man. You didn't meet Ervin Foster did you? He was cousin to Little Willie Foster, the one made "Fallin' Rain."

Didn't Robert Johnson have a cousin that you used to play with?

Oh, Lord, yes! Gray-Haired Bill! Ooo-ooo, yeah! The first electric guitar Gray-Haired Bill had was one that I had and he got it. Gray-Haired Bill, I knowed him well. Very well!

What did he play like?

Well, he was a two-key man. He was good in those keys. He worked with Floyd. He worked with me, but he only played in E and A.

Did he ever make any records?

No!

Blind Percy?

Yeah, I knowed him—Blind Johnny, too! Did you ever meet Blind Johnny? He was a wonderful guitar player. Yeah, I met Blind Percy.

Was Percy a guitar player?

Yeah. The one I know was a guitar player. 'Course I never did work with him, but I knew him. And Johnny Temple—went back to Jackson. He passed in Jackson. I worked with him—he made "Louise [Blues]" and many a records. They blackballed him, that's right. He couldn't make no more records, 'cause he made the same record for two companies. Two different companies he made the same record and they blackballed him. He made the record for [Lester] Melrose, and he made the record for another company—I forget the name of the other company. So they blackballed him. He couldn't record no more. Another great little guy—I loved to work with him; I was crazy about him—Baby Face Leroy [Foster]. I loved to work with him, 'cause he made Muddy Waters what he was. And after Muddy got up, he dropped him for Jimmy Rogers. But, oh, he was a great little guy. He played the same role that Jimmy Rogers played after Baby Face. And Baby Face and I worked awhile together there on Taylor and Paulina [Streets].

Would he play second guitar or drums?

He mostly played background or bass, but that little guy could play it all.

He could play bass. He could eat bass *up!* And they blackballed him where he couldn't play. We had a guy in the field they call Doby. You see, they used to have from the union hall—they would have men to go around, all over Chicago to catch bootlegging musicians—playing and didn't have a contract. Playing and didn't belong to the union. You get where I'm at? Baby Face Leroy, he was good at getting a job and wouldn't get a contract. And this guy Doby, he turned 'im in. And so they blackballed him and he couldn't play no more. He couldn't have a job no more and I hated that, but it wasn't no need to do that, but Doby was just a hard man. He was an ex–saxophone blower. And [Hilliard] Brown, he was out there in the field. He was a ex-drummer.

When I really started to going on the streets playing—and playing in Jewtown—was 1948. After I lost that finger, I quit. And I went to Jewtown one day and I saw a guy playing a guitar, he didn't have but three fingers and no thumb. (*laughs*) So I said, "If he can play, I can play!" Then I went back and picked it up again. I started back to playing. Well, I could play in all keys like that except one. I couldn't play in B-flat, 'cause I needed all the fingers for B-flat. Other than that—

You know I played with a lot of guys and I've helped a many guys. I worked with Moody [Jones] and I worked with Floyd [Jones]—and Snooky [Pryor]! Oh, that was back in around, I'd say, '49. After me and Johnny [Young] split. Johnny and the boss fell out. When Johnny was young he was radical. He would get whiskey in 'im, and he'd go crazy and he'd act a fool. I hit him over the head with a guitar one night! (*laughs*) I was fixing to hit him again, and Gray-Haired Bill grabbed me and said, "Don't bust that guitar!" He made me mad! He'd get up there and he'd get too drunk—and he'd jump his time! I got to the place where I'd limit him with whiskey. I wouldn't let them give it to him. But after he got older, he wasn't like that—he put that behind him. So Snooky and I worked at the 24 Club. That was in '49. We didn't have nothing but the guitar and harp. That's all we had—didn't even have a drummer. After Snooky left, then me and Moody worked there together, just two guitars. We didn't have no harmonica. He and I worked there together.

Well, when it come down to musicians, that guy could run a ring around us. He was a better musician, and practically everything Floyd made, most of the time Moody was on it. Practically everything he made. And practically everything Snooky Pryor made Moody was on. Moody was a good guitar player! I had a job with Little Walter every night in the week except Monday night. I worked with him there for two or three weeks like that. Every night of the week I was at the Purple Cat. I think that was 1920 West Madison. At the Purple Cat the bandstand was up like that. Oh, that guy could blow harmonica! At that time—to my knowledge—he was the best harmonica *blower*. The "Juke" it was [that] put him over. You've heard that, haven't you? That was his first cut was the "Juke." The guy could blow a harmonica. I declare, you have to give him credit for it. To my judgment he was the best. Some say Shakey Head Walter was the best, but not to me. Little Walter was the best.

What kind of equipment did Little Walter have when he was with you?

He didn't have nothing but a harp and a amp, that's all.

What size speakers did he have in his amp?

Oh, he'd have eighteen-inch—

You'd have one speaker in there?

Yeah, uh-huh. Because my amplifier didn't have but one speaker in it. Well, I think my amp had fourteen-inch speakers, that's what was in it.

Did he do any tricks or anything you're aware of that helped him?

No, not to my knowledge, not while he was with me. But one thing I like-ded [liked] about him, he had a harmonica to blow in any key. Now, you see, a lot of those guys that blow harmonica, you couldn't go anywhere but E and A, that's all. But he had one—any key you got in—he had a harp to fit it. So that's why I call him better. If you jumped to C [or] B-flat, anywhere you went, he'd reach back there and he'd get one to fit it. So to my judgment, that's why I say he was the best, to me. Little Walter, he left me and went to Muddy Waters. He and I and Johnny Young was at the Purple Cat. That was in '48. We's at the Purple Cat, and he and Johnny got in a little spat there. And so he left. And so the next thing he was with Muddy Waters.

Now Muddy Water[s], when he was on Roosevelt Road, I know him before he ever made a record—you know what I mean? And Muddy Water[s], to my judgment Muddy Water[s] wasn't a real guitar player—I guess you know that? He had his style, and the guy could sing, and his timing was perfect—he knowed when to break. His timing was perfect. He was a two-key man. Everything he made was in E and A. That's the only two keys he played in. Well, the biggest of the fellas, that's what they played in—E and A. And a lot of 'em couldn't play in nothing but E.

Smokey [Smothers], he would come to my house. I lived on Division then, and I was playing at the Square Deal. That was in '49, if my memory serve me right. And he was playing cross-noted, like Hound Dog Taylor. Well, I couldn't break Hound Dog Taylor of that, 'cause that was his way of life and you couldn't learn him no other way. And I told him, "You'll never get to be a musician like that." I said, "Give your guitar a 440 pitch like mine." And I made him come up there and I showed him chords, you know, on my guitar. And he'd come around the Square Deal, where I was. And that's how he come to be the kinda musician that he was. Because I pulled him away from that, 'cause playing like that [cross-noted], you can't play with any band. But when they give it a 440 pitch, any key they get in, you're right there. But with that [cross-noted] you got to put a clamp on and you can only get about three keys. That's A, E, and you *can* get G. But you got to put a clamp on it, so—I taught him to work for what he get. I say, "You'll get more harmony than you would with the strings already tuned where you don't have to chord 'em." So I started him off from that, and once the guy got going, the guy could beat me. (*laughs*)

Leslie?

Leslie, he's tall. He's his cousin. He blows the harmonica.

Lester Davenport?

Yeah, uh-huh. I helped him. 'Cause he used to come by and blow, and I gave him his time—you know what I mean. Homesick James [Williamson], did you meet him?

Now, you're not going to claim that you gave him his time—

You couldn't give it to him. You couldn't give it to him, 'cause me and Floyd used to work with him. He was a man that had [a] bad time, but he thought that he was great. Yeah, Homesick James. (*laughs*) All them boys, when they's walking around the streets, they used to come around me and Floyd Jones and Snooky Pryor. You meet Jimmy Lee [Robinson]? Now, he used to run around with us when he couldn't play nothing. He run around with us and pattern after us—me and Moody Jones and Floyd Jones. Big Boy Spires—I take him out on his first job, the first job he ever had. I went on the South Side one night and he told me—I was off; I wasn't playing that night. And they was playing on Wentworth, if my memory serve me right, somewhere on the forty-three-hundred block on Wentworth—and that was his start. Big Boy Spires, I picked him up. He went on from there.

And as far as Hound Dog Taylor, the first job he had—standard job—I give it to him. Big Boy Spires and I was playing together, at Root and Princeton. And Big Boy Spires, he worked, you know, on a Saturday night. He couldn't stay there until the night was over, because he had to get up to go to work. And so he give it up. He said, "You get you somebody else, Uncle Johnny, to play with ya." And I got Hound Dog Taylor. I got P. T. Hayes on the harmonica. And that was the first standard job that he had.

Little Willie Foster, he made "Fallin' Rain [Blues]." That was a record that went over big. The first job he ever had out in the public was with me—on the five-hundred block of Sixty-third Street. Shakey Jake [Harris]—you heard of 'im—the first job he had, he had it with me over here in Jewtown, on a street called O'Bryant—a tavern there called Mama's Place. They done tore all that down. That was his first job.

J. B. Lenoir?

Well, the fact of it is I played some with him when he first started out.

Shakey Head Walter?

Well, I played some with him. Shakey Head—that's what we called him. Some called him Big Walter. Little Walter and Big Walter. So I played with him.

The late Johnny Jones, I worked with him. Lee Eggleston, I don't know if you ever met Lee. He's a great piano player. I don't know why they don't have him in the clutch book, 'cause he's been around long enough. He and I played together nineteen and fifty. He was on the piano and I was on the guitar. We've had some good times there. You know, on a Sunday there would be guitars strung out from about Peoria all the way down, almost to Morgan. Every one of them set on Maxwell Street. That's where they was, on Maxwell Street. There was living quarters up and down Maxwell, and we would get our electric from those people's homes that were living on Maxwell. We'd pay 'em so much—have them long cords, extension cords running out the window. And we would pay those people so much for their electric. Oh, you start around about twelve o'clock. You might find a few out there at ten or eleven, but the biggest of them would be from about twelve until four thirty or five o'clock. And in the evening, you know, when people get to going and the crowd start to thinning out. Do you know we would make forty-five and fifty dollars on a Sunday, sitting out there playing, with dimes and quarters, you know. I know one white fella, every time I would be there, he would come and look for me. There was two things he liked—the "St. Louis Blues" and "C. C. Rider" [or "See See Rider"]—those two numbers. Every time he would come by on a Sunday I'd have to play those two numbers for him.

But after you got in the union it got to the place where you couldn't set out there anymore. Oh, no, no, the union didn't allow you to throw it out open in the air. But when we started out, we didn't belong to no union. The biggest majority of them out there didn't belong to no union. But after we got in the union, *well,* that broke that up. No, they'd fine you if they caught you out there. Jewtown, going south it went to about Sixteenth Street, 'cause when you get there they have all sorts of things go to a car—you know, hub caps, wrenches—they just have it out there to sell. Now, you come back going west, it went back about to Sangamon. Now, that's where all that music would be strung out—down to about that far. And back east, it didn't go too far. I wouldn't say it would go two blocks east. Right down to the expressway? Well, it went down to there. They had a lot of junk selling back there. There wasn't no entertainment over there. Back north—it didn't go too far north—because at that time Fox Brothers was on this side of the street—and B & B Tailor, 'cause I used to have clothes made there. And there was a big bank set on the north side of Roosevelt Road. So it didn't go very far, just across Roosevelt Road. That's about far as it went.

Let's talk about the records you made. Who did you record for and how did it happen?

Well, I'll tell you how it happened. Johnny Young and I made that in a house. A lady had a little tape recorder. Johnny singing "Money-Taking Woman" on one side, and I'm singing the "Worried Man Blues" on the other side. And we made that in the house, and there was a Jew there, call him Fat. And so we played it over there. We's just trying to get out there. And he liked it. He liked the beat that I had on the guitar. He said, "That's a beat ain't nobody got!" He said, "I'll record that." You know what I got? Fifty dollars. (*laughs*) That's what I got for it. So he cut it on the recorder he had, and he taken it downtown. And so it was made from that.

The guy that you call Fat, was that Bernie Abrams?

Yeah, yeah.

He had some sort of shop, didn't he?

Yeah, he was right over there on the corner of Peoria and Maxwell. He started having guitars and things in there selling—

Do you remember the name of the place? Was it Maxwell Radio Record Company?

I believe it was, because I know he used to have a music store there. Bernstein used to have that music store across from him. But I believe that's what it was. Perhaps if we'd taken down south to Melrose—Melrose didn't turn down too much. But we stopped there, so Johnny said, "Let's take it by Fat." He fell for it soon as he heard it! He liked the beat on the guitar. Said, "I ain't never heard nobody with that beat." Fact of it, I was the one brought that beat, but everybody got it out there now. But I was the one that brought that beat to the guitar. That was recorded in '47.

What was the name of the label?

I done forgot— [All the records issued by Abrams were on the Ora Nelle label.]

Did it make much of a splash when it first came out?

No, it did *pretty* good, but it wasn't what you'd call a hit, strictly because the guy didn't distribute them. Now they had record players right across the street from him, and he [Abrams] wouldn't let him have none of 'em. He tried to make all the profit for himself. He wouldn't distribute those records!

So he was selling them out of the shop?

Yeah. He sold 'em outta the shop. He wouldn't distribute them! 'Cause those people over there [at the record shop] would have bought 'em, 'cause they heard 'em. I went over there and ask him. And the guy said no, 'cause Fat was trying to make it all for himself. He said, "We would sell 'em if he would distribute 'em." But he wouldn't do it.

Did that thing ever appear on the jukeboxes?

Nowhere but on the North Side. I heard on the North Side—in other words, at that time I was playing at the Square Deal—Johnny and I both were playing at the Square Deal, 230 West Division. And he had it on the jukebox there. And a fella named Chester had a record shop right next to there. Now, he let *him* have some of them to distribute, but he mostly kept those for himself. Johnny Young and I, "Money-Taking Woman" we made that together. Johnny Young singing "Money-Taking Woman," and I'm singing on the other side.

I read an interview where you said you were trying to sing like Dr. Clayton.

They said I went like Dr. Clayton—they said I went like Dr. Clayton. Well, I admired Dr. Clayton, and I guess maybe I just took it up to carry it that way. Yeah, Dr. Clayton—I admired him.

I know that Abrams made some other records. Are you familiar with the Little Walter and Othum Brown record he cut?

Little Walter and a fella they call Otis, Little Otis, cut a record for him.

Othum Brown?

Yeah! Little fella, little guy. They cut the record for him. That's the only record I know. Little Walter had on one side "I Just Keep Lovin' Her," and "I Wonder Who's Lovin' You Tonight" ["Ora Nelle Blues"], that's what Otis had. And later on Jimmy Rogers cut it. It went over when Jimmy Rogers cut it.

Whatever happened to Othum Brown?

I don't *know*—no, I don't know!

He didn't die in Chicago that you were aware of?

No—no! He didn't pass in Chicago. Now, the number one recording man here was Leonard Chess. I was there several times with him. I put a record on tape, and he never did release it. And he never did call me back to take me downtown to cut it. But Little Walter blowed it on the harmonica, but he didn't sing it.

What was the name of it?

Oh, let's see—it's been a long time—"I'm in Love with You, Baby"—and "I'll Never Let You Go."

That's what you called it. What did Walter call it?

"I'll Never Let You Go." Little Walter blowed it—he didn't sing it. He just blowed it all the way through. And I told some of the boys, "Shit, that's the record I cut for him." I just put it on tape to see if he liked it. Now, he was supposed to call me back to cut that record. Now, I cut two records for Spencer—Sixty-third and Langley. But that guy had an outfit. His studio down there just like a studio downtown. Me and Hound Dog Taylor and P. T. Hayes. "Rock" was on one side. And on the other side was "Trying to Find a Woman (It Don't Matter Who She Be)"—and the other one "I'm Getting Old and I Believe I'll Settle Down." And on the other side was "Bebop." That's somewhere around '55 or '56, somewhere along in there. And he never did release that. Somebody broke in there overnight and moved out all that stuff out from there, and he lost everything. So I never did know what happened to those.

Of the four sides you mentioned, which sides had you singing?

All of 'em—I was singing on all of 'em. Everything I recorded I mostly did my own vocals. The fact of it, in my band that I played with I did the biggest of the singing anyway, except for Big Boy Spires. We used to split it up. Hound Dog Taylor, we would split it up.

Let's talk about the records for Chance [Records]. How did those happen?

Well, Otis [Smothers] cut those records with Spires. And there was something wrong. Chance [owned by Art Sheridan] didn't like it how the record went. So Big Boy Spires came and got me to go with him to cut it over. That's how I got down there.

Where did you cut them?

I forgot the name of the studio. It was downtown. But they never did release them. Until the Japanese label got them, that's how they got out. On "Fatmouth," Big Boy Spires and I were together on that. On "Silver-Haired Woman," Big Boy Spires and I were together on that—down at the studio.

Are those your vocals?

Yeah! He and I were together, but that's my voice.

What was the lineup for that session?

It was me and Spires and P. T., and I think it was Duke on them drums.

The two of you played a classic two-guitar style. Who played which part?

Now, this was the problem with Big Boy Spires. Don't get me wrong—he was a good guy, but his time was bad. When you playing with him you don't know which way you going. You don't know whether he's gonna hold the bass or whether he ain't gonna hold the bass, see. And that's why everything sounds so much alike. If he's gonna do the bass, he won't do it! He'll do the bass awhile and then he'll get on the lead. He was a nice guy, but that was his problem—he had bad timing. Your fingers would get up and didn't know which way was he going, but his timing wasn't good. That was all that was wrong with him, but he's a nice person. Now, he'd do better by hisself! Because he cut his time. See, where you're supposed to maybe get a whole bar, he's gonna give you a half. And where you get a half, he's liable to cut to a quarter, you know what I mean? So you had to know him to play with him! You had to be used to him to play with him.

How long did you play with him?

I only had one job with him, but we used to practice together. L. C. McKin-ley—I know you didn't meet him, 'cause I think he had done passed—now, he was a T-Bone Walker man. You put T-Bone Walker over there and put him [L. C.] over here, you wouldn't know which one to listen to, because they both sound just alike. I used to get on him for that. I told him, I say, "You never will get nowhere!" And he didn't! You can't get nowhere patterned after somebody else's already made, you know what I mean? T-Bone Walker's already made. When they'd book him they'd put "L. C. McKinley versus T-Bone Walker." But he never *did* get nowhere, because he had T-Bone Walker's style. So every man gets his own style.

I've heard that he was quite difficult.

He was the kinda guy that was hard to get along with. He's long-headed, you know what I mean—he was that! Me and Johnny Young both tried to break him outta that, but you couldn't do it! You couldn't get to him. Me and Johnny Young both used to curse him out, tell him, "You ain't going nowhere playing like T-Bone Walker, 'cause he's already made!" But we couldn't stop him. That was just his way.

Did you see Elmore James a lot?

Oh, I knowed Elmore James. My God! I knowed Elmore James from down South! I went down there in '43. That's when I got acquainted with Elmore James. And he had Rice Miller [Sonny Boy Williamson II]. I went down there in '47. Same year that Sonny Boy got killed—the *real* Sonny Boy, from Jackson, Tennessee. And Rice Miller and Elmore James were playing in a theater there. And they said, "Sonny Boy Williams here!" I said, "Nooo-no!" They said, "Yes, it is Sonny Boy Williamson!" I said, "I just left Sonny Boy Williamson. He's playing right there on Thirty-first!" "No, he's here!" He [Sonny Boy II] was going through the country telling he was Sonny Boy Williams, and people believed it. And Elmore James was on the guitar. *Them people was believing he was Sonny Boy Williamson!* Come through there when Sonny Boy Williams made "Good Morning, Little Schoolgirl." Come through there blowing that—they all believed he was Sonny Boy Williamson. But he wasn't and I told 'em he wasn't. Some of them wanted to whup me—"I know who that is!" (*laughs*) And Sonny Boy made the record "Decoration Day," and he got killed on Decoration Day. Nineteen and forty-eight, that's when he got killed.

Did you know Sonny Boy [I]?

Uh-hm—yeah, I knowed him. Well, Sonny Boy was the kind of a guy—now, just like I say at the Purple Cat, I've known him to go there with a harmonica just blowing by himself. No guitar, no nothing! He was a nice guy, but practically all the records that he made, Big Bill Bronson [Broonzy] was on those records. Big Bill was a man that, he would help you. If you was trying to get somewhere, he would help you. Take Sunnyland Slim. He may not ever tell you, but Big Bill helped to make him. Big Bill got him on recordings. Big Bill helped him. Me and him was good friends. I did have a picture of me and Big Bill, but I hate so bad that that picture got away where I couldn't give it to the guy when he come around to put in that book. I don't know what become of that picture. Me and him had a picture made together about two years before he died. So he was my friend.

And Memphis Minnie—oh, that was the worst woman I ever seen in my life. (*laughs*) That woman could drink more whiskey than the law allow, and used to cuss her husband out—her and Son Joe. She'd cuss Son Joe and then say, "Lord, I'm gonna quit cussin' my husband." Now, Minnie was all right, but you had to get used to her ways. She cursed a lot. She had a bad mouth. But you get used to her. She's a pretty good guitar player—in her style.

Now, Tampa Red, he and Big Maceo mostly recorded together. [In] fact that was practically his main man, Big Maceo.

Did you see them around town?

Oh, yeah! I knowed Big Maceo personally! He had a stroke, and that stopped him from playing. Well, Tampa Red, he picked up Johnny Jones. Now, that's who give Johnny Jones his break. 'Course Johnny Jones is dead now. Over here on Fairfield and Lake—that was in '49. I used to close up at two o'clock and they stayed open till four. So I'd come over there on Fairfield and Lake where Tampa Red and Johnny Jones were. That's who throwed Johnny Jones out there. And Tampa Red, one of the places he played on the South Side, some of the guys jumped on him and he quit playing altogether. He used to come around where we were playing at. And after his wife died, he drank, so he went kinda flicky. So he got outta that. I missed him. I didn't know where in the world he was. Nobody could tell me about him. Over here on Albany, before you get to Ogden—that's where he died, over in that nursing home there. On his birthday they tried to get him to play something. The guy told me he hit one or two licks and started crying.

Were you ever over at his house?

No, I never *was* at his house. I never did even meet his wife, but I knew *him*. Now, Johnny Young knowed his wife, but I never did meet his wife, but I knowed him. He used to play at the H & T, I think, on State Street. He played there for a good long many years. But he was a nice guy, a very nice person.

Did you ever have any dealings with Melrose?

I acted a fool. I think I made a mistake. Jazz Gillum wanted to take me to Melrose. And I wouldn't go to audition. And I think I made a mistake when I wouldn't do it. Because Melrose, them guys didn't make as much money there as the guys did with Chess, so the guys tell me. I don't know—I just didn't go. Jazz Gillum, he used to come around where I was playing at all the time. A woman killed him, stabbed him to death. After he swung out from behind Big Bill, he couldn't come up with anything new. You know, they all runs out in the long run. We all run out to where we can't come up with nothing. But "Key to the Highway," that was his best bet. That's what put him over. He made two or three records behind that, but they didn't go nowhere.

This is a mystery. Most people doesn't understand this. I'll tell you how it happened. I was to go to Ninetieth and Mackinaw to play with Floyd Jones that Saturday night. I wasn't married to the wife that I have now. I was just living common-law with a woman. And she was kind of a jealous type of woman, you know what I mean. And so she played sick that night and I didn't go. And that Sunday I was at home by myself, and I was just sitting there watching the ball game. And I got up to go get me some coffee—I loved coffee. And when I got up I heated the water. We had instant coffee. And I turned to go into the pantry to get a cup. And when I turned to go into that pantry, something struck me just like if somebody would come and tell you, they'd say, "Your mother just fell dead." Sorrow ran all over me! And I went into the bedroom and I laid across the bed, and I said, "Lord, I don't know what's wrong with me!"

I got nervous and I was shaking. I was trembling. I started to crying. Something within said, "You've gone far enough." And I laid there and I told the Lord—see, I was a turn-back outta church; I got out of church and went back to the blues world—and I told the Lord, "If you don't kill me, I'll go back! And I'll stay there until I die." And so this is how I put that down and came back to God. A person that doesn't believe in God doesn't understand. From that to the ministry. I tried to keep out of ministry. I tried to keep from preaching—I didn't want to preach. But I had to do it. I even got sick, as I thought I was sick. I went to the doctor and the doctor couldn't find nothing wrong with me. Said, "I don't see nothing wrong with you." I said, "I got an ulcic [ulcer]." He started mashing on my stomach. He said, "Do that hurt?" I told 'im no. He said, "Well, your ulcic ain't bad." And this thing would worry me so that I wasn't eating worth nothing. And I told my wife, I said, "The Lord want me to preach, but I ain't gonna do it."

And that particular Sunday I went to church. And in church my mouth flew open, so they tell me, and I been going into this ever since. Now I'm looked upon in this field with more of authority than I was with the blues. People out there, they loved me. Now, this church that I go to every fourth Sunday give me an appreciation program every year. Last Sunday was that appreciation program. I wished you could have been there. Young ministers that I teaches things about the Bible that they don't know, they were there. Mens from other churches that knowed me since I come in outta the world, and just to hear those people speak on my life and give me the honor for what I stand for. So I would say that in both fields I have been honored.

Now, the world loves its own. When I was out there in the world I never did have no problems. We loved one another. If we had a misunderstanding in the band, when we come down for intermission we'd pour a drink or set up a fifth, shake hands, and say, "Oh, man, forget it!" and shake it off. But since I come in outta the world I'm disliked by some, but I'm liked by more than I am disliked. I'm a very good Bible teacher, and if I don't know it, I don't say it. But we got some that is teaching things that is not right. And when I try to righten 'em, you know what I mean, they don't hate me, but they doesn't care for me. They say I think I know more than anybody else. But I'm just as in earnest with this as I was playing the guitar. And I did love that guitar, brother—I did love that guitar. Now I love the gospel. I love what I'm doing.

That Bible there—you take every room you go into here, you'll find a Bible—I love that Bible. I studied that Bible. That Bible is 66 books. It's 1,189 chapters to that Bible. There's 31,173 verses. There is 773,692 words in the entire Bible. There's 3,586,489 letters in the entire Bible. So I have that Bible at heart. I studies that Bible very closely. And that I don't know, I don't tell it! But that I *do* know, I teach it.

So I got a bunch of young mens that on a Monday we all go for breakfast and preaches. And they can get to discussing something, and they'll say, "Let's ask the old man. See what the old man say about it." They call me the old man! So I give them the answer. Like Monday we were talking about the creating of Adam, and I was telling them about that Adam was in the garden before Eve was. And he knew about the tree. Some people have put it to different things, but it was actually a tree. You see, there was no sex movement of Adam and Eve while they were in that garden, because it was holy. They didn't even know they were naked until he did break the laws of God and eat of that fruit. And so he was talking about the watering of the garden. You see, there was a river that run through that garden and watered that garden. And after it got though, it parted into four heads. One river was Piaza [Pishon], the other was G. I. Horn [Gihon], another was Hadakeill [Hiddekel, the Hebrew name for the Tigris], and the other was the great river Eupetus [Euphrates]. They wanted to know and I told them the name of the river. So I dedicate myself. I dedicate my time to the word of God. I'm more happy in this now than I was when I was playing the blues.

You have a reputation as a man of God, yet one who is still tolerant of the blues.

Yeah. Because I have changed—you heard me today when I was out there. I couldn't condemn Otis, because every man have a right to what he believe in. I helped him to be what he was, you know what I mean. (chuckles) I couldn't condemn him, because I did the same thing. And I loved it! So whatever a man desire to be, he can be that. And whatever a man love, you take it away from him and he ain't no man. If you keep me away from church and take the Bible away from me, I'd be lost. Same way it was when I was playing that guitar.

Now, every Sunday night, I think, the preachers tell about the blues come on. You see, I'm gonna be honest with you—I don't set and listen to it. You know why? 'Cause my mind drift back there and I start thinking deep! Because I was a part of it—and my mind go back. But I don't want my mind to get back into it, you know what I mean. Definitely your mind will go back and you'll think about how you used to do.

When they first came here and interviewed me, I was living on Parkside. And all the offers that they offered me—a man from England, all the offers that they offered me—well, if I hadn't been for real, I would have accepted it. Snooky Pryor had quit. Snooky Pryor was a Bible teacher in church. You know what happened, don't you? When they come along where he could make that long money, why, he put it down and went right back! Well, most people doesn't understand—I am for real! I'll never go back to that as long as I live. Yet it's still a part of me, because I did it and I loved it.

I'm very much thought of in the field that I am in—very much thought of! I was playing at Turner's Lounge one night. I didn't show up. I was sick. He told me, "Uncle Johnny, there's more people know you than any one man I ever seen in my life. And all of them speaks well of you!" I say, "That's because I'm regular." So what I am, I don't let it go to my head! I'm just regular.

You take a lot of preachers, they won't even talk to a wino. I got some winos up there on that corner. They all call me Daddy! And when they want a quarter or half a dollar or something, I give it to 'em if I got it. Now, I can go into the store and they say, "Wait, Reverend. We'll put that in the car for you." Those people are human beings like anybody else. I have drinked, and so why should I lift myself up above those people? Because God love them peoples just like he do me—they still living. And so I treats them nice. Any question they wanna ask me, sometimes they be up there arguing among themselves about the Bible. "Oh, here comes Rev!" I stop and I talk to 'em. If they want a quarter or something, I give it to 'em. So I'm just a regular person. I been that way all my life.

Little **Hudson**

Hudson Shower, aka Little Hudson, was a guitar player and vocalist who in the early 1950s recorded a handful of highly regarded blues sides for Joe Brown's J.O.B. label. His recordings of "Rough Treatment" and "Looking for a Woman" were classics of the era. Hudson was active on the Chicago club scene for many years—both before and after his J.O.B. sessions—but he never had another record. Perhaps there were just too many aspiring artists on the scene for Hudson to capture the attention of the major labels,

Little Hudson. Photo courtesy of Mike Rowe/Blues Unlimited.

or perhaps it was the changing style in blues or the arrival of rock 'n' roll. Whatever the reason, Hudson Shower never was able to attain major blues star status, but he takes his place among the ranks of the lesser lights who managed—with limited opportunity—to make classic recordings. In this accomplishment he joins such notable bluesmen as Blue Smitty, Little Willie Foster, Moody Jones, and Big Boy Spires. Another claim to fame for Little Hudson was his association with John Lee Williamson—Sonny Boy I. He played and ran with Sonny Boy on a regular basis and was with him earlier on the night that Sonny Boy was murdered.

I have absolutely no recollection of how this interview took place. I assume that it may have come about after talking with Jim O'Neal. I would often ask him who was still alive and might make a good interview. I know that I never ran across Hudson on the music scene. If he was in the clubs at all, they were not the same clubs I was working. I believe I called Hudson at home and made arrangements to do the interview at the radio station. We managed to stay in touch from time to time after the interview was broadcast. During one of our telephone calls several years later, I was surprised to learn that Hudson had quit the blues to join the church. He had become the Rev. Hudson Shower and was operating a small storefront church. He came by my home studio one year to record a prayer for my annual Christmas program. With this book project under way, we managed to talk again just recently. Hudson is now retired from both the blues and the church and is living comfortably on Chicago's South Side. This interview took place in September 1985.

■ ■ ▪

I was born on a plantation called Long Rise, Mississippi, 1919—September the sixth. My mother was named Ida Belle Shower and my daddy was named Elijah Shower. I got several brothers and sisters—Henry, Leo, Willie, Gert, and May Lou. One died here lately—Willie, the youngest girl, died about six months ago.

And the fact of business where I got started from, practically all my people can play music, you know. So I started when I was about, say, eight or nine years old, because there was always a guitar around—because my uncles, my mother, my grandmother, my father. I got a brother, now, that play piano and guitar. He moved back down to West Memphis. And my father, he passed away in '75, but he was eighty-two years old and he could still play. It was practically old-time blues just like you're playing today—everybody get around the campfire, the log fire, whatever you want to call it, and sit around and start playing. And the thing about it, my grandmother raised me, because my mother died at an early age. I was raised by a grandmother and so that was her husband, and that would be something like my grand-stepfather, but it still was a stepfather because my grandmother raised me. *That man was so mean!* Now, I hate to tell this, but this is true. I could be sitting down eating, he probably wouldn't even allow us at the table anyway when most of [the] time we have to sit on the floor and eat. He would just as soon come over and kick the plate out from under us, you know.

So I had another brother, but he died when he was about ten or eleven years old. Now, he liked him because he was one of them mischievous child, he didn't take nothing serious. See, I was easy. He'd say anything to him and get away with it, but, see, if I did that they would whip me. But my brother, I used to see my brother and cuss him out, 'cause he loved him. He could have thrown a brick at him and anything. Got the shotgun one time, and he would have killed him, but—how he got the shell in there backward, I don't know—he got the shell in [the] gun backward and he got it up there. Ten years old. I'll never forget. It was a pump gun and he pulled the trigger, but the shell was in there backward. It was just a miracle! So for telling this, I don't know, maybe there was something wrong with his brain. Sometimes he would be nice; he'd sit down there and tell us different stories about things, and then he would go off, and—oh, boy—he'd just as soon throw a brick at me as take a switch or strap and whip me with it. He'd just as soon do that, and I'd be ducking and all that stuff. And so my uncle would come over, and my grandmother—when he come over, my grandmother wouldn't tell him what was going on—he didn't know what was going on. And I couldn't tell. If I did, I'd get my head smashed in, see. So I had to take it.

See, Grandmother, she wouldn't let my uncle see. If my uncle had known it, he would have taken us away from there, see. But she would always keep it hid from them. And back in the days when I come along, you couldn't dispute an older person, you was out of line. And they wasn't going to believe nothing you say anyway. But one of them uncles, the younger one, he did kind of believe what was going on. But, see, when he was around, oh, we was mellow! I mean, you could put us as kings, 'cause that's the way he treated us. Finally, one day it almost come to a head, 'cause he thought my uncle had gone back down to Rolling Fork, Mississippi—he thought my uncle had gone back. But he didn't go back that day—he was in bed asleep. And my stepfather got up that morning and he started raising hell, and so, hey, my uncle got up. And that's when he began to think about what I been trying to tell, see, but that was the younger uncle, and the older uncles wouldn't accept it. See, the younger uncle wasn't but thirteen years older than I was, and he believed what I was saying.

So then he gets up and say, "Now I see what's going on!" But it didn't last long, because he [the stepfather] died in about a week or so after that. But I'm going to tell you—one morning he went out to the haystack, they were cutting hay. He put two forks of hay up on there, the way they tell me, and he fell dead. When they brought him back to that house and the doctors pronounced that he was dead, I went behind that chimney corner and if I didn't laugh awhile! (*laughs*) I patted my hands! (*laughs*) I was so glad! I was thirteen. I was so glad, I didn't know what to do! 'Cause he should have been gone a long time ago! (*laughs*) But boy, he was something!

So when I got about nineteen years old I came to Chicago, which has been a pretty good while ago. Well, at the time—I'm going to tell you just like it is—it was so bad down South between the racial. If you stepped out of line—you didn't have to step out of line, just somebody say you did—they'd just as soon kill you or take you over there and beat you up. And I just wasn't going stand for that, and I know I would have been dead, see. And that's why I left and come to Chicago. Now, when I come to Chicago it wasn't much different, if you want to know the truth, and it wasn't much different. The reason I say it wasn't much different, because you couldn't get no job. If you got a job and if you had a skill, it didn't mean nothing, because they wouldn't hire you anyway.

I started playing in the nightclubs—well, not immediate when I came. I was fooling around going from one place to another one, meeting guys. I always liked music. Lazy Bill [Lucas], now, that's where I really got my start from, 'cause he used to live right behind me when I was living at Thirty-second and King Drive now, *was* South Park, 'cause he lived on Vernon. I was working in what you call a semi-steel mill. I worked there many years. I worked there about thirty-nine years. But I was playing music on the weekend. I played music about fifteen years straight—Friday, Saturday, Sunday. And so he used to sit out on the porch, and he be playing when I get off of work. And I had to come by his house and I used to stand there and listen, and I got kind of friendly with him. And we started gathering up there together—he could play piano, you know.

The date when I first met Bill was somewhere around about '44, I think, 1944. The first place I play in was called the Club Plantation. It was Thirty-first Street Place, right off King Drive. And we made it pretty good there. I saw I was drawing a flock of people in there, I don't know why—I didn't know if I was doing it well or if they just like to come in there. I had the type of a voice—I had a high-pitched voice all the time, mostly high pitch. But not only the voice I used to have, people get on to me 'cause I could just get out there and imitate *anybody.* I could sing just like Nat King Cole—anybody! So that's why I guess I had the crowd, because I had a lot of variety of songs and different ones. It didn't make no difference if it was Lowell Fulson or Muddy Waters—someone tell me to sing like 'em, I sing just like 'em! Play just like 'em, too! This guy used to come up and say, "Who is you? Man, I can't figure you out. You play everything!" So that's why I'd always draw a big crowd and I was always interested in a crowd. That's just about the size of it. We played there for maybe six or seven months, [and] we wasn't getting nothing that amount to nothing. Just playing, 'cause I loved playing. It didn't matter whether I got anything or not!

Then I went on from there—then I started getting up bigger. Everywhere I went I had people—oh, my goodness, you couldn't get in the place—wherever I went you could[n't] get in the place—they had a chain at the door. Then I'm going to get on where the Red Devil come in. I was sitting on the back porch one day. My wife had a can of Red Devil Lye sitting down there, and I looked down and saw that can. And we were so hot at that time—drawing people—so that's where the Red Devil Trio come at. When we got that Red Devil, every sign everywhere [said] "Red Devil Trio." "Red Devil Trio," that's all they had to put on there. It didn't make any difference if we went from one club to another one. It didn't make any difference—there was still a crowd of people. How they knew it? It wasn't broadcast anywhere. They'd put it in the paper. But wherever we went the crowd followed.

So the next thing, we started off at the Dewdrop Lounge at Thirty-sixth and Wentworth. I played there for a few weeks, but I didn't stay there too long, 'cause they had a kind of a squabble there like I didn't like, you know. They had some whatchacall dancers, but they was freaks and I didn't care for 'em. So I left there and went to the Joy Box at Thirty-eighth and State. I played the Joy Box a long time. And then I had changed pianos when I got there—I had changed piano players. I had Henry Gray was playing piano, and James Banister was drumming on the drums. So when we left Thirty-eighth and State we went next door to that—I forget the name of that, but it was right next door to that—but we only played there about four or five nights. We didn't stay there too long. And the next stop was 2711 Wentworth—that was Club Alibi. And that's where I began to get the real big name there. So after I went down to Club Alibi and started playing down there, we played down there for, oh, three or four years. I played with bands such as Tiny Davis—you remember Tiny Davis? I was the added attraction to that, but I drew more people than she did. So then they switched it around and had her [as the] added attraction. (*laughs*) She was bigger than me, but I had the most crowd! We played there, I don't know, three or four years there, I guess.

Then I started broadcasting—WTAQ from LaGrange. That happened in, say, 1953. I remember just as good, 'cause I just had bought a 1953 Ford they called the Victoria, at that time. Flamingo Red—ivory top and Flamingo Red—the prettiest thing I thought I ever had! 'Cause I never had had a new car. Bud Reilly was the disc jockey at that time coming from LaGrange. And so many other things I met up on, like Big Bill Hill. I used to be with him a lot of time when he was coming from Oak Park—WOPA. When he got on that first station, I can't even call the name of that, 'cause it didn't get no further than across the street. My regular main place was— I changed pianos again. After I left 2711 Wentworth I changed pianos again and went to Eddie Boyd. Eddie Boyd used to play piano—I know you know Eddie Boyd. So that's where he and I split up at the Dewdrop Lounge at Twenty-seventh and Wentworth. So then I changed pianos again and I went back to Henry Gray. Well, Henry Gray got to the place he would drink so much, so I run up on this other fellow called Lee Eggleston. He was the king of piano players—man, this guy could play, too! He's kind of paralyzed now, though. Curtis Jones played for a couple of months with me. I forgot to mention Curtis Jones—he was in there, too! Now, I left out the other piano I had. The last piano I had was Cleophus Johnson—that's the last piano. And the last drummer I had was Willie Smith. Now, he used to play with Muddy Waters. So I been around the clock with the piano players.

And then we played at the place they called the Hob-Knob at Fifty-second and Wentworth. Now, that was the spot, the Hob-Knob. We had people stack up over there; they used to stay in line from the time we start to the time we leave. But I remember one night—this is one of the funniest things ever happened to me—in the Hob-Knob at Fifty-second and Wentworth, I was playing there. The guy come up there, they got a chain across the door, and he say, "You know one thing?" he told the floorwalker. "I been trying to get in this place all night and I ain't got in here yet!" And he said, "I'll tell you what. You wait till I come back. I'm going to get in here!" So he goes back home and he gets a shotgun and put it in one of those burlap bags. And he come up there and the floorwalker saw the butt end of that gun, and he said, "I'll tell what you do. You go put the gun away, and then you can come in here all you want!" (*laughs*) He said, "I just want to hear Little Hudson sing *one* song—that's all I want to hear!" So he sat up at that table and you know that guy bought two fifths of Old Grand Dad, and he set that table up over there and set up this table here. And he heard me play two songs—he heard me play "Shake It Baby." That's all he wanted to hear, and he walked right on out the door—just like that!

They was made for J.O.B. Lee Eggleston was on piano when that record was made. Lee Eggleston and Jesse Fowler—just us three—Jesse Fowler on drums. Well, J.O.B., he was good, but he wasn't quite strong enough, see. And the releases, what I want him to put out—I don't know if you have it, "Shake It Baby"—would have put me way over at that time. Because that thing was really rocking in the clubs—that was my theme song in those clubs. It's got a pretty good beat to it—it's a shuffle beat. And the people just went wild over that. They had got to the point where they named me every time they see me. "Shake It Baby," that's what they called me, you know. All J.O.B. wanted was the record "Looking for a Woman" backed with "Rough Treatment." Now, he thought that would have been better, but my idea of "Shake It Baby" would have been better. And then another thing—I guess J.O.B., Joe Brown, was a good guy, but he always claimed he helped me write that song. He didn't even know me when I started that song. He got his name on there, "Shower and Brown," but he ain't got nothing to do with that "Rough Treatment." I made that "Rough Treatment" myself, because that's the way I come up—'cause I come up under a stepfather—and that's what made me made the "Rough Treatment." Now, I got one thing in there about my mother-in-law. I never had no rough treatment from my mother-in-law, but I had to put that in there to make the record rhyme up. Now, there was quite a few copies sold here, but I just didn't have no interest in it. I really didn't have no interest in "Rough Treatment" and "Looking for a Woman," but the one I wanted was "Shake It Baby."

If you really want to know the truth, I was more interested in my job than I was the record. If I had just put my feet down and gone after it like the other guys did, I would have been up in there, too! But all I was really interested in was entertaining. I practically wasn't interested in records at all, but, you know, as the guy cut them, I accept the cutting them. I made some records for Chess, too, but they wasn't never released—back in the late fifties. This would have been '55 when I cut for Joe Brown, and this would have probably been around '58, something like that. I don't know what happened to those tapes. They say they can't find 'em, but I know Chess didn't throw away nothing. (*laughs*) They must have put them away somewhere they couldn't find them, but I made two cuts there. You know, I don't even know what's the name of them now—I done forgot. It was the same trio—I met him through Muddy Waters. After Muddy Water[s] was playing at the Dew Drop Inn on Thirty-sixth and Wentworth. And then he went to talking about Chess, he said, "You should come down there!" No, the first beginning of it, he told me to come down there, and then after I didn't go, Chess sent for me. He sent for me through Howlin' Wolf. He sent for me to come down to the studio. So I went down there, and they had all them—Chuck Berry and them—down there, you know, at that time. And they had us to sit down and play some numbers. Okay, he told me to come back the following week and rerecord them, but, boy, that's been so long that I don't know whether he even named the numbers, but I know I made two sides.

What Chess wanted me to play was the imitation of "Mule Train." You remember "Mule Train"? He heard me play that in the club one night—he heard me play "Mule Train." He wanted me to write a song containing "Mule Train" with the same music. I wrote that song for him. I can't think of the name of it now, but it's been so long that I had his secretary to type it out, and it went like "Mule Train." Now, he got that—he's got one that's almost like Howlin' Wolf—"Going Upstairs"? But instead of me going upstairs, I'm going down in the basement—that's what mine was. He got all that. See, Chess loved me for that "Mule Train" 'cause I had that "Mule Train" down pat, just like Frankie Laine. The only thing I didn't have in there was the whip. (*laughs*) I used to be in the studios, go down there where these guys was. I knew them all, Chuck Berry and all of them. I knew all of them 'cause we all went to the same studio. I used to go down there and listen to them all play, but—I had songs wrote and give them to other people. Muddy Waters cut some of my songs what I wrote. "I'm Going Back Home (to My Family Where I Belong)"—Muddy Water[s] cut that. I gave that to him back in the early sixties.

Anytime I heard a guitar ring, it didn't make no difference if I was laying in the bed, I'd get up and go where it was. See, that's the way I was, 'cause I loved it. In fact, I could just sit here and give a book on the fellows. I knew all those guys. I used to be around them. I know them all. I used to be out there with all of them. I tell you, the main musician back in them days was Big Bill, Sonny Boy Williams—which his name is John Lee Williamson—and Blind Davis, Blind John? Now, them was the main event—that played together all the time, that made records all the time. Me and Sonny Boy used to be together a lots—in different clubs, I used to go where he was just to sit down and listen. Now, "Bluebird," "Take This Letter Down South for Me," and "Good Morning Little Schoolgirl." That's the first one I think he record—"Good Morning Little Schoolgirl," that's what made him! Now, him and a little short guy used to be with him, play guitar, and there wasn't but them two. And they come down in the state of Mississippi when I was about, what, fourteen? And they was playing "Good Morning Little Schoolgirl" and "Bluebird," too. Sonny Boy used to go down the street and, I'm going to tell you, he was a mastermind. He could go down the street and see something and then make a song out of it. We was walking down the street together, down Thirty-first Street one day, and he saw a guy walking down there staggering, you know, drunk. Three weeks later he come out with the record "*I was walking down on thirty-first Street*" ["Alcohol Blues"], and I said, "I knew you was going to make that record!" He say he drank so much his eyes couldn't even give a peep. But that was real funny record and we laughed about that awhile. He said, "I told you, Junior"—he always called me Junior. "I told you, Junior, I was going make it!" I said, "I know you was!" Because that guy was walking down the street staggering.

He would get a big kick out of me singing, sound just like him. (*laughs*) Now, I was with him the night that he got killed. I was playing at the Plantation at that time. Sonny Boy came up there and made a record with us called "Cold Chills (Run All Over Me)." He would give me the mic sometimes, let me sing it, 'cause I could sing it just like he could. Then he blew the harmonica, and I'd say, "Hey, Sonny Boy," and you know when womenfolk come up to him, he's the type of guy quit playing and go to hugging them—it didn't make no difference. And I told him, "Man, let me tell you one thing. You don't do that, 'cause you don't know who the old lady's husband or boyfriend. They might get other thoughts about what you doing." "Oh, Junior!"—he used to call me Junior. "Oh, Junior, they aren't going to hurt me! They aren't going to bother me!" I say, "Don't put nothing beyond people today." Because in the same night before he came in there, it was a lady come to the bandstand and brought her husband there with her. She had told him that I was trying to make love to her, make a date or something with her. *I didn't even know the woman!* Then when she gets up there, she tells the man, "Oh, I was just joking to make you jealous!" I said, "Look, lady, you don't do that, 'cause there's no telling what this guy did." Then he took her on out. I don't know what happened behind it.

But the next night Sonny Boy come in. We was up together till around about—I think he left me about twelve o'clock that night. Well, I didn't go nowhere that night after we got off playing at the Plantation. I went straight on home. And when the news come out the next morning, he was *dead!* And I just couldn't believe it. I say, "Well, me and the guy was together about four or five hours ago!" And they said, "Well, he's dead." He lived on Rhodes—Plantation was on Thirty-first Street—he lived on the thirty-third hundred block on Rhodes. But they found him outside. But I'll tell you one thing—it was more than one person, 'cause that guy'd whup two or three people. He was fast as a cat. Now, him and Big Bill Broonzy? They used to get into it all the time, but, see, Big Bill was six foot, 200 pounds, too, you know. Sonny Boy was five eleven—he wasn't quite six. He wasn't no big fat guy, but he was kind of tall and 190 to 195 pounds, so he wasn't small. If he would have listened to what I had to tell him about them women, he probably be living today.

That club over there on the West Side called Ruby Gatewood's [Tavern], that's where I saw Big Bill over there on Lake Street. It was right there on Lake Street—Jim Martin owned the place—and that's where I met him [Big Bill]. Now, he set down—he tried to fool me downtown to the Blue Note. They had a band there, and he said, "You can do it. Don't be afraid." But I had never played too much onstage, and I was afraid to go on at the Blue Note. He said, "Well, I couldn't go myself, but I had to get somebody and I wanted you to go down there." He said, "Oh, you're a handsome-looking guy and you can fake it anyway. Just go out there and strum a little bit—you can *sing!* That's all they want—you won't have to do but a couple of numbers!" And that's why today I sings a lot of his songs and got his old records at home. "Cell 13" ["Cell No. 13 Blues"], I got that at home. Sometimes I sit down and sing "Cell 13" and record it and see how it sounds, just by myself. And "Old Man Blues"—I got "Old Man Blues," "Evening Blues" by him. And I said I was going to go back and learn all the lyrics and words in them, and get them boys together and try to see how it sound. Because I liked that guy. He was the first one started me up on the stage that first day, but Lazy Bill Lucas, he's the one that made me really interested in it! But Big Bill Broonzy was the first guy called me on the stage—I'll never forget it—Thirtieth and Indiana, at the Harmonica Hotel in the basement. He was a real outstanding guy.

Also, Big Maceo—he was, too! He come down to the Plantation after he got paralyzed and played a few numbers with us down there. Tampa Red—oh, yeah. I remember when Tampa Red was down there on Twenty-second Street—him and Johnny Jones playing down there. I went down there several nights. Tampa Red was a pretty good guy, but he was a guy he talked slow, he walked slow—he looked like an unconcerned person, you know. But the guy—as many years as I knew him, I didn't even know he could play piano. I always thought he was at the guitar, but he could play piano just as well as he could play guitar. But him and Johnny Jones used to team up. Now, before him and Johnny Jones it was Big Maceo and Tampa. Now, they made some good records, like "Worried Life Blues" and all them kind of records. Tampa Red, I could hear old Tampa in the background. I know their sound, see.

And Nighthawk—that's another guy I used to sit up all night long, had to go to work, sit up everywhere he went to hear him play. He's a nice, easygoing guy. Had a girl sing with him—I guess was his old lady named Anne—but she died with the pneumonia a long time before he died. He used to play there in a tavern at Thirty-first and Indiana. Right behind there used to be a theater called the Terrace Theater. And I was at that time working in a grocery store. I was a young boy at that time, too! I wasn't but about twenty, twenty-one. I used to go sit up down there and listen to him play, and I had learned this song from Big Bill Broonzy, "I'm Gonna Make My Getaway" ["Makin' My Getaway"]—"*Bye-bye Arkansas, hello Missouri. I'm going up north and join Rogers too. If I feel tomorrow like I feel today, I'm gonna pack my suitcase and make my getaway!*" I used to go down there and I had a lady used to come in the store, and I told her I was going to go down there where Robert Nighthawk and them was and sing "Make My Getaway." Sure enough, she was down there that night! I couldn't sing so well. I could do all right, but just nervous, you know.

And they had a little guy about this tall (*laughs*), used to play drums. This guy was so little till you couldn't hardly see him behind the drums. He had something going. That was "Porkchop," Eddie Hines. Now, I can't leave Sunnyland. I used to see Sunnyland—he was the oldest one out there, but I never had him on the stage with me in no public in different places. Now, that's a guy if you can play with him, you can play with anybody, because his style of playing is so difficult than the average piano player. I don't know whether he's on the style of Leroy Carr or Roosevelt Sykes, but anyway, Sunnyland Slim liable to be singing about tomatoes and maybe wind up talking about pears later, see. So that's the type of guy he is. But the best record he ever made was "Brown-Skin Woman," to my concern. Same time as Dr. Clayton—remember Dr. Clayton? I just saw him once. At Thirtieth and Indiana at the Harmonica Hotel. He was down there when Big Bill Broonzy and Big Maceo was playing at the Harmonica Hotel.

Now, people can say what they want to about B. B. King, but B. B. King is one of the most generous people that you want to meet! He's a nice person. Muddy Waters was also a nice person. I'll tell what I did one time, when we was playing at the Club Patman—I forget, Club Patman on the North Side. It seated about two hundred people, and it used to be standing room only. We was playing there at the weekend, like Friday, Saturday, Sunday. Howlin' Wolf was playing there on Sunday evening, you know, giving a cocktail party or something like that. And sometime I would go to work early, because I was supposed to start at something like nine, so I'd go just before the cocktail party be over with and may sit in on a couple of numbers. I'll never forget that the longest day I live! I was up there singing about "So Many More Years." And he got so jealous of that, he told me he didn't want me on his bandstand no more! (*laughs*) Okay—that's all right! I left—I didn't come back, but when I didn't come back, the people didn't come back! This is the truth. Now, he's a big boy and the people didn't come back. He sent word by my piano player to tell me,

"Come back, sing anything he wanted and I give him fifty dollars just to come back!" 'Cause he didn't have no crowd, 'cause I was playing on the weekend—they wait until my time come on. So we used to have a lot of fun, and he and I would laugh about it after then.

Now, I'll tell you another guy was kind of on the stuck-up side, too—Little Walter. He was kind of on the stuck-up side, too. Now, I knew him when he was over there blowing in Jewtown and he didn't hardly have pants to wear. The guy was so proud of himself, do you know what he'd do? He'd go and get some shoes—and I'm not lying—and cut 'em out and make believe something wrong with his feet. But when he got up in the music there and started making [a] little money, his shoes always was enclosed all the time and they wasn't cut no more. So I asked him one day, "How come your shoes aren't cut now?" "Don't give me the publicity—I don't want the publicity!" (*laughs*) I said, "I know the reason they was cut before. You wouldn't tell nobody, but I know why they was cut before. 'Cause you didn't have no more to put on!" And we went over there—Jimmy Rogers, we was over there one Sunday evening and I'll never forget. Jimmy Rogers was playing with Muddy at that time, and Walter was just like a devil anyway, a lot of the things he'd do. Jimmy went to sit down and he pulled the chair flat out from under 'im, and he sat flat down on the floor. (*laughs*) And all the peoples in the place—B. B. King was there that evening, Howlin' Wolf, Memphis Minnie, Son Joe, and all us, J. B. Lenoir. Well, Jimmy didn't say nothing. He got up and brushed himself off. But Muddy Waters kind of got triggered about it. "You guys is too old to be doing things like that!" Well, we wasn't old then—twenty, twenty-five years old—but Muddy, he didn't like that so well, see. But I had a lot of fun with those fellows. None of them ever mistreated me!

So I has lots of fun in playing music—I loved it. I still love it, but I figured today, the way things set up today that the people don't react no more like they used to. I'll tell you one thing, music is not easy to play. People think it is, because you up there on the stage wailing away. But when you up there on that stage—I never did get used to it. I was always afraid, you know—big crowd of people standing there—'cause when you meet a big crowd, you standing in front of this mic and you standing up there and all those people looking at you. That's not easy! And I'll tell anybody that I don't care who it is, the only way what it get easy is—at that time I used to drink a little bit, you know—and that's the only thing that bring it up! 'Cause I have had people come and says, "Now, you aren't doing nothing tonight. I know you can do better than that! What you want to drink, son?" So I get a drink—then there I go! But in other words, you'd be shaky up there, sitting up there sweating and everything. And that's another thing. You come out on the bandstand—you done played in there, and it's nine below zero, your shirt and things sticking to you—it's harder work than where I was working, honest to God! Then you liable to catch rheumatism, anything you want to name, 'cause you come out nine below zero and your shirts is wet! Now, you know what you expect out of that? I really don't have to do anything if I don't want to, because I worked all them years. I worked thirty-nine years on one job, so I get a pretty good pension from that, so I really don't need to work!

Part Three **Esoterica**

Tommy **Brown**

The Atlanta blues and R & B scene was small almost to the point of non-existence—Titus Turner, Billy Wright, and Tommy Brown, plus throw in disc jockey Zenas Sears at pioneering R & B radio station WTES. Ironic, then, that a scene with such a limited cast should exert such a tremendous impact on pop music. Zenas Sears was one of a handful of trailblazing disc jockey/star makers, among the first hosts who broadcast blues on the radio and brought R & B of the late 1940s and early 1950s to the postwar generation. Billy Wright, a dynamic vocalist and quietly gay was the template and firsthand influence on the frantic, flamboyant, and fabulous Little Richard, while vocalist Tommy Brown's pioneering stage show, with his spins, splits, and microphone tossing, was the acknowledged role model for the Godfather of Soul, James Brown. Tommy, in fact, ran the gamut—starting as an R & B vocalist, making Chicago-style blues records with harmonica virtuoso Big Walter Horton, trading wives with bandleader/guitarist/producer/icon Ike Turner, taking time out to write the classic "Honky Tonk" for Bill Doggett, dabbling as a stand-up comedian, and finally producing the very first recordings by a local protégé named Gladys Knight.

Tommy Brown. Photo courtesy of Tommy Brown.

As of this writing, Tommy is largely retired from show business (he will take an occasional festival gig or overseas engagement) and until recently operated a private nursing home in the Atlanta area. Members of the Atlanta Blues Society got in touch to suggest that Tommy would make a great interview, and they were right! This interview took place on May 31, 2003.

■ ■ ■

I was born 1931—May 27, 1931. I'm what they call a Grady baby. That's the city hospital. Grady Hospital, in Atlanta. Well, really what happened was my mother would make me stay in the house. I was so small that she'd make me stay in the house. I couldn't get out and play football and baseball and stuff with the other kids. And she'd make me sit in the kitchen and watch her cook. And so I thought that she was going to make a girl out of me. So I started listening to the Major Bowles program and the people tap dancing. And so I'd come home from school every day and put on my Sunday shoes and get on the porch and make my feet sound like they did on TV. And I had an uncle who was a buck dancer and I'd watched him, and so I got into that. And just, as a dancer, which gave me good rhythm.

When I was a dancer, Cab Calloway's brother, Elmer Calloway, was teaching at the school. And so he was doing the show for the school. I was about seven years old then—between six and seven, because I started at six. And he had this show at the Royal Theater on a Saturday morning for the school. And I got on that show as a dancer. And I danced on that show, and somebody saw me and hired me to do a show at the YMCA the following week and paid me seven dollars, which was *big* money then. And the following week, I danced at the Peacock and I got paid. And from that down to a club called the Five o'Clock Supper Club, which was a white club my uncle worked in as a clean-up man. And so I guess that started my professional career right there.

Later on, my mother got me a piano and I played that for a year. And then I lost interest in that, because I didn't want to take lessons. So I got interested in playing drums. I didn't get to play them, though, until I got to the sixth grade in school. I decided I wanted to get into the band when I got into the sixth grade. And I went down to the band director's in the band room and told him I wanted to play drums. He said, "Well, we've got all the drummers we need." He had a kid named Paul Magahey was playing drums and playing the cadence on the drums. And I said, "I'll play anything he play." He gave me some sticks, because he didn't believe me. Well, I had the rhythm, because I was a dancer.

But I didn't know how to hold them, but I played everything and he showed me how to hold the sticks. He said, "Go home and take you an old inner tube, cut you a square out, and take you a piece of wood about an inch thick and about a foot square and stretch it over that. And take these sticks and practice." He showed me how to hold the sticks. So I came home and I practiced on everything I could find. And the next day when I went into band to show him that I could do it, he put me in the first band right away. That was my start. That was the high school marching band.

Well, the second day, I put *my* band together. I had got a saxophone player, and my mother bought me a set of drums about a week after that. And so I had got me four guys and we started my band, and we would play there at school during recess and for dances to raise money to buy band uniforms, and high school proms, and played for Georgia Tech, the University of Georgia, Emory University frat parties, and stuff like that. That was called the Maroon Note. And my name was Sweet Poppa TB.

They had the first black radio station here, was WERD. And the way that progression went, Zenas Sears used to have a show called *Diggin' the Discs*. It was on at WEST. Every evening they played black big band music. They didn't play any of the blues or nothing. Blues wasn't being played on the air. So eventually a guy named J. B. Blayton bought WERD and made it a black station. Well, Zenas Sears turned around and opened WAOK as a black station. And he had mostly black jocks. He had one or two white jocks, but they were mostly black. Well, the former governor of the state, Ed Rivers, had a station—a country western station in Decatur which is seven miles, right in the metro [Atlanta] area. WEAS. He brought Ned Lukens from Philadelphia down here as Jack the Bellboy. And Ned Lukens really set it on fire. So I had a show on Saturday for about thirty minutes on WERD, and then I had to leave there and go to WEAS in Decatur and go on. And I had a show there for about twenty minutes. Well, my band would play. Okay, if my band didn't show up I would have my drums and my sock cymbals [high hat] and I would play the piano and sing as my set. The one me. Whatever way I had to do it, I'd do it. Sometimes a guy would say, "Well, my wife say I can't go. I got some work to do and I can't be there." But I never missed a show. And I just did it, you know. And I was determined. And I loved it and I got plenty good jobs out of it. I played for all of the major colleges. And a lot of the high school proms.

Who were your main influences? When you wanted to sing and perform, were there people that you saw that were the people that you wanted to emulate?

Ivory Joe Hunter. That was my main man. Ivory Joe Hunter.

When you were in Atlanta, before you hit with anything and you were just scuffling around with the band, you knew both Billy Wright and Little Richard. Would you talk about them and their careers and just them personally?

Yeah, well, Billy—I understand Billy came to Atlanta as a chorus boy. And he used to work at the Point Sienna Club. And then when Billy was singing and emceeing over there, and that's when my band first backed him, before he got his own band. And when he would do little tours out through the little country towns, my band—I would take him in my station wagon. Until he got his own band, my band would back him. Well, Little Richard came into town and he hooked up with Billy and he really copied Billy. He styled himself after Billy. Well, his walk—he walked like Billy walked. And Billy, he's changed his hairstyle a little bit now from what Billy wore, but he had his hair the same as Billy before. And we used to do a little southern tour down through Georgia with a guy named Snake, had a little vaudeville show. And Richard would sing on that show. And he would give him a dollar to buy him a bowl of beans and a muffin. And sometimes he would sleep in my station wagon. And we would tour Anniston, Alabama; Birmingham, Alabama—a place outside of Birmingham called Foot's Place—and then come back to Atlanta, the 81 Theater. And then go down to Macon, the Douglas Theater, and on down into Savannah to a little theater down there in Savannah. We toured around like that, Billy and Snake and myself and Little Richard.

How did Billy Wright make records, and were you the band behind him?

On some of his first ones my band backed him. And then he got his own band. He got with a fellow that—you know, Billy was gay, and his man was a drummer. Older fellow. Way older than Billy. And Harper put a band together for Billy. He played drums. And that was after Billy had started recording. And he took over running Billy's business.

Didn't Billy have a nickname of some sort?

Prince of the Blues! Prince of the Blues, yeah. He was called Prince of the Blues. He was one of the best-dressed people in the nation. Billy was always dressed. He dressed like a man. He didn't dress like no gay person, you know. He dressed like a man. But he didn't hide the fact that he was gay. But he was one of the nicest people you would ever meet. He passed away a few years back. Richard came to his funeral. I guess, ooh, it's been five or six years since he passed away.

I know that you were out there and you had your share of success, or tasted a bit of success. What did you think when you saw Little Richard take off?

Oh, I was proud of it. Happy for him. He toured on the Show of Stars with us at one period of time. I rode in the car with him for a while.

Herman Lubinsky came through to record Billy Wright. Zenas Sears hooked him up with Billy Wright. And my band backed Billy Wright on his first recording. That was around 1947. And my band backed him. So the second time Lubinsky came in to record Billy, he talked to me to record me. And, of course, we came to terms. Hey, he recorded—sign anywhere! Because there wasn't that many people around here recording then. And so I signed up with Lubinsky. That was around the late part of '47, early part of '48.

What kind of material did you have for him?

Well, I did "Atlanta Boogie," and I called it "Women in Cadillacs." They called it "V-8 Baby."

You had a tune called "Double Faced Deacon." Would you explain what that was about and the complications that went with it?

Well, back then you couldn't talk about preachers and deacons and tell what they did. But I had seen something happen in the church that I was going to. My father at one time was assistant pastor. It was the biggest church in the area, in the Methodist Church, called Big Bethel. And I'd seen people in there arguing and fighting and stuff, going with this sister and that sister, and the pastor accused of going with this woman and that woman. And I just wrote the song, "Double Faced." *"Let me tell you about a deacon. Top hat and long-tailed coat. . . . Preach his best while winking at womenfolk. And he preached against gambling, said it was a sin and a shame. . . . Then met me in the alley, shot seven for my watch and chain."* And it just come to me like that when I'd sit down and decided to write something. They banned it. It started to hit and they banned it. They wouldn't let them play it. They'll play it now, but it's old-time stuff now. That's vintage stuff now. (*chuckles*)

Zenas Sears was doing a commercial for 20 Grand Ale. And I wrote a commercial for that and I recorded it for him. *"Twenty Grand's a man's best brand in the land. Pour it in the glass. Pour it down fast with the bubble in your glass and cool off your—."* But when it came out, two months later, it came out with Billy Wright singing it. Well, Zenas—I found out recently that Zenas had a bone to pick with me, because I wouldn't let him manage me and handle me. So when I wrote "Fat Hardy's Tardy," I recorded for Zenas, and I never knew he released it until last year when Brian Baumgarten had told me he had a copy up there in Canada and sent me a tape of it.

Well, Fat Hardy was a bootleg liquor manufacturer in the area that sold liquor to the local clubs, because, see, we didn't have pour licenses here then. They couldn't pour—black or white clubs. But the white clubs would get a license through the mayor's office, and if they were going to raid them the mayor's office would call them and tell them that the state was coming. But the black clubs, you brought your own liquor or they would sell you bootleg liquor in the clubs. They'd sell you ice and Coca-Cola. And so this one particular club had bought some of that liquor and 138—or 139 people died. And so when those died, I immediately wrote the song "Fat Hardy's Tardy." *"Don't want no Fat Hardy's Tardy at the party."* And he tried to sue me. Well, Zenas Sears put it out on some—I don't know what label he put it out on, because I just got a copy of it and not the record, but a tape of the song from Brian last year. And he put it out as "Roy Mays Boogie." Roy Mays was the trumpet player playing on the record, who was Villa Mays's brother. She was the local disc jockey and singer. And he put it out as "Roy Mays Boogie," and I never knew what had happened to it. But he and Otis Redding's manager, the road manager, collaborated and put it out on some label. And I don't know what label it was. It was about six or eight months after I recorded with Savoy when I did that, you know, because Savoy wasn't going to do anything to Zenas, because Zenas was the top deejay here. And he was hooking Lubinsky up with everybody, and of course Lubinsky wasn't paying anybody, you know. So that's how my recording started. And after he gave me away to Dot [Records] and I had the two hits with Dot, then he came back and wanted to record again. And of course everybody wanted a crying record. And that's why you got about three or four of them on there that's crying. And later when I worked with Laverne Baker, she told me that she took Johnny Ray in and taught him my act.

Do you remember Johnny Ray?

She told me she taught him my act. That he came into the Flame Show Bar in Detroit barefooted and cold in snow. She taught him how to do the crying thing. But there was nobody that did the falls. Didn't nobody. I fell out of the balcony of the Apollo Theater, out of the balcony of the Cow Palace in San Francisco. Well, I danced and I'd sing and I did splits, and the thing with the microphone that James Brown does, he got it from me. Spin it and catch the mic and go into a split and come back up. Of course, mine was more refined. Now, he does the thing catching the cord. And then Joe Tex would slide off the stage. Now, Joe Tex told me that he used to follow me and watch me. And James Brown stopped the show, his show at the Palms Café in New York one night. Liz Lands and I was there. And he started out, and he saw me and he stopped the show. And he called me up and he told them, he said, "This man is responsible for my career," because, truthfully, all the dance steps he got, he got them from me. I used to dance on the bar. Dance between glasses and spin and turn and split and all, on the bar. But when I got out of the service, the agencies kept me in a small circuit and these guys would watch me and then go do my act someplace, and then when I'd go there, people thought I was copying off of them.

How about the crying stuff on stage? Tell me about the crying on stage. I know that was the big thing that went along with the hit, right?

Right. Okay, the way that came about, I was singing Ivory Joe Hunter's "Blues at Midnight." (*sings*) "*When the midnight hour's chiming, I was in my bed alone.*" I was dating a young lady that is known as Dot Willis, who supposedly married Chuck Willis. Well, they were common-law married, but they weren't married at all when I was dating, because we were engaged. And I was at the Peacock—Royal Peacock—on the stage and I was doing that song, and she came in with another guy. And I—when I come to myself, I was on the floor banging on the floor and crying. And I ended the song, and when I went up front I passed by her, wouldn't speak to her. And Ned Lukens, this same Jack the Bellboy, stopped me at the bar, he said, "Tommy, why don't you keep that in your act?" He said, "That's a good act!" I wasn't acting, but he said, "Why don't you keep that in your act?" But I didn't think about it. But I left there and went to Hopkinsville, Kentucky, the next week. And musicians don't really like to play for singers. They didn't then and they still don't. And I got to Hopkinsville, Kentucky, and I told them I wanted this song in B-flat, and they started it in E-flat and I couldn't sing it in E-flat. So I made up the lyrics to "Weepin' and Cryin'" as I went along. And then I put that back into the act and it went over, so I kept doing it. And I still do it today.

They sang blues. I liked them. And B. B. King and I had worked together starting back around '47 in Nashville, Tennessee, at the New Era Club. He was coming in. He was a disc jockey then in Memphis, Tennessee. And we used to work at the New Era Club there down on Fourth Avenue in Nashville, Tennessee. And Fats Domino would come into the theater—the Bijou Theater, I think it was called. And so, like I say, I worked with all of them. And as a kid, my band backed people like Roy Hawkins.

What can you tell me about Roy Hawkins? Because almost nothing is known about Roy.

Only thing I know is somehow he had lost the use of one of his arms. He had either had a stroke or been in an accident. And Roy came to Atlanta and then he had some dates booked through Texas and stuff. And my band—I traveled with him and my band backed him up. And we had a guy named Freddie Jenkins. Used to play with [Duke] Ellington, used to play trumpet with Ellington, had half of his fingers on his trumpet hand was cut off at the lead joint on his fingers. And we did some dates with T-Bone Walker, and we had T-Bone's Cadillac while T-Bone was in jail! And we played Memphis and we got over in West Memphis, Arkansas, and had a wreck. And we came back into Memphis to get a car the next morning. We were sitting there in the car asleep, and this big cop banged on the door. A guy, Nat Foster, the piano player, rolled the window down. "What you black son of a bitches doing sitting up out here asleep?" So he asked everybody their name, and I was sitting behind the driver. When he got to me, I just raised up on the seat, with my Masonic ring hit him in the face, and his attitude changed just like that. He said, "Yes, sir. Can I help you? What's your name?" I said, "Brown." He said, "Can I help you, Mr. Brown?" And I was a young guy. He said, "Can we help you in any kind of way?" And that's the way it was. And so we went on down through Mississippi and we went into a Billups station, and the guy there had about eight white guys working on the car at one time. And Freddie Jenkins got out of the car. The guy says, "Nigger, where the God damn hell do you think you are?" And so I told him, "From now on, you don't say nothing! You just let me handle it." I was a teenager, you know. And we went all through Texas with Roy Hawkins, and we came back and he went on back to the West Coast.

You know what? I don't remember what he sang, it's been so long. I don't remember what he sang. Whatever his hits were, we backed him on them, his hits. He played here and then we went on tour with him. Let's see. Who was booking us? Jimmy Liggins. It was Jimmy and Joe Liggins. There was two of them. And Jimmy stayed here and had set up a little booking agent here. And, you know, we worked a place down in Savannah, a guy named Gus Hayes had it. Tommy Small, a deejay out of New York, was working for a station down there, WJIV. That's how he got the name Dr. Jive. And he was the emcee. But when Gus would get drunk, he would come up and take over. (*laughs*)

And I was working there, and that night he came up and took the mic away from Tommy Small. Tommy told me that night, he said, "This is my last night going through this." And the next day he left and went to New York, and the next thing I knew he was Dr. Jive in New York. But then he didn't copyright the name and the station took it away from him. Oh, man, I've been around with these people.

You know, one thing I've always wondered—and I've never been clear on this— was Zenas Sears black or white?

He was white. He was a Jew.

And so all the big—there was like Hossman in, was it Nashville?

Hoss Allen.

These were all white jocks who were playing black rhythm-and-blues records?
That's right.

Except you said Zenas Sears didn't start out—he was playing big band.
Zenas Sears was playing big band music. They had a show called *Diggin'*
the Discs. And he played big band music. And on Sunday they would play
gospel music on that station. But wasn't no blues played, because blues was
called dirty music. Nobody played blues on the air during that time. When
Billy started recording, that's when Zenas started switching to play some black
music, but he couldn't play it there. That's why he bought and set up the other
station, WAOK.

What was it that you liked about Ivory Joe Hunter?
His performance, his mellow, his songs. (*sings*) "*Since I met you baby, my*
whole life has changed." They told stories. They told good stuff, you know? "*I*
need you so." When I started singing, I was singing like him. That's why when
"Tra-La-La" first came out, most people thought it was Ivory Joe. I had him in
mind when I was singing. (*sings*) "*Tra-la-la-la.*" I had his tone, you know? It
might not have come off that way, but a lot of people thought it was Ivory Joe,
especially here. And Ivory Joe was my main man.

I was playing a Tuesday night dance for teenagers at the Royal Peacock in
1951. The Griffin Brothers came through and they played at the Peacock that
weekend. And they asked me if I would join them for two weeks—leave my
band, because I was singing from behind the drums—and join them to sing,
because Margie Day had to have an appendicitis operation. And so I accepted
and the next week we were in Jacksonville, Florida, and Randy Woods, out of
Gallatin, Tennessee, came in with a song he said Tommy Ridgley had recorded. I
think Dave Bartholomew wrote it. And he said that he had an order for twenty-
five thousand if he could get it recorded right away. Well, Margie wasn't there,
and I tried to teach Thin Man, the saxophone player Noble Watts, how to sing.
I couldn't do him. Jimmy Griffin couldn't sing it. Buddy couldn't sing it. So he
said, "Well, if Herman Lubinsky don't let us use your name, we'll use another
name." Because I was under contract to Savoy. Well, Herman Lubinsky said,
"The kid's no good." And when he did that, he released the record—he flew it
back to Nashville and put it on the air that night. And the record hit. That was
a song called "Tra-La-La." (*sings*) "*Tra-la-la-la, la-la-la-la-la-la.*" It's on the CD.
And it was done in a radio studio; had no acoustics or nothing. And a couple of
nights later I was in Virginia, and I heard it on the radio there. So that record
hit. And then, as we went back up the East Coast, we got to Washington, D.C.,
at the Howard Theater. While we was there, he came in to record the "Weepin'

and Cryin'" song that he had seen me do. It went over quite well and he heard about it. And he came in and we recorded that in Washington, D.C.

We left there and we went into the Apollo Theater. Well, when we got to the Apollo Theater, we had our rehearsal that morning, Thursday morning. And Frank Schiffman sat down and he charts everything. So we were going on first. And so after we went on and they called me on, and I did the crying thing. I fell off the stage and down through the audience. After the first show, Frank Schiffman readjusts his shows to put the strongest acts in closing. So he told them, he said, "I want Tommy to close." And the Griffin Brothers said, "Well, we're the stars and we're not going to let him close." He said, "This is my show, and if he can't close the show, you're fired and he can work." So they went on and played for me. We opened on Friday night. And the following Thursday was when I was singing a song, and I can't find anybody that remembers that song. And Dot don't have any records—that they had—says (*sings*), "*I'm going to join the army if I have to volunteer.*" And they walked out on the stage and handed me my draft papers. (*chuckles*) And everybody cracked up. And that was on a Thursday night. And I left there the next morning and came into Atlanta. And Monday morning I was drafted. I went into the draft, into the Marine Corps.

"Weepin' and Cryin'" hit right after that, which became the number one record of the year. Which I didn't know until last year, this past year, in October, when I found out it was the number one record of '51 and '52. And both records hit about the same time. Because when I got out of service in August of '52, it was still number one. And while I was in there, I'm reading in the magazine, *Jet* magazine, where I'm appearing in Chicago. But that was Carlton Coleman working under my name. And like I said, recently I found out that Roy Brown worked under my name. I didn't know that until recently. But I knew there were about five people working under my name. And I was in there for nine months. So when I got out of service, the agencies basically kept me out of circulation and made their points, because they had other people there working as me. And incidentally, Randy never paid me anything for "Weepin' and Cryin'." So last year, in October, when I called BMI to find out about the royalties, they said, "Well, we don't go back past '71. And we've been trying to find you since '75." But prior to that, I kept in touch with them and they never gave me no money. And so then that's when the lady said, "Oh, yeah, that was the number one hit. You had got an award for that!" I said, "I did?" She said, "Yes." I said, "Could I get a copy of it?" She said, "Oh, yes. But it will take a little while, because the president has to sign it." Well, it took them about six weeks, but I got a copy of it. And he wasn't supposed to have been in my publishing firm. I got an award for both of them. One for me and one for the publishing company. But I never got no money. See? So that's about the round of "Weepin' and Cryin.'"

I came out of service. The day I got out of service, I was coming home. The Griffin Brothers were playing the Auditorium here in Atlanta. And the club owner had called my mother and asked her when was I coming, because he couldn't sell the tickets. And so I told her, "Tell him I'm on my way home now." And he said immediately after that, he—before he died, he always stopped to tell me, he said, "He sold out after that." And then they didn't want to let me sing "Weepin' and Cryin.'" He told them, "If you want to leave this town in one piece, you better let him sing it." So I did it in my Marine Corps uniform. I was stationed at Camp Lejeune after I finished at Paris Island in the Marine Corps. And they used to play Kingston, South Carolina, about every eight or ten weeks. So one night I got some bodies and we went over there. And when they saw me, they wouldn't let me sing "Weepin' and Cryin,'" because they said I wasn't with them anymore. So Buddy tried to do it from behind the piano. He was blind. And he sat there behind the piano and sang it. So they finally called me up to sing another number, but they wouldn't let me do that one. So I did another number and went over real well. And from that point on I never saw them again.

My first date was at the Showboat in Philly, where I had worked with the Griffin Brothers. And of course I didn't know that Carlton Coleman was working across in Trenton as Tommy Brown. So when the club owner saw me over there, he brought Carlton Coleman over to confront me, because he thought I was still in service and that was just another fake. And when Carlton saw me, he says, "Oh, baby, don't spring on me." I says, "I don't care. I know who I am." So this club owner went to the guy at the Showboat and says, "Hey, that's not Tommy Brown; this is Tommy Brown." He said, "No, I got Tommy Brown, because he worked for me before he went in the military." That's when they found out I was out of the service. So I called Lubinsky then about royalties and he sent me a check for $1.75. Yeah, he sent me a check for $1.75, and from that point on, Carlton Coleman went back to being Carlton Coleman.

And it got to a point in New York, they wouldn't book me. And I was laying around New York, and Jack Archer called me in one day. He was one of the guys in Shel's office, and he said, "Tommy, you've been branded." I said, "Branded what?" He said, "You're a smart nigger." I said, "What's that supposed to mean?" He said, "They're not going to book you." Because I wouldn't let anybody manage me. I wouldn't let anybody handle my money. I said, "You pay me and I'll pay you." You know, they booked me on a job out in Cleveland at Gleason's Lounge. And they told me, they said, "You got a week and possibly a week option." Well, they knew I didn't have an option. But that's the way to strand me out, because most entertainers, after the first week, they're broke. But I didn't drink and I didn't gamble and I wasn't married, so I didn't throw away no money.

And so at the end of the week, when I called to find out where was I supposed to go, they said, "Well, Jack Archer's in Florida. His father died." He had more deaths in the family. And that was going to leave me stranded. So by Thursday, when I contacted him, he said, "Look, kid, I got a gig down here in Newport, Kentucky, I can send you on, but I couldn't get you but $250." Well, my thing is this: that's better than nothing. But I went down there knowing that they were booking me for more than that. And I told the guy when I went in. He said, "We won't charge you no commission on this trip." But when I got there, it was a gangster club. They had gambling and stuff. So I told the guy, I said, "I left my contract in Cleveland, Ohio, in the desk drawer. Could I see your contract?" And it said $1,750. (*laughs*) So I said, "That's what you pay me." He said, "Well, they told me you owed them a lot of money." I said, "I don't owe them a damn thing. You pay me if you want me to work." Well, nobody talks to the gangsters like that, but I did. And so I said, "Now, if you want me to work"—and it's time for the show to hit—"you will pay me what you're supposed to pay me." So they did. And that's when I got hip to what they were doing up there. They were double contracting and would tell me one thing and send me one place. They'd tell a man $1,700 or $2,000, and they would take it all and give me a check for—a contract to pick up $500.

Who was your band at this time, Tommy?

I didn't have a band. I was working with house bands. I was singing with Bill Doggett. Well, the office had asked me to team up with Bill Doggett—not to work for Bill Doggett, but to team up with him—because they wanted to get Bill out of New York. I had the hit records; Bill didn't. So we left as a team, but when we got on the road, it ended up me working for Bill. Bill was handling the business. So it ended up me working for Bill, because he didn't want to play for me; he wanted to do his thing. He played "Tara's Theme," and "Autumn in New York," and that type of music. He didn't do no blues. But he had to back me up. And when we went on the road and we ended up at the Flame Show Bar in Detroit, and I was going over quite well. And Bill started to catch on. We were in Cleveland, Ohio—it was at Cleveland, Ohio—and they didn't want to pay a singer to sing. They had to pay the ten percent surcharge tax if you sing. So I didn't work that week, and if I didn't work I didn't get paid.

But we had two weeks at Loop Lounge and we had a Sunday off, which we went to Lima, Ohio, to play a dance. Well, we got there and those people didn't want to hear "Autumn in New York." They weren't going to dance by that. So he would hit on my number, and I'd get up and I'd dance and sing and they'd start dancing. And he'd cut me off and go into his stuff and they'd sit down. So at the intermission, I sat down at the piano backstage and I started playing "Honky Tonk," which I'd been playing for years. And I said to Billy Butler, I said, "Come on, Hank Snow." He said, "Yeah, like I used to play on the back porch with my uncle." And he started playing. And Shep's sitting on the drums at intermission, wiping his face with a towel. He kicked in on the drums. Said, "Come on, Scotty." Scotty got in and we rocked that house for thirty minutes. It jumped. Well, when we finished, Bill said, "Don't you ever do that again to me. You're not giving me respect as bandleader." I said, "Bill, why don't you record it. Name it 'Honky Tonk.' It ain't nothing but honky-tonk blues. Why don't you record it?" "No! That's not my type of music." So we went back to Cleveland. Loop Lounge. All week long that week, he couldn't get the house up. I kept saying, "Bill, play 'Honky Tonk.'" So the last night, we had a forty-minute set. He said, "Well, we've got a little old hand-clapping thing here we're going to do." From the first note, the house jumped. He couldn't play nothing else for that whole thirty minutes, forty minutes. We left there and went to Buffalo. Same thing happened. He wouldn't play it all week. So that last Sunday—that Sunday night, I said, "Bill, come on; play 'Honky Tonk,' man." And he tried it again. The house come down. I mean, he couldn't stop playing it.

So when we got through, he said, "The bus leaves at seven o'clock in the morning." Okay. Seven o'clock in the morning, I go down and I jumped on the bus and Red fired up the bus to pull off. I said, "Hey, Red, you're leaving Bill here." He said, "Man, Bill is in New York recording." I said, "What?" He said, "They're at Bell Sound Studio recording." So we got there about four o'clock that evening and went in the studio, and they were recording "Honky Tonk." And he was arguing with Syd Nathan about recording "Honky Tonk," an instrumental. "Syd," he said, "well, if you don't want to do it, I'm going to do it myself." So then I sat down and I played conga drums on there. And you hear me in the background, saying, "Oh, yeah." Well, I got forty-one dollars and a quarter for that set. When the first royalty check came, it was eighty-seven thousand dollars. He gave all the musicians seventy-five hundred dollars a piece. He didn't even speak to me.

And after I left him, about two years later, he ran across me in Chicago, "Hey, baby. Come on, let's get another hit." I said, "You're outta your mind, '*let's* get another hit,'" you know? So "Honky Tonk" was mine. Now, he and Henry Glover stole the vocal "Honky Tonk" from a girl named Cleo Bradford out of St. Louis. I was in the studio when Glover told him that he got it from this girl. And Glover was going to try to sing it, and Bill Doggett said, "No. You can't sing. Tommy's going on the road. Let Tommy sing it." But I see on the record, they put Bill Doggett as the vocal.

In the instrumental version of "Honky Tonk," do you have a composer's credit on that at all?

No, I got nothing on it. The title will give you twenty-five percent! But I got nothing on it. And of course nobody really knew I did it except me telling them that I did it. Because he just ignored it, you know? But he knew, because when he came to me and said, "Let's get another hit," he wasn't talking to Scotty or Billy Butler or Shep. He was talking to me. Nobody there but he and myself, you know. (*chuckles*)

Well, what they did—Irving Fell out of Washington, D.C., that owned the Super Drugstore there, he organized a thing called Super Attractions. And he had Clyde McPhatter—he was managing Clyde and he put all of his acts together—and we met at the Apollo Theater to go out on the road with the first show.

How many of them were there altogether?

I believe it was three. I'm not sure, because we were doing ninety one-nighters, I believe, twice a year. And the first one went out, it was all black. Then the second one was mixed and the third one was mixed. And the last one was all white.

Now, in the first one, the all-black package, who were the performers and who was the house band on that?

I believe that was Choker Campbell. I'm not sure. I know Paul Williams had one. But I think the first one was Choker Campbell, if my memory serves me right. And there was Clyde McPhatter, Laverne Baker, the School Boys, Frankie Lyman and the Teenagers, the Bobettes. It wasn't quite as big as the one that went out after he mixed the shows, because it was eighty of us on the show after he mixed the shows.

Now, how many numbers would you do on this?

About three.

Where would you come up in the order here?

He finally put me to closing the first half. I would close the first half of the show before intermission. He finally moved me to closing the first half because, you know, I was going over real strong. And really getting most of the publicity. But what really happened, I was signing my check every week for them to deposit in the bank, two of them. And they weren't depositing it in the bank. And I didn't know that until I got ready to leave them, and I had no money in the bank. Because I wasn't using any of my salary, because I was making enough selling programs to send money home and then have money. So after I left them, the IRS came after me for about fifty-some thousand dollars—fifty-five thousand dollars—and I told them I didn't get it. My managers got it. So they said, "Well, we'll just write it off." And I wanted them to go after it, but they wouldn't.

You said that you were selling programs. I don't understand.

Oh, you know, the program for the show with the pictures and everybody in it and all of that? Well, me and the Drifters and all, between shows, when we'd come off, we would go out because people would buy them from the entertainers. You'd autograph them for them. And we got ten percent. So I was selling a beaucoup of them. I had a little spiel that I went through with them, saying, "Get them while they're hot. I've only got a few thousand left." And they'd laugh and they'd buy them up. And so I was making good money doing that. You know, we were happy to do that, because we made extra money. Because everybody was on a weekly salary. Everybody was on a weekly salary. But while I was signing my check every week for them to deposit in the bank, they weren't depositing it in the bank. And I didn't know that until I got ready to leave them and I had no money in the bank.

When you did the mixed packages, who were some of the white artists who appeared with you?

The Everly Brothers. The Crickets. And Buddy Holly was very, very racist when he came on the show, but I broke him down and treated him so nice, he was real nice before he left the show. The Diamonds. Those were the major ones. I think the Silhouettes were white, out of Canada. I'm not sure. But I think they were.

And how did the audience—what was the mix of the audience at that point?

Oh, the audience was mixed except when we played in the South—in, like, Memphis, Tennessee—they had an auditorium with a stage between two auditoriums. You know, the big auditorium on the right side, the whites was there. And you looked to the left and the blacks was over there. Now, we were playing facing the wall. The band set up and we played facing the wall and got to dance from one side to the other to entertain both of them. But when we played in Columbus, Georgia, there was a white line down the center of the auditorium—little bitty auditorium—all the way up on the stage. And the white musicians couldn't even sit on the same side of the stage as the black musicians. And that was the system.

And, see, I got Paul Anka through Irving Fell in Montreal, Canada. He came in and he wanted to meet Fats Domino after we had done the show. And he was telling me about "Diana," the song that he had coming out, "Diana." And I took him in and introduced him to Fats Domino and Irving Fell. And Irving Fell signed him up that night to tour with us for a hundred dollars a week. And he would fly while everybody else was riding the bus. Well, the guys didn't like him for that, but I didn't care. And Paul Anka and I became friends. But when he became a millionaire, Irving Fell was doing things with him that he wasn't doing with Clyde McPhatter and myself. So Clyde invited me up to his apartment in New Rochelle, New York. And I got up there and he's staying in a sixty-nine-dollar-a-month apartment, and I said, "Something's wrong and he's getting twenty-seven hundred dollars a week." But he wasn't getting his money, like I wasn't getting mine from Irving Fell. So I said, "Clyde, I'm going to get out of this." "Man, he can do this for you; he can do—" I said, "But he's doing it with Paul; he's not doing it with us." So when I got back to New York, I went to Washington and I said, "I want a release." And he had Allen Blue come in there with the contract for me to sign the release and put it up on a file cabinet where I couldn't hardly even see up there. I had to reach up to sign the release. I said, "Now, where's my money for—the checkbook for the money in the bank?" They gave me a big checkbook but had only put five hundred dollars in there when I bought a '58 Ford. And all the other money that I signed my checks for them to deposit, they never put it in there. Irving Fell was cold. His son later bought Ringling Brothers Circus and still runs it. He owns it and runs it.

We was in San Francisco at the Cow Palace on a Saturday evening. We were going to work there Sunday. His wife died. He flew to Washington and buried her and was back there Sunday. And that was, you know, that was a shock to me.

Oh, that was the first time that I went into Chicago in the early fifties. I worked at a place called Martin's Corner over on the West Side. And then I worked at the DeLisa when Mike DeLisa and them had it. I first went into Club DeLisa about '52. And that's where we worked six nights a week. Actually we worked seven nights a week. We would rehearse Sunday morning. They had a breakfast show Monday morning. And they had a chorus line and they had some beautiful dancing girls. And there was a group called the Dyrettes. These people don't know nothing. Those girls could dance! And they had a full show. Red Saunders had the band then. Who—on the corner of Twenty-second and Madison—a guy named—what was the guy? A policeman—a mechanic and a cop had bought it, because they had run Jim Martin out of Chicago to Mexico. He was a kind of underworld figure, I understand. I don't know. And so they had bought it. And what would happen, the guy would—they would take all the money home and split it up on Saturday night and then try to pay off out of what they make on Sunday. And so I watched the bartender, and one day the bartender went in there and he just laid his gun on the table and picked up all the money and took his out and said, "Now, you all see what you can do with that." (*chuckles*) Well, Dennis was a musician. He was a musician. He was the one head man. And so I asked him for my money. And I grabbed him and I told him, "You put your bouncer over here and I'll break every bone in his body." And he's a kind of husky guy. And so Fats Jackson and I were working together then. Fats Grady Jackson. He weighed three hundred pounds, and he would blow his sax and I'd stand on his stomach and sing while he would be blowing. And he'd get up on one knee like he couldn't get up. And I'd go around behind him like I'd kick him in the butt, and he'd jump straight up in the air and just break up the house. And Fats kept saying, "No, Tommy. Be cool. Now, be cool." I said, "No, I've got to get my money." So finally the cook, the one that owned the restaurant, his wife was cooking. He said, "Tommy, my wife likes that crying song you do." He said, "Go up there and sing that song, and I'll steal your money from her and give it to you." So I went up there and I sang that song, and he got my money from his wife and gave it to me. And I left there. Fats never got paid.

And then when I came back to Chicago and went back into DeLisa—see, I was instrumental in Joe Williams getting with Count Basie. They had a little guy that worked the lights. A little light guy by the name of Wesley. About four feet tall. Alcoholic. But he never missed a cue on the lights. And so that I had a two-month contract. I finished the first month, and I went in that Monday morning to get paid. And I'm standing in the office, and this guy Wesley, the light man, he came up the steps and came in the office. And Mike DeLisa kicked him in the ass and—called him something. And I said, "Wesley, why you let that cracker kick you?" He said—Mike DeLisa looked at me and said, "You no satisfied?" He's an Italian. He said, "You no satisfied?" I said, "No!" He said, "Why you work?" I said, "I don't; I just quit." So he called Joe Williams to do my other month. Count Basie and Lionel Hampton was sitting there at the table eating neck bones and collard greens at seven o'clock in the morning, because they had a café that stayed open all night in the club. And so Joe Williams went up and was rehearsing, and that's when Count Basie heard him and hired him. But he had to finish my month before he could join Count. And that's basically that story.

You and Joe were friends, weren't you?

Yeah, we were very good friends. Yeah, we were very good friends. In fact, you know, I sit down now and think about all of the famous people that I worked with and that I knew and that I had been around, even from Bob Hope and on down. Otis Redding came to see me the night that he died. He came to the DeLisa to see me. And we sat and talked. You know, all of these— I'm one of the luckiest people in the world. I came through an era and had the chance—by me doing comedy and singing, I got a chance to work with a lot of people that just a singer wouldn't have got the chance to work with. Or just a comic wouldn't have got to work with. I worked with Redd Foxx and Slappy White and just on and on. The list is yay long. Pigmeat Markham, I worked with him at the Apollo. Pigmeat, I didn't know him well. I know they shocked me when I got there and saw how Pigmeat and Freddie and Flo were living. And they were supposed to be big-named artists. That shocked the hell out of me. They were living in an apartment back of the Apollo Theater. They tore those down. But there was an apartment building there. And, you know, when Count Basie and the band used to come through here, through Atlanta, and I'd go catch those guys and these were big-time people to me. And Lucky Millinder. And I get to New York and these people are working as window washers and stuff during the week—get a leave of absence to go on the road. I was shocked. You know? But I got over it, because I realized they've got to live. And Lucky Millinder couldn't read a note of music big as this house! But they had him front the band, because he looked like he was Indian or white. That's why they did it. You know, he's standing up there waving the baton and didn't know what he— And the last time I saw him, he was an alcoholic, falling down backstage at the Apollo Theater, begging for pennies. And Span, the guy working back there, said, "I'm not going to let you be back here like this, as big as you are." And took him away from back there.

They did put a guy on me one time. I went back in there and worked after that. And they had a guy they called Dummy working there. And he called himself going to put him on me to whup me, and I rammed him through a jukebox. And they backed off. I wasn't scared of the gangsters. I just wasn't scared of them. I worked Kansas City at the Rose Room, and this guy Marty Graham—we were off—couldn't work on Sunday. But New Year's came on Sunday. So they was going to open at twelve o'clock and close about two. And he asked me if I would work, and I said, "Yeah, but you've got to pay me so much and so much." And first he said no, and then when I started to get my stuff and was going to tell the people I was going home for the weekend, and he said, "Okay, I'll pay you." Well, that night when we got through, he didn't want to pay me. So the place was full of people and he told me he wasn't going to pay me. I just reached across the bar and grabbed him in the collar and pulled him across the bar, and reached in the box and took my money out and put the rest of it back. And everybody was, "Man, they're going to kill you! You're dead! Them gangsters. They're going to kill you."

Well, six months later I was in Chicago and Carl Wright of the Three Leggers, who had gone to school with me in Atlanta, he stopped me and he said, "Man, what the hell did you do to Marty Graham?" I said, "Nothing but take my money." He said, "Man, that cat's crazy about you. He said you and Jimmy Witherspoon can work for him anytime. You all are the only two niggers ever stood up to him!" And so even like in Chicago, I said to Vince one night, I said, "Vince, I don't understand one man being scared of another." He said, "Well, kid," he said, "it's knowing it's coming and not knowing when." I said, "But that's the way it is anyway. I don't know when it's coming. Why should I be afraid? Crazy, come here and let me show you something." We went through the door. Right in front of the door was an Oldsmobile, '53 Oldsmobile. And one of the top men, the gangsters, was in it. On each corner, he said, "Come with me." And on each corner on the four corners was a limousine with three guys in it. And on the backseat, the guy on the backseat had a Thompson submachine gun in his lap. And he showed me that. And I said, "Well, I *still* don't understand. It's coming anyway." But we got along. We got along. When at night, when I be in the club and Jimmy Allegretti walked in, all I had to do was slap my face.(*slaps his face three times*) "Strong as a tiger! Strong as a tiger!" That was one hundred dollars for me.

You know, one night I was sitting there at the bar singing, and they were having the furniture dealers convention in Chicago. And this guy from Carolina came in, and I'm sitting there besides this beautiful white lady, singing—I'm singing at the piano bar. And he said, "By God, I ain't never seen a nigger sittin' with white folk before." He says, "I'm goin' to give this boy some money." And he gave me a hundred-dollar bill and I wouldn't take it. So Jan, the hostess, she came and picked it up and stuck it in my pocket. She said, "Take the money!" Said, "We'll get him." And they sold him eight hundred dollars' worth of water that night, in champagne bottles! Everybody was drinking on it. And so finally one of the guys told me—I won't call no names—said, "Come here, Tommy." The toilet, the bathroom was way down a long flight of stairs, straight down. He said, "When I call him over, you knock him down them stairs." I said, "No, I'm not going to do that." I said, "I'm not going to do it." He said, "I'll do it." And he called that guy over there and he got that cat, and he went down them steps, man. And I felt sorry for the guy, because he hadn't really done nothing, you know?

I worked in Chicago. They booked me in Chicago at a place called the Vanguard, which was a syndicate club up on the North Side. It wasn't when I went in, but one guy came in one night and told me, he said, "Look, my people are going to take over this club in two weeks, and you're going to be all right." So he became my manager. When they came in, I stayed there for about a year and a half in that club.

About what year are we talking about?

About '53. And that's when I met people like Gene Connor and Marlinsky and, you know, Jimmy Allegretti. They sent me up to Milwaukee to work. And, well, they told me to go to Milwaukee and I refused to go, because I didn't have a contract. So two weeks later I got a phone call saying, "What the hell are you doing down there? You better get the next thing smoking and get up here." So I took the train and I went up there that night, that evening. And when I walked in, the owner said, "Go to work!" That was a guy named Frank Ballusteri. So when I got dressed and came out, Johnny Carson was the emcee.

When I came off the first show, a real distinguished-looking guy with some horn-rimmed glasses on came up to me and introduced himself. Said he would be out at the military that night at twelve and couldn't, you know, we want to hang out? He said, "What do you think my rank is?" I said, "Well, you look like an officer." And he said, "Well, I'm a colonel. But I'm a dentist and I'm thinking about putting my practice up in the black community and la, da, da." We went on. So finally he asked me, he said, "Do these girls go out?" I said, "I don't know. But most of them look like they do." They were strippers! So I went to Johnny Carson and asked him. He said, "What does the guy look like?" I told him. He said, "That's the fuzz. Stay away from him." So when I came off the stage that night, he met me at the door. And said, "Baby, let's go hang out." Well, Frank Ballusteri told me, he said, "Take off!" That's when the guy threw his credentials on me. Federal Bureau of Investigation. So I just got my stuff and went on and got on the train and went back to Chicago.

Well, my wife at that time was living in St. Louis. We were separated. So she was managing a club for a guy named Manny Rucker over there. She asked me to come over there and help him get the club off the ground. I took off and I went over there, and I worked for him and helped him get his club off the ground. Well, first of all, I went into a club on a Saturday afternoon and a white guy walked up and said, "Hey, Tommy, baby. What's happening?" So I figured it's somebody I met someplace. He ended up being a federal agent, which I didn't know.

In the meantime, I went back to New York and did a show for Christmas. And when I came back from out of town, I said, "Where's Smitty?" He said, "Well, you go talk to his wife. Your buddy was a federal agent." Well, I had asked ——(??) what did he do. He said, "I work for the Chicago syndicate." I said, "No, I worked there and you don't work there." But it ended up he was a federal agent. So that's when I stayed in St. Louis then for a period of time.

What kind of a show were you doing at this point? Had you quit singing and dancing, and were you doing just strictly comedy? Or were you singing?

I was doing singing and dancing and throwing comedy in.

Okay. Now, this was the early fifties?

Yeah. Um-hm. Yeah, '53.

What kind of audience also? Was this a black audience? A white audience?

In Milwaukee it was white. In Chicago it was white. In St. Louis it was mixed, black and white. Mostly black. Then I started working over in East St. Louis at the Manhattan Club. A guy named Booker and that was around '58, after I left the Show of Stars. And Booker backed my band, which I took on the road then.

Who was in your band at that point?

Benny Smith played guitar. Jackie Brenston played sax—baritone sax. A guy named Sam Rhodes played bass. Raymond Hill, whose father fathered Tina Turner's first child, played saxophone.

Those are all familiar names from the Ike Turner band, right?

Right. Right. That's right.

The real Anna Mae that they talk about—the real Anna Mae, I married her. (*chuckles*) Yeah. And we were together a couple of years. And then Ike drew a gun on me, hit me with a gun, and I took it away from him and whipped him and gave him the gun back and told him to keep her.

Wasn't there sort of a story on Ike Turner? Didn't he have a reputation for pistol-whipping people all the time?

Oh, yeah. But he had his band to back him up. And, see, they wouldn't back him up with me. And I was in his house! But, see, he didn't weigh but about ninety pounds, ninety-five pounds then.

I heard everybody in his band hated him!

They did, but they would help him. He was a ruthless person. But they would back him up. His just being around would scare people. But the day I whipped him in his house, they stood there in the door and looked at him.

Well, what happened was Anna Mae had been with—I met her with Ike. Okay? And I left and I went on the road, and when I came back a year later they had been separated a year. So she and I got together. She could book my band. She was a helluva salesperson in booking. She was wearing miniskirts back in the fifties and stuff. So she booked my band and we left. I got Booker over there, was managing and was backing my band financially. So we were in—we came back into town. About seven o'clock that morning, my phone rang. And Ike asked to speak to her and I said, "Okay." So I gave her the phone. A few minutes later some jumbled-up old telegram came in, because Ike couldn't read and write. But it was supposed to have been in code. So I heard her say "about two o'clock." Well, we were going to rehearse at two o'clock in East St. Louis at the club. And two o'clock, we pull up at the club and we went in and started rehearsing. She said, "Can I use the car?" I said, "Sure. You got your key, haven't you?" She said, "Aren't you afraid I'm going to get into something?" I said, "No more than you're going to do anyway sooner or later if you want to." And it wasn't a love thing with me. She was a good businesswoman. And we had only been married twenty-seven days at that time. But we'd been together for about a year and a half. And so she went off and she was gone. She said, "I'll be back in about thirty minutes."

Well, after two hours, when we finished rehearsing, I had a friend of mine take me out to Ike's to look for my car. When I got there his car was parked outside of his garage. So I went up to his garage and looked inside and saw my car. So we got back in this guy's car and went back to the club. About twenty minutes later she showed up. I said, "You got lost, didn't you?" She said, "Yeah, a little bit." So we got in the car. She said, "Where we going?" I said, "We're going back to Ike's house." She said, "I don't want to go out there." "Well, you're going." "Well, you're going to hear something you don't want to hear." I said, "I might as well hear it now and get it over." So, now, Ike and I are friends, so I'm not here to fight; I'm here to talk to him. When we walked in the door to his bedroom, she sat down by the door and I walked around on the other side of his bed by a bay window. And I said, "Ike, we got a little problem here." I said, "She's my wife but we got a problem. She can stay with you or she can go with me. If she stays with you, you won't get no phone calls, no messages, no nothing. If she goes with me, I don't want any more from you." He said, "Is that a threat?" I said, "You can take it the way you want it." And I'm laughing.

So she threw his shirt on the bed, because he was getting out of the bed, but his gun was in the shirt. So when he stood up, I was talking to her sitting over by the door. And when I went to turn to face him, he hit me with the pistol. But I was heavy into judo and automatically reflexes made me give him a judo chop across the neck and knock him down. And so he dropped the gun and I knocked him over on top of her. And I'm hitting him. And she came out from under the bottom and grabbed me from behind and said, "Don't hurt him; I've hurt him enough." I said, "Do you realize you're my wife?" She said,

"I don't give a damn." So then I turned and reached for her and she ran behind the bed, and as she fell across the bed, he picked up the gun and he shot down by my foot. And I said now I know he ain't going to shoot me, because if he was, he would have done it then. But he had his gun pointed right at my stomach. He said, "You know, I can shoot you legally. You're in my house." I said, "Yeah, you're right." But I had to pass him to get out. I had my hands up, like I was getting them up in the air about chest high. And as I got up on him, I hit the gun with my left hand and grabbed his wrist and elbowed him across the neck and judo chopped him and hip tossed him and he tossed the gun. And I picked the gun up and took the bullets out, laid the gun on the dresser, and told him, I said, "Ike, this is your woman. It's stupid of us to stand up here and fight over her." And this is what I said: "And one of us could be dead, the other in the hospital or in jail; she's going to get another nigger and go on about her business. This doesn't even make sense. We're friends. Let's shake hands. That's your woman. You pay for the divorce, you've got her." So he said, "Okay." And I walked outside and he called, "Tommy, come here." I went back and he asked her, he said, "Does he mean that?" She said, "Yeah, he mean it." I said, "Shake hands, man." I said, "Meet me in your lawyer's office in the morning and you pay for the divorce." So we met at his lawyer's office the next morning. And he paid $175 for the divorce. And that was the end of that. And he and I hung out together that night. And word had got around about the fight, so people were looking at us kind of strange. But, you know, I don't believe in fighting over no woman. I don't fight no woman, and I don't fight over 'em! So he and I are still friends together to the best of my knowledge.

How did you leave St. Louis then?

Well, the guy that was backing my band, Booker—well, Little Milton was working there, too. And finally I just decided to expand the band and leave and come back to Georgia, because, you know, I wasn't making any money— couldn't make any *more* money there. I could only stay right there in that one level. And that's the same reason I left Chicago in '72. It came to a standing point. I was doing all right, but I couldn't do any better.

And how long did you actually spend in St. Louis?

About three years. Well, first I was in there around '52 for about a year. Then, when I went back there around '58 and '59, it was about two years I spent there then. When I left St. Louis I came back to Georgia, because I'd been playing around here. Came back to Royal Peacock. I worked the Royal Peacock and a couple of clubs down through this area. Then I went back into New York. And I went back into the Apollo Theater. See, because after I come out of the military in '52, I worked the Apollo at least twice a year for the next six years. I was one of the few that worked there twice a year. But I worked there twice a year until—let's see—until '58.

And so I came home to do a show at the Royal Peacock for Henry Winn with Arthur Prysock. And I brought Liz down here, too. I had met her there in New York. I knew she was an alcoholic, but I didn't know she was on dope. And I saw a guy misusing her. I saw this beautiful talent just being wasted. And so I brought her down to Atlanta and showcased her at the Royal Peacock, and they went crazy over her. Well, my father was a minister, and he said, "Well, I know you're sleeping with this woman. I don't want you to bring her back here unless you're married to her." So we went back to New York, and I was due back in Atlanta for Thanksgiving, which was two weeks later, to go back to the Peacock and was bringing her back. So we got married in New York.

I was at the Apollo Theater that week. And I wanted to leave that Thursday night—be here that Thursday night for Thanksgiving—but Bobby Schiffman said, "If you can get somebody to take your place, you can go. But if you can't, you have to stay." So I couldn't get anybody, so we stayed there, and when I finished that night we left New York driving. Got stopped in South Carolina. Got a ticket. The judge said if the money didn't get there by the next morning, he was going to let us go anyway. But the money got there and I paid the ticket and we came on to Atlanta. And Henry Winn said he'd canceled it out because we wasn't here Thanksgiving night. But we worked the next week.

And from that I went to the West Coast. And I took her to the West Coast. And we worked out there at the Parisian Room in L.A. with Red Holloway. And Liz went over real well out there. And Dionne Warwick was a dear friend of hers. So Dionne wanted to record her. In fact, she signed up with Dionne. And that's where I got her booked in the Playboy Club. And the drummer knew Bob Hope and got Bob Hope to come over. He came over and he caught her, and he flipped out behind that. He told me, he said, "Tommy, I want you to quit what you're doing. I'm going to pay you $5,000 a week just to keep her happy. I'm going to pay her $10,000. You all's money worries are over. Don't tell nobody. But it's over." And she got high a few days later and blew it in New Orleans. A $780,000–a-year job. He said, "Your money worries are over. This is for life!" And she blew it.

You heard the last record that Minnie Ripperton had out? That's Liz Lands, really. E. Rodney Jones had recorded her and Minnie had died, so they put it out as Minnie Ripperton so he could get his money back out of it. But Liz had one of those peculiar voices. She had better than a five octave. She could hit notes so high you couldn't hear, but the needle would peak on the recording equipment. She was good. And she was kind of unique. Because she would have three or four different rhythms going at the same time with her feet and hands, and musicians loved her. Because her voice was an instrument. Now, that's one person that I know musicians loved to play behind. But other people they didn't like to play behind. I've got some stuff on tape on her. I quit working for two years in Chicago just to push her. And she got so I couldn't send her one place and I'd be another place, because she was going to get high and drunk and mess it up. I was trying to keep the public from knowing that she was a dope addict. In fact, a lot of times I had to make them take her to get me. But the way people want to say, I wouldn't work if I didn't work.

But it cost me in the long run, because I didn't want nobody—Dionne Warwick thinks today that I put her on dope. She was on it when I met her. And I found out she wouldn't make friends with nobody who wouldn't get her some dope. And I stopped a lot of people from giving her dope. "You say you love her; how can you do that and you're killing her?" Because I've never used any in my life! I married Liz in '59, and we were together one month short of fifteen years.

How did you make the comedy records?

Just record them. I had a tape recorder and I recorded them live, most of them in Chicago. And I got one I'm going to release next—I had cut in the Parisian Room in L.A. in '72. And I just found the tape on it. And I was mastering them out and just mastered out. Went to Leonard Chess of Chess Records up there and had them pressed. Then this guy, Vic Lavelle, was supposed to distribute them for me. And I found out, I don't know how many thousands he sold, and I never knew he'd even had them pressed. Five. I think I took the first one around '69. And the last one around '72. But the first one was really the best one. ——(??) Somebody in California has mixed it with one with Mantan Moreland and they're selling it. I've got to find out what company that is, because I've never given anybody any rights to do that.

I was working in L.A. and Redd Foxx came in one night. And he asked me, he said, "Tommy, can I come up and do something?" I said, "Sure." And I brought him up and he went on, and I went right behind him and did my thing. He came off, he says, "I want you to come out and be on my show, because these niggers won't let me come on their stage and you do." I said, "Why not? You do your thing and I do mine." I don't see these people being jealous or scared of something like that. I've never been afraid of losing a job, because if you're good, you're good. And I tell you you're good. But I tell you one thing—if you come behind me, you're going to have to work, because I came up with the old-timers and I know the tricks of the stage. I know how to get to an audience. I know how to hit them hard, make them laugh, make them cry, make them laugh, and leave them.

I don't think it's a lower kind of blues, because blues is blues to me. But you use different instruments to tell a different phrase or a different kind of story. But I notice in England, in Europe, they told me that they were kind of surprised that I did some blues with the harmonica. But that was Leonard Allen's idea to use the harmonica, because he was real tight with Willie Dixon. Well, he caught me—I believe he caught me at the DeLisa—and he asked me to come up to his office, which was I think on Forty-seventh and Cottage. Right on the corner of Forty-seventh and either Cottage or South Park, right there by a park. I think it was South Park. And I went up there and met with him and we talked. So he asked me about doing the recording, you know, recording for him. I said okay. And we got together and we did it, you know? And most of it was already tracked. Most of it was already tracked. And he had a building on the corner and he had his own studio in there. That's where we recorded. He decided on the material except for "Stacked Deck," which was the card thing. Billy Wright had recorded it. A kid out of Chicago named Tommy—what's that boy's name? Tommy something else wrote it. And Billy Wright had recorded it. And he had seen me do that. I used to do that with some great big cards. He wanted me to do that and I wanted to do it. So we did that. And "Southern Women," I think Willie Dixon wrote that. And I did "Remember Me." I wrote that. It seems to be catching now. Most people, a lot of places I go, they'll ask me to sing that. Especially if I go to white places. That and "V-8 Baby"—they called it "Women in Cadillacs." In fact, "Women in Cadillacs" is going to be in the next CD that I'm doing in Pittsburgh now. I've got to go back there on the sixteenth, seventeenth, and eighteenth to finish it up.

What about this, too— "Nosy Neighbor"? Where did that come from?

Oh, I wrote that. I wrote that. Usually I write about things that are going on that I see about people and stuff. One of the tunes I've got in there now says that "*if you spend my money, I'm going to spend your time.*" You know, I've got stuff like one says, "*How you going to leave me when I'm already gone? I heard you tell your best friend talking on the telephone that you were leaving. But you can't leave me, because I'm already gone. Where do you think I am at three o'clock in the morning when I'm not at home?*" In other words, the story is you tell your best friend everything, all our business, and that's who I'm with. These are the kind of things. One says, "*My pastor says I'm living a sinful life. Last week I caught him in bed with my wife. Now I'm in jail and he's in hell with my wife.*"

How did you leave Chicago? What caused you to leave Chicago?

I had a little record company going there. I was producing talent shows and I was doing all right in Chicago. But Chicago, I never went there to live. Chicago—I couldn't go any further in Chicago. I couldn't grow anymore in Chicago. It was my town. I could do what I wanted to, but I couldn't make it any better there. And I didn't want to get locked in there. And the clubs were dying out, you know. Pervis Spann had finally taken over the Club DeLisa. Then they had the High Chaparral, because the DeLisa burned. And then they had the High Chaparral. I worked there for them. I worked Barber's Peppermint Lounge on the West Side. And I did a couple of things down Old Town Chicago. I did one—a couple of shows down there with Miles Davis. Then Liz worked a lot of places down there. I worked on the North Side at some clubs that the organization had. I don't even remember the name of them.

And one day they asked me to come over to this hotel over near the lake. And, you know, I wasn't thinking anything. I went over there, because I figured up north you go where you want. Man, I walked in that hotel and that cat said, "We don't let no niggers in here!" And I said, "What?" And I picked up the phone and called upstairs and told Vince. I said, "Vince, this man says I'm a nigger and I can't come in here." Vince came down, "You mother . . . This is . . . We brought this so-and-so up. This is my boy here. You don't talk to him like that." I said, "That's okay." And I left. And, no, he kept— I said, "No, I've got to go. I don't want to come in here." And I left. And then it dawned on me. It was always a lifesaver. They had set up, up there. They wanted me to come up and freak off with some women, and I wasn't going to do that, no way. That wasn't my game. These were the gangsters. And, no. (*laughs*) I wasn't going to do that.

There was always something that kept me from getting put in those tricks. I guess I'm always thinking and I'm not trying to get anything for nothing. And that keeps me out of a lot of problems. I realized that most people that get put in tricks are trying to get something for nothing. None of the stuff ever appealed to me, and I've seen too many of my friends go down for dope and alcohol. I've never tasted beer or liquor in my life. I've never used dope in my life.

You had a hand in the first recordings with Gladys Knight. What was that about?

Okay. We were working at a little club here called the Builders Club. And I wanted to start my own record label. And I talked to the club owner because he was a number banker and had the club and liquor man. And I wanted a partner because he had some money. So he told me, he said, "Yeah, I'll go in with you, buddy boy." He stuttered when he talked. "Yeah, I'll go in with you." So I kept on saying I'm going to get the license, and he never would show up. So I went to city hall, got my license, and came back. I said, "I've got my license." "Awww, I'll go down there with you; we'll put my name on it." But it didn't happen.

So I told Gladys and them that I was setting up a record company. And I started lining up people that I was going to record. And so they did "Every Beat of My Heart" in the club. And I said, "That song is a hit. I'm going to record that." So then we started rehearsing. We rehearsed for six months! And I rehearsed—I had nine artists. Grover Mitchell. Local people. Little Clarence. And anyway, we rehearsed for six months. And on a Sunday morning I took them in the studio, a national recording studio here. Felton Jarvis was on the board. And the boy that did "Streakin.'" What's his name? But all these guys was in the studio. And we did "Every Beat of My Heart." My piano player, I fired him five times because he didn't want to play it like I kept telling. That part of—*dum, dum, dum* (*makes bass music sounds*), and he didn't want to do that. And I said, "Messing up my record." I said, "No, this is *my* arrangement." I said, "I'm paying you to do it and you do it like I want it, because I know what I want." So we finally cut the record.

And in the meantime, the guy I took in as a partner for five hundred dollars without ever putting his name on anything, handshake agreement, he was trying to steal the label out from under me. And I didn't know that. He had told Gladys's mother not to sign the contract with me because I would be in and out of town doing shows and he was going to be right there. Well, when I got ready to release the record, I said, "Clifford [Hunter], they need to either be with you, me, or the company. Because there are people that can offer them more than we can at this point." "Oh, oh, no, buddy boy. See, them niggers ain't going to do nothing, because, see, they owe me money. I done owed them money." I said, "That doesn't matter. There're people that can offer them more than we can." "No, no, no." Well, he knew what he had in mind. Well, I went on and released the record. Now, there were over fifty-nine disc jockeys that owed me a favor, because when we were touring with the Show of Stars we would go in town and do record hops. They would give you fifty dollars to come over and do the record hop and sign autographs. I would never take that fifty dollars. I said, "Keep that." Well, I kept a list of the disc jockeys. So I sent it to all these radio stations and all these disc jockeys across the country and asked them to all play it on the same day. It was either the second or nineteenth of August, I believe it was. I'm not sure on that date right now. But I asked them all to play it the same day. And that's what they did. And the record broke. In three days we were getting orders for fifty, sixty thousand records a day!

He had the phone cut off in the office except for the pay phone which was in his building. And all of a sudden he started coming into the office. Well, I came home from the office that afternoon and I laid down to take a nap. About six o'clock my phone rang. And it was Steve Clark out of WBJ, and he said, "Tommy, you know, I made a deal with Clifford Hunter to buy 'Every Beat of My Heart.'" I said, "You did? How did you do that? He can't do that." "But they said I can't get the masters unless you okay it, because they don't know him." I said, "That's right." So I said, "I'll call you back." I got up and went to the club. I said, "What are you doing?" He said, "Well, buddy boy, see, they offered me a thousand dollars and three percent. And that's a lot of money." I said, "It's fifteen hundred dollars and five percent." I said, "But that's no money in the record business. That's chicken feed you're talking. This is a hit! And you're throwing away a million dollars." "Oh, no. No," he argued and we argued. I said, "Clifford, don't do it." So the next morning, he came into the office and the phone rang downstairs, which was the pay phone. And he grabbed the phone. And he said, "Uh, Steve say he going to be late. He can't get here at ten o'clock. If you want to go get some breakfast, you go ahead." I said, "No, no, no, no." Well, at ten o'clock sharp, Steve rode up. He came in with the check. I said, "Steve, I didn't say we was going to sell this record." He said, "Well, he made a deal with me." And then he went on. I said, "Man, I'm going to sell out to you to keep from killing you," I said, "because you're throwing away a million dollars right now." I said, "You go cash the check and bring me a thousand dollars and you've got it." And that's the way it went down.

So, now, when the record hit, disc jockeys thought I made a bundle of money and didn't give them any. But I had no more control over it. It was on T and L [Records]. And we changed it to HunTom [Records]. Then sold to Vee-Jay. Bobby Robinson was trying to reach me by phone and he couldn't. So they called the radio station. Zenas Sears and Ida Pat told them that we didn't have a contract. So Bobby Robinson sent Zenas Sears and Allie Pat two thousand dollars a piece and Gladys and them eighteen hundred dollars and flew them into New York and cut the record identically the same. Well, if I had still been involved, I would have taken it away from him. But I wasn't involved anymore. See, had I been involved, I would have sued them and took both records. So he's real sick now. So he told me the other day, he said, "Well, you can do what you want with it, because I'm not going to be in that anymore." So I will probably rerelease it as a part of local artists of Atlanta along with Liz and some other people that I got stuff on.

Now, how did you make those records in New Orleans? How did that happen?

I worked at—Frank Pandy's place down there. I've forgotten what the name of that club was. But I was approached by—who was it approached me down there? It wasn't Dave Bartholomew. Wow. One of the record company executives approached me and asked me about recording down there while I was down there. It was over in the French Quarter, we went over and recorded.

For which label?

Imperial.

Okay. So it wasn't Dave Bartholomew. Who was in the band?

I don't know.

What tunes did you do for them?

You know, I'd have to look and see. (*chuckles*) I know I did something for them. I never really got all the way out of it. What happened was my mother died in '77 and I came home to take care of that. The night she died I was in Washington, D.C., at a club called the Executive Club. And so I came home and she had a business of a personal care home, taking care of elderly people, mentally retarded, mentally ill people. And I had to come home and run that. So I was going back and forth. And the young lady that I later married was a practical nurse, I had her running it. I run into some problems with my brothers and all about the business. So when I left Atlantic City and came home—my father died in September after—my mother died in May, my father died in September. And I came home to bury my father, and I took over running that business. And I would go out once in a while. I worked locally. But the business was such I couldn't be gone long. Because I'd run into a lot of problems, so I had to stay here and run that. But I would go out and do shows, and then later on I opened my own club. And I had it for about a year. One day I met a guy at the post office from the license bureau. He said, "How'd you make out on your dope case?" I said, "What dope case?" He said, "Didn't they raid your place the other night?" I said, "Not to my knowledge." And I went back to the club and found out that they did raid my club and got the manager. They were selling dope. And I said, "It's closed as of now," and closed the club up. But I was still running the personal care home, which I had moved into.

I had bought a school building from the city and enlarged it, and renovated and made it a home. I had forty-seven people which were taken care of. So I would still go out and do shows periodically or whenever. But if didn't nobody call me, I didn't go looking for them. And that's same true today. If they don't call me, I don't go looking for shows.

Two years ago they were doing a photo shoot of all the blues singers around.

But nobody told me about it. So when they got to do the photo shoot, they had about two hundred people there. Somebody asked where was I. And this gentleman friend of mine that was a friend of Roy's say, "Well, Tommy, I know how to get in touch with him." And so then he called me and asked me if it was all right to give him my number. I said, "Yeah." Then another gentleman called me and said, "Is it all right to give Brian Baumgarten your number up in Canada?" I said, "Sure." So Brian and I got together. He came down and he did the juke blues story. And I am available for dates.

Well, before Liz and I got to Chicago I had started doing comedy here in Atlanta. Because this gave us both a chance where I could be where she was rather than if they wanted just a girl singer. I could be there as the emcee and do comedy to keep her straight. So when we left and went to Anchorage, Alaska, I was singing and doing comedy with a guy—we met him in California; he was out of Michigan—a guy named Danny Gibson. And he had a club up there called the Mermaid Club. Well, we went in there in October. We went in there in October, yeah. And one of the strip girls there pulled my coat to him. When I got there, she said, "Be careful, because what he'll do, he'll goad you into quitting. And then once you quit, you got to come back and work for him on his terms or you can't get out of Alaska." So it went on.

Came up to Christmas Eve, he wanted to know if I'd let Liz go shopping with his wife. I said, "Sure." She went down and bought Liz a lot of new gowns. Well, Liz thought she was paying for them. But she's charging them back to Liz. And we don't know that. So Christmas Eve night he come in, and I said, "Well, we're going to wear—" I bought me some new stuff. He said, "No, don't wear that tonight, because ain't going to be nobody in here." Well, we got there Christmas Eve night, man, and the line was a block long in two feet of snow! And the place was already packed. He said, "Man, go back and put on your—" I said, "No, we're not going to do that." He said, "Well, I want you to wear it." I said, "It doesn't matter. I bought it and I'm not going to wear it." He said, "My wife, Ruby, wants you to wear it." I said, "That doesn't make any difference." "Is she your boss?" I said, "She's not my boss. You signed my contract." And he said, "Well, you—you going to—" I said, "No." And I said, "Tell you right now. If you fire me; you pay me tonight." Because what they do, we get paid—Sunday night's the last night, but they don't pay you until Tuesday so that you won't leave. And so I said, "But if you fire me, you pay me tonight." "I don't keep that kind of money here." I said, "You always keep enough here to pay me. And don't you ever forget that."

He said, "Well, damn it!" I said, "Damn it to you! Don't you cuss me in front of customers." I said, "Don't you cuss me!" Well, I was doing a quick-draw act with a Colt .45 single action. It was a real gun, but I was using blanks. But this time I went and loaded it. And I went on stage and I told —— (??) —he was behind the bar, leaning on the counter, right in front of the audience. Because everybody heard us arguing. And I told him, I said, "Look, Danny, if you bend down behind the bar, stay there until I finish, because if you raise up, I'm going to blow your God damned head off! And when I get through, I want you to have my money ready." And he laid there. When I got through and come off, he came and apologized to me. A guy named Good Rocking Brown had the band. He told me, he said. "Man, you wrong, Danny. You wrong." He said, "Well, they tell him what to wear in Vegas." "Yeah, and they pay for it, too." So we stayed there. He figured we couldn't leave. But I wasn't blowing no money up there. We stayed there until March. We came out in March. "You all can't go nowhere." I said, "Watch me when I close." I closed that night and got in my Cadillac and pulled out of Anchorage and drove all the way back home. But that was—

And while I was there, one night I was up there performing, and I was using the words "nigger" and "honky" and "peckerwood," and this voice came out of the audience and said, "By God, you remember when Herman Talmadge—he knew I was from Georgia—said he didn't want no nigger to vote for him" and everybody wanted —— (??). I said, "Leave that man alone. We've heard that before." So I said, "I'll be over there in a minute." So when I came off stage, I went on and sat down and talked to him. And he said, "You know who I am?" I said, "No." I said, "I'm the half brother of Senator Herman Talmadge. I'm from that great Georgia. I've got as many half-black brothers and sisters as I got white." He said, "You know who this guy is here?" I said, "Who?" He said, "This is George Wallace's baby brother." He introduced me to him. He said, "Tommy, when you come to Washington, here's my number. You come to my house and stay." (chuckles) I met all kind of people.

And then I had been working at a club here called the Gypsy Room, a strip club. And one night, Georgia Tech played Auburn. And George Wallace's wife, Lurleen; his brother; and Richmond Flowers and his wife; a couple of ladies from England came, but Wallace wouldn't come in, because I was working there. He said he couldn't come in because of his stand on race. They came in and they sat down. And Richmond Flowers, when I came off stage, he said, "Can you sit down here?" I said, "Sure." And I walked over to sit down. He said, "Tell me something." He went into—I don't know if you want to go into the race thing or not, but he went into all of that. And I told him, I said—he said, "Why would you want to live in a neighborhood with white people?" I said, "It's not a matter of living with white people. If I see a house and I can afford it, I figure I ought to be able to live in it." Anyway, to make a long story short, when we got through, Lurleen said, "You know, I'd be proud to live in a neighborhood with you." I said, "Why me?" She said, "You've proven yourself." I said, "What do you mean I've proven—you haven't proved yourself to me!" She said, "Well, blacks have so low morals." I said, "Let me tell you something, lady." I said, "You look around this club. You got nine strip girls up here. There are 250 men in here other than these two with you and your party of women. They are the only other women. There are some priests over there. There're some politicians." I said, "Now, what do you think they're in here for?" "Well, I—" I said, "Let me ask you another question." I said, "How many young white girls in your neighborhood in the middle of the school year took a vacation?" "Well, I can think of about ten." I said, "Where do you think they were?" I said, "They went to have babies! Can't you understand that?" "Oh, I never thought of that." I said, "Yeah, you thought of it, but you don't want to face it." And Richmond Flowers said, "He's telling you right. He's telling you right." I said, "Richmond Flowers, George Wallace is using you because you're a good man." "Well, when I put on my—get in office in February, I'm going to put my gun on. If they come on my marching—" I said, "No, you wouldn't, because you're an educated man." I said, "You're smarter than that. They're using you." He said, "Tommy, would you quit doing what you're doing and come work for me? Work with me in Alabama?" I said, "No, I can't do that." I've had plenty good offers. (chuckles) But I tell them like it is. You know? And I don't have any reason not to. I look at things, I observe, and I'm an entertainer. I'm not a black entertainer or a white entertainer. I'm an entertainer.

Ralph **Bass**

Ralph Bass was a famous record producer and A & R (artists and repertoire) man in the world of blues and rhythm and blues. He's credited with discovering James Brown and Little Esther Phillips. He produced a gigantic hit record by tenor sax man Jack McVea with "Open the Door, Richard." He worked with Etta James and Little Milton, produced the comedy records by Moms Mabley and Pigmeat Markham, and was responsible for a variety of respected jazz sessions, including the classic recording "The Chase" with Wardell Gray and Dexter Gordon. Over the years Ralph worked at the Black & White label, the Savoy label, the Chess/Checker labels, and the King and Federal labels. In fact, he did so well for Syd Nathan and the King label, it's rumored that Syd started the Federal label strictly for artists produced by Ralph—his own personal vanity label.

Ralph Bass with Lacey Gibson.
Photo courtesy of Jim O'Neal.

I actually met Ralph Bass several years earlier when he was managing the Chess studio in its final days. He was a short guy with tousled hair in a belted safari jacket and sandals with no socks, middle-aged cool for the era. He seemed distracted in about a half dozen different directions but managed to lay out the conditions and price, took my money, and gave me a receipt—then turned me over to the recording engineer Malcolm Chism.

Several years later I found out that Ralph was still living in Chicago. He and his wife were operating the Katherine Dunham Dance Studios on South Michigan Avenue. I called him and asked if he would be interested in doing an interview with me for the radio program. He agreed and we set the date. The interview was done at the dance studios. When I arrived Ralph was in the studio, wearing a nylon two-piece workout suit and running laps to keep in condition—at seventy-six years old! He was diminutive and hyper, twitchy—constantly shifting the Rubik's cube in his mind, seeking the proper angle in reply—and laughing at his own jokes.

Ralph Bass is the only white person interviewed in this book, yet he had abandoned life in white society many years earlier. As he immersed himself in black music, he eventually immersed himself in black society. He married a black woman, and worked and raised a family in the black community.

This interview took place on June 11, 1987. Ralph Bass died on March 5, 1997.

■ ▓ ▒

Well, I was born in the Bronx in New York. And being a half Jew and a half Dago (*chuckles*), I had to fight my way out of the school every day! Well, I learned when the non-Jewish boys were going to pick on me, I'd say, "Hey, baby, I'm Italian!" I wasn't lying. Well, then of course I've been a rebel all my life. And I wonder why was I a rebel. In other words, my first wife—I have two white sons by my first wife. I have a black daughter by my second wife. And my parents sent me to a Baptist prep school in Pennsylvania. We had a Baptist church. And I rebelled. At all times I just rebelled against things. And I got it from my parents, because you must remember, an Italian marrying a Jewish woman—way back then! Of course, you know how old I am [he was born on May 1, 1911]. That's where I got it, subconsciously.

And I gave my first concert—don't call it a concert—World War I, I was only about five years old. And the parents—the PTA, or whatever they wanted to call it in those days—was raising money for war bonds, liberty bonds they called them. And my mother dressed me in a sailor suit and I was playing violin. And I gave my first solo performance (*chuckles*) then. And from there I played in bands—well, those days the society bands. I didn't like the idea of playing society bands, but it was just doing something. I was fifteen, sixteen years old playing in the roof gardens of all the hotels and whatnot in New York. And of course another buddy of mine, another violin player, and I decided to stop off in Harlem. And there I saw Chick Webb, and I saw people dancing the blues. You know, playing the blues. I said, "I've never heard of the blues." And I said, "Look at them! They're making love on the floor, dancing!" And what it was, it was that feeling. Here we go again. It's a feeling! And from that time on it grabbed me.

Then I started collecting jazz. I was into jazz in a big way. I went to Colgate University. I just didn't dig what was happening there either. There was only one other Jewish boy—it was a Baptist university—only one other Jewish boy. They didn't know I was Jewish. They thought I was a Baptist, because the prep school I came from was a Baptist prep school. So they thought, well, he had to be Baptist. I was accepted. I didn't have to take an examination, no nothing. And his name was Hy Bergan, I never will forget. But his parents owned the big department store in Utica, which wasn't too far—about twenty-five, thirty-five miles from Hamilton, New York. And his father had given money to the university, so they accepted him. And I didn't dig the fraternity life. They were ostracizing this young man. And I felt something, because, being a Jew myself, I had the feeling for him. So I cut out from the fraternity and we roomed together. And then I didn't go back, because I just didn't dig the prejudice—even way back then at the university, this is the way I was.

Anyway, when I got married I went to California then with my wife, my first wife. And I had two sons, but then I was—baby, it was during the Depression and you did anything to make a living. And I was selling bottled water, and one of the bottles—five-gallon bottles—fell off the truck, anyway, and it broke in my hand, my left hand. And it cut my fingers, and one finger is stiff—the middle finger here, as you can see. They operated on me and put it together. And I couldn't play my violin anymore. I used to turn the radio on and play with the bands that were playing, play with them. Not in person, of course, but you know.

And I got to collecting jazz big bands. That big band sound was in my ears. And then during the war years, the second war, I was working in the war industry. And we were making synthetic rubber. I was working for Shell Chemical, a subsidiary of Shell Oil. And we were having our big outing and they couldn't get a band, because they couldn't get bands during World War II. Most of the musicians, good musicians, were in the army or the navy. So I said, "Hey, I'll be your disc jockey!" They didn't even call them disc jockeys. I said, "I'm a record collector. I have a lot of records and I have a PA system, and I can bring it to the picnic." Because we were about—oh, it must have been about five hundred of us. And I played the music and I looked at them and I said, "Hey, that gives me an idea. I can make records better than these"—playing the records for the audience. And, you know, I wrote letters to all of the record companies. I got a copy of *Billboard* and the addresses of the record companies.

I got one answer from a company in Cleveland, Ohio—Black & White Records. And they had another label called Comet, which the jazz was on that. They had Art Tatum. And the man's name was Paul Reiner, and he said, "I'm coming to California because I'm moving my operation to California from Cleveland, and I'd like to interview you." So! What I decided to do, I said, "Hey, I've got to know something about musicians in Los Angeles—who's in here and who are the good ones." (*chuckles*) And I went to the black union. There were two unions, one was white and one was black. Musicians union. And there was a woman there named Florence Cadressa. I'll never forget. She was the secretary. And I told her what I was about to do. And I said, "Can you give me the names of all the best black musicians in L.A.?" And of course you must remember that Los Angeles during the forties was not overpopulated with blacks yet. They hadn't moved in in numbers. It was just pockets of them. And she did. And I went to see them. She told me all the places they were working and gave me the phone numbers. I called them and they told me they were working. And there was one band that struck me because I was on the big band kick. Name was Sammy Franklin. And I said, "Hey, I like the sound of your band."

So when Paul Reiner came into town, he had his office there. Of course, he distributed his own records. He said, "If I hire you, what would you record?" Well, there was a record that I dug by Joe Liggins, "The Honeydripper." I said, "'The Honeydripper'!" He had heard of "The Honeydripper" because a company called Exclusive had it out with Joe Liggins. And it hit him. Yeah! I'll tell you why. Even though it was out and it was making some noise, in those days there were practically no black deejays playing or no deejays of any color playing black records. So if you had a hit on a black-orientated record, it took six months to a year to go from California to New York, the East Coast from the West Coast, because the jukebox operators would play it. We would work with the jukebox operators and say, "Hey! How many boxes you got?" He'd say, "A hundred." "Okay, if you buy fifty, I'll give you fifty." That was our means of promotion. And he put them on the box. And then especially the people—the men who worked at the railroads, in other words, a black pullman or a waiter or whatever—they would be visiting and would hit one end of the coast; he would hear a record in a club or in a bar, in the jukebox; and then he would buy it and bring it back to them. It would start—in bits and pieces. That's how records got started in those days. So that's why they lasted so long. It took so long for a record to last. So he figured that he would put it out in areas, because he had connections in the Middle West. And so he figured that he could get the record—we did "The Honeydripper," he would be able to sell it. So we made a deal. I called Sammy Franklin up and said, "Hey, I'm going to record your band! I want 'The Honeydripper.'" And he said, "Okay. Great."

Now, there was only one studio in Los Angeles at that time—one good studio: Radio Recorders on Sunset—on Santa Monica Boulevard. And you couldn't get in, man. Everybody—Capitol was using their facilities. They had it tied up most of the time. But then they had good clients, and so they had priority. They were working around the clock. We couldn't get in. There was a studio—I think it was on Cuhuenga, right before you got to Santa Monica Boulevard, right across the street from Technicolor. And it was a radio station, but they had a studio. And I went in there an hour before the session started and talked to the engineers and said, "Look, man, I don't know a damn thing about recording (*chuckles*), okay? So if I act crazy sometimes, don't mind me. Why I say that is because I'm going to sit in the control room and let you guys take over. And I'm just going to see if the take is a good one or not. That's all. I'm not going to make any comments to you about what to do." In those days we were recording directly on acetate. You couldn't mix it. There was no two-track, four-track, sixteen, thirty-two. In fact, it's a great sound doing that.

Anyway, so I sat there and I said, "Now, I expect my boss to come in. If he comes in, have him announced." The studio was in another building from the reception room. "If they come in the reception room and ask for me, tell them to wait five minutes, to give me five minutes to get in my act. And if I act crazy, don't mind me, now. I'll tell you when to tell them to come in." So, sure enough, after about an hour, here it comes: Mr. Reiner and Mr. Cookie—that was the salesman. "Okay, give me five minutes." And I went out there, tussled my hair, took my jacket off, took my shirt—I had my shirt down and everything and rolled up my sleeves. (*chuckles*) I said, "Okay, let them in!" And when they came in, they said to me—they were sitting down. And I said, "Man! That's not what I said!" Yelling at everybody. "That's not the way I want it done!" (*laughs*) I didn't know what the hell I was doing. Because I told the band don't pay no mind to me. They were all cued in. So after a while, after about a half hour of me screaming and yelling and carrying on, Mr. Reiner said, "He looks like he knows what he's doing. Leave him alone." (*laughs*) It worked. Well, from then on, the rest is history.

In my early days I started doing a lot of jazz for him, recording Dizzy [Gillespie] and Charlie Parker. Dodo Marmarosa—all the greats. And we couldn't sell them. Great musicians. Couldn't sell them. Well, jazz was only—you know, like New York, Chicago maybe. L.A. wasn't really hip to jazz yet. And we couldn't sell them. I said, "Oh, boy, I better do something else. I better get another area. I better get into—I better do some blues." And then there was a band there, a small group, Jack McVea. He used to play lead saxophone with Lionel Hampton. And he had quit the band and he had his own little group. And he had a drummer named Rabon Tarrant who was his drummer. And Rabon was a blues singer. In fact, Orson Welles was a blues freak. And he used to hire Rabon to come into his wagon in the back of the studio and sing the blues for him. He had a trailer.

And I signed Jack up—in those days in order to get a good musician under contract, exclusive contract, you had to give him twelve, sixteen sides a year! Guarantee it. They were all in the army, the armed services. Anyway, I had done a lot of blues with him. And it wasn't really making any big noise, but it was selling a little bit. And then I had to do eight sides to fulfill his contract. And I only had three hours' time at Radio Recorders, this famous studio. I finally got in. And we did seven sides of blues with Rabon singing, you know. Bing, bing, bing, bing. And then I only had about six minutes left, studio time left. Of course, in those days with Radio Recorders being at that studio, when you booked three hours, right on the button you had to get out! Because a half hour later they had someone else coming in. I said, "Jack, everything's sounding alike, man. Let's do something different." After you hear seven sides of blues—bing, bing, bing, bing, you know—they all start sounding alike. The same. "What'll I do?" I said, "Hey, I've got an idea. I heard you at the club one night and you were doing a thing that was different! You were doing this song and it was a rap." It was the first rap record that was ever made, incidentally. He said, "Well, I've got a new band. They don't know it." I said, "Look, man, I've got four minutes left! Let's do it—for good or bad! It can't be any worse than what we've done." He said, "Okay."

So they played the vamp and they went on. And in those days all records had an ending. So I said to the engineer—his name was Valentino; I never will forget—I said, "Val, how are we going to get out of this thing? I ain't got time to do another take." "Well," he said, "I'll fade it." (laughs) And that was the first time a record was ever faded. "Ooh, great!"

Well, the record was pretty bad. One take and, you know, half the cats didn't know what was going on. They were just making up things. Improvising. Not song-wise, rap-wise! They had the lead line, the song lead line. But otherwise the rest of it. And I bring that up because it was so bad, it was a number one hit. I didn't release the record, that side, those two sides. The first two sides I released of Jack McVea, I didn't release that. And my oldest boy was about five years, six years old. And of all the records that I had, even his records, he would pick on one record. And when he and his friends would be walking down the street, knocking on doors and singing, "*Open the door, Richard!*" That was the song.

Dusty Fletcher hadn't made it yet. He made it after ours became a hit. It was taken from Dusty Fletcher's act. Now, Dusty Fletcher was a great black comedian. And I saw his act at the Apollo in New York. It was all about this girl that was upstairs with his friend. His woman was up with his friend, and he was knocking on the door and yelling, "Open the door, Richard! Why don't you open the door?" And that was the whole story of the song—in his comedy act. It was no song when he did it; it was just an act. "Open the door, Richard."

Anyway, I went to the jukebox operators with the record. I said, "Hey, put this on. I'll give you whatever you want; you won't have to pay for anything." The operator said, "Man!" He listened to it. He said, "Man, ain't nobody going to put a nickel in the jukebox to hear someone talk!" (*laughs*) Well, you know, with the bars, they want to hear somebody singing. They wouldn't pay any real attention to the jukebox. It was just background music as far as they were concerned. So it got to me—I've got to do something now. The disc jockeys wouldn't play it. They wouldn't play any record. They used to call our records off-brand records. (*chuckles*) Solid black, off-brand.

So I went to a friend of mine, because I recorded a lot of his big bands. He was in charge of the big band department for William Morris Agency in California—Charlie Wick, who's in charge of [President] Reagan's communication department today. And I said, "Charlie, this record has got me crazy, man." And I told him what had happened. "Can you help me with this? I've got to get it played. I've got to get it started." He said, "Leave the record." He says, "There's a cat named Stillman Pond, he's a millionaire. And he's got big bands. And I'll make an appointment for you to see him." And then I went to see this cat. I met him in Hollywood. He listened to it. He said, "I don't play that junk. I've got big bands. What would I want with that piece of junk?" "Okay." I went back to Charlie. I said, "Charlie, no dice." He said, "Wait a minute, Ralph. You've got something here. You know something? Everybody in this big office is singing that song. 'Open the Door, Richard!' I know you've got something."

Well, there was a cat named Al Jarvis in L.A. who was the number one disc jockey. *Make Believe Ballroom* he called his show. He had a cat who programmed all his stuff for him. He just read—the program cat would make up this list. You know what I'm talking about. And he'd just read off the records and everything was programmed for him. But he was a good salesman on the air. And he had a way of getting people—he had that personality. So I went to this cat and I said, "Hey—" and I told him about this record and he said, "Hey, I dig it! That's something there. I'm going to program it." That was a big station. KFWB, I think the name of the station is out there. I can't remember, but as I recall it was a big station. So Al Jarvis gets the record. He said, "I've got a record here!—'Open the Door, Richard.'" Next record. Puts it on. The switchboard lights up. Now, you know why the switchboard lighted up? On the rap, the one that says, "*What did the lady say?*" And instead of one cat answering, three cats jumped for answering at the same time. (*laughs*) They wanted him to play the record over to hear what the lady said. It was so interesting up to that point, you know. If I had time to do the record over again, I would have corrected it, you know. But because I didn't, it just shows you what can happen with records and with music, with the arts by mistake, by error, by lack of time, by being so bad!

That put me on one thing. I don't ever want to be a perfectionist. And I'll tell you why. Eighty percent of the people don't know that much technically about music. If someone played a bad note, they wouldn't know it from a hole in the wall. But it's a feeling. Here I go again! They've got to feel something. I don't care whether it's opera, hillbilly—it's a feeling. You've got to feel music. Music is a basic emotion. That's what it is.

Let me ask you some more about Black & White. I know you had a lot of artists there. I'll run down a list of people that I can think of off the top of my head, and then you can add to it. Were you responsible for sides by Ivy Anderson?

Yeah, sure. I did that.

Helen Humes.

I produced that.

T-Bone.

I produced him. "Bobbie Sox Baby" was the first hit I had with him. Then "Stormy Monday" came next.

How did T-Bone come to Black & White?

I'll tell you how I got him. I got all the artists for them. When you say Black & White, you're saying how did Ralph Bass get—(*chuckles*) Now, this took off, as I say—*bang.* So I say, "Hey! I'm going to do the blues." It was the first black record to cross over. Whites and blacks. I'm going to do the blues. That's what I'm going to do. Well, I'd heard about T-Bone. T-Bone was from Texas. And he is probably the most underestimated guitar player in the history of music. T-Bone gave the guitar a new different sound, blues sound. See, T-Bone didn't come from the deep South. You must remember that most of the guitar players in the deep South, they didn't play with bands; they played by themselves. They went in and got five, ten dollars to play all night or something, or whatever. And they played mostly rhythm to themselves. Once in a while they'd make a fill, but they didn't have any band with them, no rhythm section. So they had to play rhythm to themselves, a blues rhythm

And when T-Bone got it, T-Bone had a band. He had a rhythm section. He got started playing fills, and he had that slur that gave the guitar that sound. Everything else after that came from T-Bone. To me, anyway. So I heard about him. And I said, "Well, I'm going to go to his manager." A booking office. A cat named Harold Oxley on Sunset Boulevard. And I went to him and I said, "I'd like to sign T-Bone Walker." I had never met T-Bone! I had heard about him. And he said, "What's the deal?" We made a deal. He said, "You got him! You know why you got him?" There was another cat who was representing himself as T-Bone's manager who was a phony. He was out to make that money. And all the record companies were dealing with him. He said, "Everybody's dealing with him. You're the first one that came to me. I'm the only one—" (*laughs*) That's how I got him! And then we went to the studio. And "Bobbie Sox Baby" was a stone hit, and that set T-Bone off. So, anyway, that's part of the early history of Black & White.

I'm a different kind of a producer when it comes to blues. As I said before, blues is a feeling. I'm not interested in the technical thing with blues—or with the singer. As a producer, an A & R man, my whole theory has been blues is a feeling. If you don't have it, you ain't got nothing. So when I bring a band in the studio—no, I don't have any rehearsal. We have heads. And then we go from there. And if the singer is singing his buns off and it's so great and I start feeling something, I know I've got something. I don't stay in the control room. I'm in the studio with the band, and with the singer, trying to get everything out of them. I try to create the atmosphere of a joint late at night. And if you go into a club sometimes at nighttime and hear a band or a singer performing—"Hey, he sounds a lot better than the records. I mean, why can't they get that kind of thing out of them?" Because they've got an audience. They have to react. A great, great blues singer has to react to audiences. These days of putting a pair of earphones on and listening to it, I mean, you know, how do they react? They can't. It's too mechanical. Like everything else today getting so darn mechanical.

Well, most of those things that T-Bone would come with, if he had a working band, he already had arrangements, right?

No! There weren't arrangements. These were all original songs!

So these wouldn't be things he was playing on a bandstand?

No, no, no. These were the first time that we'd do them. We'd do them right in the studio. That was the first time we played them.

Ralph Bass with Sunnyland Slim. Photo courtesy of Jim O'Neal.

***Any anecdotes that you remember concerning T-Bone being in the studio, that
kind of thing?***

T-Bone was—he was a great guy. He was straight, a businessman, and I'll
tell you a story about T-Bone, funny story. He was so successful. I only signed
him for a year with no options. And I went out to sign my new contract and I
was told by Harold Oxley, his booking office, where he was playing in Texas a
certain day. I said, okay, I'll meet him in Texas. So I took the contracts with me.
Got to Texas. And this town that he was playing in—now, you must remember,
blacks in the South didn't have any place for recreation except clubs unless it
was a big city. Didn't even have a movie house to go to, unless it was a big city,
that had a section roped off in the balcony for the blacks to sit in, or to have a
theater that was nothing but blacks. In the smaller cities they didn't have any,
or the towns.

So music was an important thing for blacks. Every black had a radio and a
phonograph. I don't care if it was wind-up phonograph. That was their thing—
music. And you see, this statement about blacks got rhythm. Hey, man, you
know why they got rhythm? When they say that? Their mothers, when they go

to church, they take their little babies with them. And they hear those choirs with that beat, or when they're home they hear music. They're tuned in from the time they're born to the sound of music and the beat. They get it from the time they're born through their early stages of life. So when a big artist had a big record, a black had a big record and he would come into town—I couldn't believe it, because I took Little Esther on the road, she and Johnny Otis, when Esther was at her height. She was the biggest black attraction in the country. And I wanted to see the South through the eyes of a black, not through what they wanted me to see, to see what the South was really like and why people came to buy these records. And let me tell you, they came in and I'd say to the promoter, "Man! You're paying so much money for Esther. Where are you get-ting the money from? There's only maybe two, three thousand blacks in this town and maybe four or five hundred of them would come." Man, they'd be coming from 150 miles. He had placards 150 miles away. They would come in to hear this attraction, okay?

So T-Bone in Texas—I came to the club to see him. And the place was jam-packed! It's a funny story now. And I noticed there were stiff women. Most of them were women in the audience. And they were very stiff; they weren't drinking. So I said to the promoter, I said, "What's going on here? These people don't seem like they're having a good time. Why?" Well, he said, "I'll tell you what. All those women out there were church women and here's what happened. When T-Bone was here about four months ago and played, when he left town the preacher's wife left town the same time! (*laughs*) And all the women in the church want to come out and see what T-Bone was putting down." (*laughs*)

Now, T-Bone was a performer as well; he was a show man. And depending upon the nature of the club, he would perform—he would fit his music to the club or his style or perform—"showmanship" is the word I want to use. Well, this club, the first thing you know when he came along and he was introduced, he wasn't there. All you heard was *bing-bing, bing-bing, bing-bing*—his guitar sound coming out of a long, long corridor going into the bathroom. And he started playing the first chords in the bathroom. And people were wondering, "Where is T-Bone's sound coming from?" And T-Bone wore glasses, you know. And he would put teardrops or something to make his eyes glisten when the lights hit him, so he would look very sexy. And then he'd slowly start walking out and start playing. Well, you want to know something? Now, I was there! After the second or third number, those women were having a ball and throwing dollar bills out on the floor! Because that's what used to happen in those days. They used to throw money out on the floor. They made the extra money that way. So that was T-Bone's showmanship in his performance. He was great. He was a great—

***Talk about Helen Humes. How did you hook up with Helen? How did that hap-
pen?***

Well, with Helen, it was just the fact that she had a record before, and I just
wanted to do another record with her.

Those were Buck Clayton sides, weren't they?

Yeah.

Was that before Buck went in the army or after he came out? It had to be after.

Yeah. Yeah. Yeah. I remember Helen was up in the hotel. I went up to sign
her in the hotel. And she was sitting there playing cards while I was talking to
her. Wanted to record her.

How about Ivy Anderson?

She had just left Duke Ellington. That's when I was still on that jazz kick.
(*chuckles*) With the big bands and everything, you know. It was before I got
into the guts of the blues. And I got an idea, "Hey, let me do—"

Ivy was one of the greats. She was still a little on the jazz side being with Duke,
you know. I wanted to get some *raw* blues singers. The rawer—I mean, the *guts*
of blues. That's what it came to. That's what it came to. And then, of course,
from there I went on to rhythm and blues, which was the big moneymaker.

I want to tell you what happened. I decided to go in business for myself. (*laughs*)
And, you know, here I am with all this young—all this ambition. And I had a label
called Bop, B-o-p. I don't know whether you ever heard of Bop. In fact, there's
one big record I had on it, "The Chase." Wardell Gray and Dexter Gordon. It was
a hit, a jazz hit. I did it live. And they were in town on Central Avenue, played
some big club. Central Avenue was the main drag for L.A. blacks, for nightclubs
and whatnot. And there was a big ballroom there. Wardell and Dexter were there.
And I had a hell of a time because I had to do it remote. There was no such thing
as coming in there with disc. We were putting everything on disc, you know. And
Radio Recorders made arrangements with the telephone company to put it on a
number one-A line. That's a special telephone line that would equalize everything.
And they set it up. And they were miles away. So they had to record everything
that came out. You couldn't talk to them. And I did Wardell and Dexter in a jazz
thing called—we called it "The Chase." And it was a big, big jazz thing.

Well, talk about getting the feeling of the club, that was the ultimate, wasn't it?

Yeah, it was! Same thing. Something about doing something live. For example, even when I did Etta James, for example. Chess, I did all their hits. I
remember Etta from a group—she had a group that went way back. And had a
song called "Dance with Me, Henry," which was a take-off on a song that I had,
"Work with Me, Annie," which was a big hit that I did. She wasn't doing too

well. She was at the Regal Theater. I brought her into Chess's office and signed her. And one thing about a producer, an A & R man—you have to know your artist! You can't just sit there. You have to play up to their strength and play down their weaknesses. You have to understand them. And I never familiarized myself, or got that close or that tight, with any of my artists. We got to the studio—it was a thing, a together thing—but I wanted the respect and I didn't want to be on top of them at all times. And we'd get in the studio, that's when we were together.

And knowing Etta, it's difficult to get a male writer to write for a female. Naturally, how does a man feel the emotions of a woman unless he's a woman himself (*chuckles*) is all I'm talking about. There was a girl in New York named Pearl Woods who used to sound like Etta. And she was a good writer and she lived the same kind of life as Etta. And she knew Etta. Not that she ever met her, but she had a thing for—a common bond with Etta. I brought her in from New York to write for Etta. And she wrote this song "All I Could Do Is Cry," which was a number one hit, R & B hit. And I had the big band down here in Chicago. And we had two-track at that time. Unh-uh. Not me. I don't want no two-track. I wanted Etta on one—I wanted Etta on one track and the band on the other, I said. I didn't want no—because people weren't buying stereo. They didn't have any stereo sets, so I didn't care about getting a stereo sound. So Etta, I knew Etta had to hear things. She was a great singer. She had to be—inspired by what was going on, as all great musicians and singers, or all people in the arts are. And Etta, one take. And she was so great, after she got through singing, she was crying! And Murray Watson, who just passed not too long ago—a great trumpet player here in Chicago—Murray came up to the control room and said, "Ralph, let's make another take." It was after I had heard the playback. I said, "Why?" He said, "I hit a wrong note." I said, "Murray, do you buy records?" "No." "Do musicians buy records, these kind of records?" "No." "I ain't making them for you; I'm making them for the public." I said, "Do you realize how great Etta was? That's what they're buying—Etta."

And you know something? It was a number one hit, and Etta was making it in all the theaters. There were the five theaters—the Apollo, the Regal, the Royal, the Howard, the Uptown—you know, in the country that black acts could only work at. Vegas wasn't open to them. Miami wasn't open to them. The clubs, the black clubs. And I was at the Apollo Theater recording Moms Mabley or Pigmeat Markham, either one of the two great comedians that I put on the Chess label. She didn't know I was there. And she was on the same bill. And Etta was about maybe a year after she had the hit out. She came off the stage with tears in her eyes again. No matter how many times Etta sang that song, she always cried. It was so personal to her and her performance was so great. And Etta was a performer who didn't have to go out there and dance and jig and dress in all those sexy gowns. Etta sang. The audience was as quiet as could be. She had that thing, she had that magic. So here we go again—it's a feeling. Rhythm and blues is a feeling, coming from the blues.

Would you backtrack for me and talk about leaving? You went into business for yourself. You had Bop. Did you lose your shirt trying to—

Right, I lost my shirt trying to distribute the records (*laughs*) and get my money. So I recorded one other act, Errol Garner. Now, Errol—a great jazz musician—was also commercial. He had a sound. Errol had a sound. I mean, you don't have— For example, I tell great musicians when I hear a musician, a musician in order to sell you have to have an identifiable sound. When a disc jockey plays your record on the air, if he plays an instrumental, he doesn't know who the hell it is unless you have a distinct style that belongs to you. And Ramsey [Lewis] had that funk sound, which I told him that's what I wanted. And musicians, they have a sound that's identifiable without seeing them. And Garner had this thing. Garner couldn't read a note. In fact, he told me—because I used to use Errol on a lot of sessions that I had. And he would sit down by the piano player and listen to what he's playing, and he'd sit down and play, you know. I said, "Why don't you learn how to read, Errol? You can get a lot of gigs." Because, you know, times were tough. They weren't really making it, these great musicians. He said, "I tried that. You know what I did? I started changing my sound, my style." And that's what sold Errol.

Anyway, I had this record with Errol Garner, "Stairway to the Stars," and I went to New York to try to get the Bop label distributed and also the Garner record, okay? And I played the Bop record for a store around Forty-second Street, one of the better stores, and the cats flipped over it. Anyway, there was a cat in Jersey named Herman Lubinsky who had Savoy Records. He'd heard about me. And he said, "Hey, I'll make a deal with you. Put the record out." So I figured, you know, he had the distribution. I'm naïve. Well, I gave him a label I had called Bop, and then I had a label for the Garner called Portrait. And there was one cat in Los Angeles that was a percussion player. He was right around the corner from Radio Recorders. Jack Rosen, his name was. I used to come in and say, "Hey, did Herman send my tapes in yet? I mean, the masters?" "No." Then he called me one day, he said, "Hey, I got it, but it's not on your label; it's on Savoy." I called up, man. Oh, I mean, I couldn't prove anything, because, you know, when I recorded Errol it was during the ban, the recording ban. I had no contract. And Petrillo had a ban; no musicians could record back then [referring to the Petrillo Ban of the American Federation of Musicians, led by union president James Petrillo]. I was helpless. I didn't want to get Errol in trouble. And when Errol found out it was on Savoy—because he was on Savoy before he came with me—Errol came in and, man, he blasted me! "I thought it was on your label!" I said, "Errol," and I told him the story. He said, "Why—that—mother—" I said, "What happened?" He told me. He said he was going to record for Herman and there was an elevator strike, and he made him walk up eighteen, twenty flights of stairs. (*laughs*) Well, anyway, the rest is history. And we made a deal and worked for Herman Lubinsky. (*laughs*) Well, he was a hand—

See, look, I'll tell you in those days. There was a handful of record companies, independents. The independents were in black music or country. The majors were completely ignoring black music. Completely. There was only four record companies, majors, then. Columbia, RCA, Decca, and Capitol. Capitol was just starting to get big. And, my gosh, who could you go with? Who was there left? And the independent record companies were family affairs. Like the Bihari brothers, that had Modern Records, you know. There was Aladdin Records with the Messner brothers. They were all family things. And the only ones that made any money were the family. (*laughs*) And so you get hired as an A & R man, you were lucky. You got flat salary. There were no royalties, no nothing. No deals. So that's what it came to. And I've always been a bad businessman anyhow. My thing was in creativity. It's very difficult to have both at the same time. So it was a struggle, survival of the fittest, and if you didn't produce, baby, you were out.

Who did you produce for Herman Lubinsky?
Well, I gave him Little Esther—Esther Phillips—and Johnny Otis. She was the biggest black attraction in the country. At the age of fourteen, fifteen. They couldn't believe that anyone thirteen, fourteen year old could sound like that. They could hear teenage, young girls singing—they sounded like young girls. But Esther had a Dinah Washington sound! And they couldn't believe it. In fact, the promoter—one of the biggest promoters in the country, in Atlanta, Georgia—in his placards he had a question mark where Esther's picture should have been. He had Johnny Otis's picture on the placard. People came out there wondering what this girl looked like that singed like that.

Johnny Otis had a club called the Barrelhouse out in Watts. Now, Johnny Otis was a Greek. He was a white boy. But he was into black music real heavy. He was married to a black woman, too, but during way back then—and he had to pay some dues; I know, okay? He was devoted to black music, Johnny was. Johnny had a big band before that. His manager was someplace. During the war years, they couldn't get good musicians and good bands. Anyway, his manager ran off with the money and stranded them someplace in the West. So Johnny had this Barrelhouse with a man named Ali Baddou. And that's where I met Johnny. And Johnny impressed me. The reason I went there, he used to have an amateur show once a week, Monday nights. That's why I would come there, because I was out every night at all-black clubs, listening to talent. Finding out, you know, who I could get. They didn't know where to go, especially in the deep South. They didn't know where to go. Nobody was there. They didn't have representatives there. I lived out of the trunk of my car half of my life. And he had Esther on the show and I couldn't believe it! There was a theater in Watts, a black theater. And she won an amateur show there. I said, "I want to sign her, Johnny, with you." Well, California had some rough laws, you know, for teenagers. They had what was called a Jackie Coogan Law [to protect child actors]. You know what happened to that. I guess that's all history. So the state of California passed some very rigid laws about minors. So we had to get her mother to sign the contract, or a legal guardian or her mother. And so we went to her mother and her mother signed the contract.

And Johnny and I used to write at nighttime, thinking of songs, writ[ing] tunes, ideas. And we came up with a song that someone had given him. He had changed the lyric. And what gave him the idea, there was a comedian working at the club, and they had a line in one of their comedy bits about the "lady bear." Now a lady bear—I didn't understand what a lady bear was either. [The term is black slang for an ugly, sexually aggressive woman.] I know you're looking at me and don't understand what I'm talking about. We put that bit into this song. A lady bear is going to grab a man; she's going to get him! There was a line "*You've got to watch out. There's some lady bears out in the forest. There's some lady bears out there.*" (*laughs*) So he put that in the song. And you want to know something? I was recording a group called the Robins, and we had to have a male part in it. So I took the bass section. After the session, I told Johnny bring the girl down to the Radio Recorders. Bring Esther down. And I will make an audition of it and send it to Herman Lubinsky. I want to sign her. So we did. So after the session was over, we only had about ten or fifteen minutes left, and I had the bass singer of the Robins sing with Esther on this thing about the bear. And we didn't have a title. We didn't know what to call the song. It had no title. [It would be named "Lady Bear Blues."] I just sent the dub to him, to Herman. And I said, "And send me twenty-five dollars. I want to pay the male singer of the Robins some money for singing with her, and I want to pay Esther's expenses coming down to the studio." Twenty-five bucks, now. He called me up and said, "Wire me twenty-five dollars. I can get anyone to do-wop, ooh-wop. Twenty-five dollars. What are you recording? Children? Kindergarten class?" I told him she's only thirteen years old. So he wouldn't send me the money. (*chuckles*)

Anyway, a cat named Bill Cook, he was a big deejay in Newark, and Savoy's office was in Newark, New Jersey. He came in the office and said, "Herman, ain't nothing happening. I need a record. Got anything that's new that ain't released? I need something." "Well," he says, "my man in L.A. made some records with a group called the Robins." So while he's playing the Robins dubs, he played the thing on Esther. He [Cook] came running, he says, "Who is this girl? What's her name? This is something!" He was excited. Herman looked at him like he was crazy. "What?" He calls me up in the middle of the night. "Ralph, that girl you got, sign her! She's something." And he told me what happened. "Oh," I said, "now you realize it, eh?" "Sign her."

I woke Johnny up. Johnny was working over at the bar. It was about three o'clock in the morning. I woke him up. I said, "Johnny, let's sign Esther up. We'll get to her momma; sign the papers. We've got to have her." I told him. He says, "You mean that thing is great?" I said, "Yeah." He couldn't believe it himself. (*chuckles*)

Well, we were in the studio and I had two writers, [Jerry] Leiber and [Mike] Stoller, they were young kids who wrote "Kansas City" for me. I was the first one to record it. And that was the first hit on Kansas City. (*chuckles*) Anyway, there was a storm out there. We were in a studio recording. And it was thundering and lightning, and so I said, "Hey, write a thing about the storm!" So Leiber and Stoeller said, "Okay." They were right in the studio. I had to have some sound effects. And I didn't know, what the hell, how to get rain sound. So we took the microphone into the bathroom, the men's room, and we were flushing the urinal (*laughs*) to get sounds. So, you know, it has to come to you.

And I'm going to tell you one more story and that's it! A great story. James Brown. This is a classic. I'm in Atlanta, Georgia, and I hear—we had our own branches. King Records had their own branches. He didn't believe in having distributors. He said they're nothing but pimps.

Was King Syd Nathan?

Yes! In Cincinnati.

Anyway, I'm in Atlanta, Georgia, looking for talent. And I'm seeing the deejays, you know, and whatnot. And I went to our office branch there. The branch manager said, "Hey, I've got a dub I want you to hear." So he played it for me. I said, "Who is that?" "I don't know. Some group down in Macon, Georgia." "Where? What's their name?" He says, "Well, they call themselves the Famous Flames." So I got one of the deejays in Atlanta to drive me down. I'm going to find him—what do you do? You go to a radio station and find out who—of course, a Macon, Georgia, deejay at the radio station probably knows all—that's not a big city. So we head for a radio station and I go up there. I said, "There's a group here in Macon called the Famous Flames. Do you know where I can reach them?" "Yeah, there's a man named Clint Bradley who manages them."

Now, you must remember that—the Bible Belt—there was always one black cat who controlled everything across the tracks, what we used to call across the tracks. You know, he had the gambling and so forth and so on. And the nightclub. He worked with the white power structure in the town. Now, I'm going back to 1952, '53. Especially in those smaller areas like that. "They work at his club. And he can tell you about them." So I says, "Can I reach him?" He says, "Yeah. I'll give you the number." So I call. He gave me a house number and I call and his wife answered the phone. And I explained to her why I was there. She said, "Stay by the phone." She asked me where I was and I said, "I'm at this number." "And I'll have him call you right back." And he did. And I told him. And he said, "Okay, I'll tell you what I'll do. You got a car?" I says, "Yeah, I've got a car." "Eight o'clock tonight, I want you to meet me at this place. There's a barbershop right across the street from the railroad station. And park your car there at eight o'clock in front of this barbershop. When the lights go on and the Venetian blinds go up twice, back and down, come on in. The door will be open." We were trying to figure out why he was that secretive. Well, only one reason. Here I am, I'm a strange white cat. And he doesn't want the white power structure to think that I'm dealing with a stranger. (*laughs*)

Anyway, so we did. Eight o'clock. That's what happened. Lights came on and the blinds go up and down. I said to a friend of mine, I said, "Hey, babe. If I don't come out in twenty minutes or so, come on in and get me." (*laughs*) Anyway, I come in. He was standing there and "Well," he said, "There might be another record company interested in him." And I didn't know that Chess Records—because Leonard Chess told me later on, he said, "I always hold one thing against you, Ralph. You took James Brown away from me." He'd heard about it, too, from this cat, you know, that we were going to sign. But he was going to come down there and listen to him. I listened to him first. And then there was a rainstorm or something and they couldn't get a plane out. (*laughs*) Anyway, I said, "Look." I had two hundred dollars in my pocket. Now, two hundred dollars in '53 was a lot of money. It was like a thousand dollars today. I said, "Clint, I've got two hundred dollars in my pocket." Now, this is how sure I was of this thing. "It's yours. I want him now. I want everybody now and sign them in the barbershop." He said, "Deal!" So they all came down. I didn't know James Brown from a hole in the wall. Just the Famous Flames. I had them all sign. Now, he says, "Come to the club. Tonight at my club. They'll perform so you'll know what you have." I said, "Okay."

Now, in those days I wasn't interested in the performance. I used to tell people I used to audition, "Hey, stop working out, man. Just let me hear you sing." This was before the days of video, of course. I ain't selling no picture; I'm selling the voice. I came to the club and they came out. There was James on his stomach, crawling on the floor with the microphone, going from table to table where there was a pretty girl, singing one word, one song. "*Please, please, please.*" I said, "Oh, my God. That's the thing. I know I've got to have this. I've got to have that." So we made arrangements. I said, "I want you to come up. How soon can you all get away to come to Cincinnati?" We had our studios there. We got, I think, two weeks ahead. I said, "Okay, I'll pay your expenses. Clint, you come. You bring them up in your car. I'll put you in the hotel and everything. Don't worry about nothing, okay?" So I did. I put them up in a hotel called the Manse Hotel, which was in Cincinnati, a black hotel. Because Cincinnati was that way, too. (*chuckles*) And brought them in the studio. Syd Nathan wasn't in town. I did this with him being away. And then I put in for my—I went to the bookkeeper and I said, "These are my expenses. Pay off the hotel, two hundred dollars, food, gas, everything." I don't know what it was, but whatever it was they gave me a check. And I took off. They took off.

And I was in St. Louis and my buddy Henry Glover, who was another A & R man for Syd Nathan for King. Syd gave me a label called Federal, and I produced everything on Federal. The only thing I ever produced for King itself was Earl Bostic. Made a big thing out of him. But, anyway, I'm in St. Louis at the Atlas Hotel, I think it was called. There were two black hotels in St. Louis. And all of a sudden, here come Henry Glover. They knew where to find me. (*chuckles*) There was no problem. They knew I always stayed at black hotels when I could, because I wanted my friends up there and I didn't want anybody—no big deal, no nothing. They think I'm in the drug business or something, you know, some phony business. What's a white man doing in a black— Nobody believed me. The police. Nobody. A lot of stories, okay. But I'll have it in my book.

Anyway, Henry Glover comes up with a cat named Andy Gibson, a great writer and arranger. He looks around. He says, "You better call the old man up." "What for?" "Well, he told me if I found you to tell you that you're fired." "For what? What'd I do?" "I don't know. Call the old man up. Don't tell him we found you." (*laughs*) So I call him up. I said, "Syd? What's happening? What's going on? Anything wrong?" "How could—are you all right? What kind of—what are you on?" He always thought—everybody thought I was on drugs, because they never thought a white cat could do the things I did. Even the people I worked for. And I'm going to tell you something. I never smoked a joint in my life. Not even a joint! I mean, if you got caught with a joint down in the deep South, baby, they'd put you in jail for two years. That and the fact of my upbringing—whatever it was, I just couldn't do it. I got high on music. I didn't have to—well, maybe a couple of bottles of beer. So he said, "How?" "What do you mean? Who are you talking about, Syd?" "Sounds like someone's stuttering on the record. All he says is one word!" "Oh," I said, "you mean '*Please, Please, Please.*'" "Yeah, that's it. Worst piece of shit I ever heard in my life." (*chuckles*) I said, "I'll tell you what, Syd." Now, I knew what I had. In fact, I had made a dub of it before I left Cincinnati and I—after a club date, I'd have the musicians come up with their girls, you know. And the girls would go crazy listening to this thing. I knew what I had. I was 110 percent sure of what I had. I said, "I'll tell you what I'll do, Syd. Put it out in Atlanta. If it don't sell in Atlanta, don't fire me. I'll quit." "I'm going to put it out all over the country to show you what a piece of bleep this is!" So that's what happened. The rest is history.

I have a sequel to the James Brown story. Now, the record's out now and about three months later, you know, it was a strong hit, number one hit in the country—R & B–wise. And I'm in Cincinnati, having another session with some artist anyway. And the studio was in another building, another part of—not where the offices were, but another building. And he had his pressing plant there as well as the studio. And also he had his branch office, his sales branch for selling records for Cincinnati, for the area there. And he had about five or six booths where the dealers could come in and the salesmen would play the records there. When they came in to buy records, where they'd pick up records. So here comes Syd Nathan. And Syd was half blind. He had these great big, thick glasses and he couldn't see but just so far. And I was sitting down there, waiting for the musicians to come. He didn't see me. And he was talking to this man he was with. He said, "You know why we are so successful here at King Records? That's because we don't do things like anybody else. We do them differently! I'm going to show you what I'm talking about." And he goes and he puts him in the booth there and he puts on "Please, Please, Please." (*chuckles*) I was cracking up, you know.

You see, what I'd like to put an end to what I was saying. An A & R man has—he has to believe in things, in something. And even though other people might say, "Oh, why are you doing that?" That's the same as when I found Moms Mabley. My gosh, Leonard Chess almost had a fit! Going down to New York and giving Joe Glaser some money to sign her. And what's the cat's name—the black comedian that was on that health kick? What's his name? Gregory. He wanted me to sign Dick Gregory. And I didn't want to sign—and I went to the club to hear Dick at the Roberts. And I listened for about twenty minutes, a half hour, and I said, "Man, who wants—" Every joke he had was a racial thing. I said, "People don't want to buy no record—they maybe want to hear a racial thing every now and then. But not a whole record of racial things," I said. No. And everybody was after him, Dick Gregory. I went to New York and signed Moms Mabley instead. So, you know, you have to believe in something. Even though the people you work for are against it. I don't believe—like I told you—James Brown, the Moms Mabley thing. Because Moms became the one—we sold more records on Moms and Pigmeat Markham—my gosh, LPs. But you have to believe in something. And even though it might be different to you—you might hear it and say, "Aw, that ain't nothing." But you've got to believe in it. Truthfully.

You're going to make mistakes. Of course, you're going to make mistakes. My gosh, nobody is perfect. Like I always say, a great baseball player, his batting average is over three hundred. He's a great baseball player. You don't expect him to make everything a hit. If your performance is three hundred, you're a batter, you're great! So you had to believe in it. And you have to be a little different. You have to have something that's going to capture someone's ears, because as I say, you know, the record today—and I'll tell you something about today's thing. Today's thing is both a visual thing. A lot of the records that—if it depended upon pure audio, it would never be hits. But a lot of them are hits because of the fact that they see the video and they see the weird costumes and the choreography, whether you really want to call it choreography, the band itself and someone, you know, acting like a lion on a stage—performance-wise. That's great. There's nothing wrong with it except the fact that in my era it was completely audio. And—

You still had James Brown with his fabulous performances. Is there any way you could capture that in audio?

No.

And you weren't concerned with that?

Never. I always told him, for example—I told the acts when they came in, "Look, these companies can't pay you a big sum of money for recording. But you know where your money is? In the clubs. In the performances. The record is your publicity. It gets you started. And from there on, you make all the bread playing the big theaters, playing the big clubs, playing the one-nighters. That's where the bread is." Which it was. And then I said, "Get a good act and you perform." And then they didn't care too much about performers. You had to perform, but it didn't have to be way out.

James—you know where James Brown got the crawling thing? From "Big Jay" McNeely, who I recorded, with a saxophone. I did a thing called "The Deacon's Hop." And when he used to perform—I had a big jazz concert in L.A. at the Shriner Auditorium, and I had all these great musicians on the ——(??) jazz. And I had Big Jay on as an added attraction, he and his brother Bobby. And Big Jay got on his back and crawled on his back with his saxophone, and the audience broke up! They cracked up! They were out of it! And when the intermission came, and you know what happened when the curtain came up? Everybody was laughing! I was in the backstage. I didn't know what's happening. And I walked up to the side curtain because I was getting everybody ready. I was downstairs in the dressing room. Come on! Intermission's over with. And I was busy getting everybody together to get on the stage after intermission. And I heard this roar of laughter. And the whole band was dressed in skirts, women's clothes. (*chuckles*) Where they got them from, they found—the women who used to clean up the auditorium—and they went in the closets and put all these dresses on. And I wanted to know what the hell was going on. They said, "If they want comedy, we're going to give them comedy!" They thought that Big Jay—(*laughs*)—so you see what I'm talking about? Audiences are like that today. That was the forerunner. Those were the forerunners of what's happening. (*laughs*)

Cadillac **Baby**

Narvel Eatmon was known to blues fans around the world as Cadillac Baby. He was the owner and operator of Cadillac Baby's Show Lounge, one of Chicago's premier blues clubs of the 1950s, and the owner and operator of the Bea & Baby record label, which issued records by Eddie Boyd, Sunnyland Slim, L. C. McKinley, and many others.

By the time I met Cadillac Baby all the good times had passed him by. The club and the record label were both long gone, and he was operating a neighborhood candy store, Aladdin's Cavern, at 4405 South State—directly across the street from Chicago's notorious Robert Taylor Homes. He sold candy, pop, potato chips—and the latest 45 rpm records. I compared notes with several fellow blues enthusiasts and found that we each had good

Cadillac Baby in his La-Z Boy. Photo courtesy of Cadillac Baby.

times and great adventures in his company and under his guidance. It was a great place for a novice blues enthusiast to step into the world of blues.

My introduction to Cadillac took place in 1971–1972. I believe I heard him being interviewed by Amy van Singel on her radio program, *Atomic Mama's Wang Dang Doodle Blues Show,* which aired on WNIB in Chicago. I know for certain that she was plugging an LP he had issued. The LP, "Colossal Blues," was a story in itself.

According to Jim O'Neal, the entire sequence went down something like this: Jim and Amy van Singel were husband and wife at the time. They were owners and editors of *Living Blues* magazine. In one of their earliest issues they ran a feature on Cadillac Baby, his blues club, and his record label. As it happened, Cadillac still had copies of the original 45s issued on his Bea & Baby label, and so they ran a small ad in *Living Blues* magazine to sell the 45s he still had on hand. He had success selling them and decided he'd like to release an LP, a compilation of the sides originally released as 45s. He placed an ad for his LP in *Living Blues*—and started receiving orders from customers—even though he hadn't yet produced the LP. When the orders started coming in, he decided—with encouragement from Jim and Amy—to go ahead with production of the LP. But instead of a simple compilation of the sides on his label, he decided to present the original studio recordings as though they were live performances captured at Cadillac Baby's Show Lounge back in the 1950s, with dubbed-in club ambiance and Cadillac in the recording studio re-creating his role as master of ceremonies, introducing each artist in turn. And typical of Cadillac's bargain-basement production values, he sought to create club ambiance with only a handful—five or six at the most—people, including Jim and Amy! This all eventually turned into the unintentional kitsch classic "Colossal Blues." In the words of Cadillac Baby himself: "Colossal—it means bigger than the world!" I heard the plug for the LP and read the article on Cadillac Baby. I phoned Jim O'Neal to ask him if Cadillac Baby was receptive to visitors—and if it was safe to go where he lived. With Jim's assurances, I made a visit one winter weekday afternoon. It was January 22, 1973.

Cadillac lived in the back of his store, where most activities took place around a potbellied wood-burning stove and a La-Z Boy recliner that sat directly next to the stove. Here Cadillac would play host and entertain for hours at a time. On my first visit we were joined by a pair of his longtime friends—blues pianist Sunnyland Slim and record label owner/producer Joe Brown of Chicago's famed J.O.B. label. That afternoon I had my first Champale—a malt liquor popular with African Americans—and somebody brought in raccoon meat, which was cooked in a pan of water on the wood-burning stove. I drank the Champale; I passed on the raccoon. A few nights later Cadillac invited me to come along on an outing to a local blues club, the High Chaparral. This was a real blues bonanza, as the featured artists that evening were blues mandolinist Johnny Young, Lee Jackson, Winehead Willie Williams, Sunnyland Slim, and Hound Dog Taylor.

This was the first of many visits over the years and the start of our friend-ship. Through our early conversations Cadillac helped expand my knowledge of the artists and their records and of the history of blues in Chicago. During this time I began hosting my first blues radio program and Cadillac agreed to do a series of vocal drop-ins. Using his best master of ceremonies voice, he recorded a program introduction and various station IDs. The only prob-lem was that he couldn't remember my last name; he kept calling me Steve Schikel, which was the name of a local TV reporter. That was even better and I just went with it. Several years later I was doing the *Blues Before Sunrise* radio program at WBEZ, Chicago's public radio station, and invited Cadillac to come down for the interview that follows.

During the 1980s I started doing speaking engagements with a presentation called "Voice of the Blues." It was a slide/lecture presentation that included interview segments with five different blues people, including Cadillac Baby's story of "Cryin' Shame." Whenever I had a speaking gig in Chicago I'd be sure to let him know. And after I played his interview segment we'd turn on the house lights and introduce him. He loved to come out and see and hear himself—and he loved to be introduced to the audience. It was a small taste of glory for all the kindness he sent in my direction over the years.

In the last years of his life Cadillac gave up the store and operated his final hustle, selling used hubcaps at Fifty-ninth and State. We did this interview on September 9, 1983. Cadillac died of cancer in 1991.

■ ■ ■

Steve, I was born in 1910—October 8, 1910. Cayuga, Mississippi. I had six broth-ers, six sisters. We had three younger children, my mother did. I was the "Baby," and my sister, Alma, she's still alive, and the next brother was Armon. We call him "Boy." So my mother named the three children nicknames—the Baby, the Gal, the Boy. (*laughs*) You know how the old folks do—"He da Baby, you da Gal, dat's da Boy!" We three younger ones—*I* was the Baby! So the whole town knew me as Baby Eatmon. My correct name is Eatmon. My father died at an early age—I guess I was four or five. I hardly remember him. He was a church man—a deacon and all that kinda stuff. My mother, she was left with all the children to raise. Like all women, they fall somewhere by the wayside. They can't do a good job raising children. But she was determined to raise her children after the old man passed, and she did. The girls didn't go astray, and the boys listened to her. After a time the brother older than me died—pneumonia or something—he got sick and passed. She came to me and she said, "You the man of the family." That made me feel big! I'm already smart, but that made me much smarter, knowing that I got an obligation! I said, "Okay, you don't have to worry. Whatever I can do."

We owned our own little home, and usually during WPA [Works Progress Administration] time, if a person had a home they couldn't get much help. If you was able, you wasn't entitled to this benefit. But since we had no father, I had to be the father. The government gave me the privilege of being the leader. So they said, "You can work and support the family." We made $40.10 a month. And that was big money. We did such work as road work, grading, and, you know, there wasn't much machinery—had to do it all by shovel and pick and hand. We cut ditches and ran the ditches through town they call sanitary district and all that take the water off the city. And slope banks and good roads—hard work. More like penitentiary work, but—they was very nice. After all, your leaders knew that you was working for a living and small support, and they didn't push you too hard. But I'll tell you, all men actually felt like working. There wasn't no shirking, you know. You went home every night. You transported the men to work each morning, and that's where I happened to buy a big car to transport a lot of the workers. I was working part-time for—it wasn't like a steel mill—more like an iron-yard place. So I worked in this iron yard and from there to the WPA. I'd switch off—so many days here and so many days there. This was back in the thirties. We started about '33 and I worked up until '37 or '38 doing the WPA. Just about the time Social Security cards came in around '35 or '36. Somewhere during those years Social Security came in. You didn't have Social Security numbers when I first started. Then the Social Security numbers came out. That meant someday you could draw Social Security, like I'm drawing now!

See, the town I lived in, it wasn't like there was rich soil. You couldn't live off farming too much. You could only garden and raise a little stuff to live on, but you couldn't make a big living on planting stuff to make a big crop, like cotton and corn. You just made enough to survive on. You had to maneuver and hustle. It kept you shifty. I think this kind of thing makes a great person when you come the hard way and have to think fast to make a living and survive. This is how I had to be thoughtful all the way through life.

In my home, since I was the leader of the family, we take a part of the home and made a kinda—not exactly juke house—but it was more like an eating party. Saturday night fish fry like Louis Jordan sang about. Where people could come and entertain theyself. So we had this fish fry, and my mother, she invented this thing. Lindbergh got sunk in the ocean or somewhere—so she started it was like a punch, like they say Coca-Cola started from liquid; it wasn't bottled. So my mother she invented a—well, it wasn't nothing but like "pop-aide," now—but she invented an awful good drink, Lindbergh Punch. And it was good, 'cause I drinked it myself. We sold that. We sold fish. And we got bands like Walter Jacobs, the Chatman Boys, you know. They had a string-band instrument, violins and guitars. Wasn't electrotized—had that old steel guitar—beautiful music—Mississippi Sheiks! They worked for me! I hired them. 'Course I made pretty good little change. I guess if I paid them eight or ten dollars apiece—that's like two thousand now. So I'd hire them to work. We even started by lantern light. In later years we got electric. We had candlelight, lantern light, Coca-Cola-bottle light—and had these parties. And it was so smoky, but we could see. I went to another city and got a juicebox [jukebox] entertaining music. Well, they call 'em nickelodeon then. See this thing, it played more like whatever top blues tunes we had, and this is the way I raised money to feed my family. And that's where I start listening at the blues.

A funny thing about it—I was in Edwards, Mississippi. This wasn't at my place, at a place joining me down in town. They call the old guy Pocket. Pocket ran a place. He ran a fish shack and an all-night place. So I'm a young man and didn't understand the problems of a real man, and here was a man from Jackson. So this man had a great problem. He's a nice man—he provide his home, but, anyway, his wife or somebody wasn't satisfied. They kicked him out. It was just like that record on Eddie Boyd: *Five long years in the steel mill for one woman—she had the nerve to kick me out!* They kicked the man out. So he came to our town—visiting, I don't know, probably just stopping through on his way passing through. And there was a juicebox—we call it a juicebox. He started playing the box. He found a record on there he liked. I wish I could think of the artist [Blind Boy Fuller], 'cause this was in 1937. So this box was playing a record that he heard: *My baby went away and left me—Ain't it a cryin' shame!* But the basic of the record—*Ain't it a cryin' shame*—that was the punch line! Do you know, this man spent one week—*he had money*—playing one record. He wore the record out. The juicebox broke down. They had to call another town and get the juicebox repaired, 'cause he stood there and he'd go to sleep playing it—he had that much money. "*Ain't it a cryin' shame.*" He felt like it was such a crying shame—all he had did—this is true! (*laughs*) This is true and I got witness. This man stayed there night and day—for one week, playing *one* record! After he found a record he liked! 'Cause he was hurt.

See, I never saw a person in love at that time. I didn't know nothing about no love. This man was in love, and after the woman kicked him out and he had to worry about it—and he found what soothed him, what give him relief—I think he put about four or five hundred dollars, at five cents a throw—*one nickel*. Why, you take playing it for a week (*laughs*) all day and all night. "Ain't It a Cryin' Shame." So, anyway, the next three or four days people would come through, and they'd hear the door open and they'd hear the record playing. *They named the man*—now, this is no lie—they named him Ain't It a Cryin' Shame. Everybody come through there say, "That's ole Cryin' Shame." He worried that much. I never worried that much. I been slightly in love, but not that much.

This is how I got to hear the blues. They sung such songs as "*So cold up north the birds can't hardly fly.*" I hadn't been north. They say you spit on the street and it'd roll like a marble. Man, I was so scared. I'm telling you the truth. I said, "If I go there I'll freeze." You know, in a hot climate you hate to hear about all this temperature business. And everybody would talk about how cold it was. The birds'd fly and their wings would freeze up. I learned better—you hear all kinda tales. We thought money was shook off of the trees. People living so good you can shake the trees and get dollar bills. Now, who in the heck is gonna get dollar bills flying in the air? But fantasy, fantasy—no kidding! Oh, back in the twenties and thirties you believed anything, 'cause you hadn't seen it. This is how I wanted to really get here to see what was really happening. Now, I'm telling you the truth! I didn't get here till '39. In 1939 I came to Chicago. My older sister was already in Chicago back in the twenties and the thirties. I been wanting to come here for eight or ten years. Every time I'd get enough money to come to Chicago—I don't know, a young man, young boy—I'd blow the money! Several time I saved enough money to come on, but I never made it. Until all of a sudden I said, "I'm going."

So at that point I didn't have any money, not enough to come on. I left and I had to stop on my way. I live in the hills—I live in Edwards, between Vicksburg and Jackson. "Jackson the capital—Vicksburg the hilly town." So I was coming up—I believe it's the 61 highway—and, Steve, I didn't have enough money to get to Chicago. I was hitchhiking and catching the bus for a few blocks. And I got off where I saw a lot of people were working. I said, "This is the place I can make enough money to get on the Chicago." I got off there and—I worked one day! So I didn't even get my pay, to tell you the truth. And that night I stayed in some kinda flophouse. And I couldn't rest—and I didn't wait to see the bossman. The next morning I say, "I'm gonna get on my way away from here." So I went up there on the road and hit the highway. Somebody take me into Memphis—Memphis, Tennessee. And I counted up my change. And say, "Let's see. I got enough money to take the bus to Chicago. But I ain't got enough to eat on." I had people here if I could just get here. And that's all I had to worry about. So I counted up my change and I had enough money to come to Chicago—nothing to eat on. After I get here, no bus fare, no cab fare—but I wanted to get here! That kept me from hoboing all the way. I got off at the Illinois Centrals. I got off somewhere at Sixty-third, and I got off here and called my people, 'cause I was lost. And they got me and carried me to the house. But I was determined! You know what I did? The next day I went to work. I started lugging beef. It was a small place they called Guggenheim at Thirty-ninth and Iron Street. This was a meatpacking place. And I worked there and got a little start, and then I went into construction work. See, I can build—I can wreck, foundations. I had to learn it the hard way, and that made me pretty mean. I was a nice person until I had to work so hard. (*laughs*) I got mean behind that.

I had a sister. She had worked in Chicago even before I came. She had scrubbed floors and worked around for the white folks, maid and everything. She was a mixologist, serving for parties. After I got here I found out the family had paid rent for—well, they were about fifteen years ahead of me. They came here, as I say, in the teens. I talked them into the notion. I say, "You paid enough rent to own this building." You know, just like you sitting down talking, and you say, "Why you still paying rent? Why don't you buy you a home? Or buy a building?" So, anyway, my sister, I talked her into it. She say, "Well, what can we do?" I said, "I'll take my money and put it with yours and we'll buy a place." We really bought—Forty-seventh and Dearborn—a big old building. It needed a lot of repair. It was almost condemned when we bought it. See, the building was a double building. It was 2929 and 2927 West Forty-seventh Street.

The building had a standard income—you understand what I'm talking about? There was a beauty shop there and on the twenty-seven side was a store. That was a meat store and a grocery store. I was afraid to mess with the income of the building. If I did, we would have lost the building. So I started in the back. To tell you the truth, I started from a garage. Now, the garage had no income. I could get out there if I wanna. If I didn't succeed—if I didn't have no luck, my sister and I could still pay for the building. After the beauty shop moved out then I went straight through from the back to the front. But the real interest was from the back. The club was set up at 4708 South Dearborn. So by me being a younger man, I decided I could do a lot of handiwork, and so I was working every day at the building. People was saying, "Whatcha gonna do?" And just like you ask me then, I say, "I don't know." I kept working at it and I kept working.

Cadillac Baby outside AMVETS Club. Photo courtesy of Cadillac Baby.

So here was a friend of mine came along. He said, "You don't know what you're gonna do? Why don't you open an AMVET club? You don't have money to get a tavern license. Get you some members and chart it and get yourself going." That sounded pretty good. This friend of mine on the garbage truck—he was the garbage truck driver—he was taking up commercial law. Big Emmett. So he told me, he say, "I'll find you a hero." See, the only way you can chart[er] a club is to get a hero, a hero name. I thought about other AMVET posts—Colonel Boswell was at Fifty-fifth and Garfield, and the old Giles post and other posts. So he searched the book and found me a name—Corporal Henry "Buck" Rogers. That was me—they called me Corporal Henry "Buck" Rogers. He was the man that grabbed this gun on some hill in the army—in World War II. That was shortly after Pearl Harbor. He grabbed this gun and mowed down so many of the enemies. They killed him, but then he was a hero. So his name was available for me. And I registered myself as Corporal Henry "Buck" Rogers Post 193. It's on my book [the charter for his AMVET club] there now.

I went around and asked all the veterans. They said, "We'd like to join, but we don't have the money." Oh, Lord—I'm back on the same train. (*laughs*) I said, "I'll tell you what I'll do." I told each one, I say, "Will you pay me?" They say, "Yeah." I said, "I'll put the money up for you." I'm the one trying to get going;

they're not interested in nothing but another drink or whatever else. Do you know that I put the money up for—let me see, to charter—I want a national charter. To get a national charter it's either twenty-five or fifty people. You have to send the names in nationally, not state. 'Cause just a state charter I didn't have enough privilege. I wanted enough privileges to make me some money. So, okay, I paid each member's dues. I paid their fare—I paid their way. Probably four or five dollars at the time, but for coming out of one person's pocket it was quite a bit. But I figured this—it was still cheaper than $465—$465 at that time for a tavern license. And I know it would last longer, 'cause your tavern license is every six months or something. 'Cause later I had to get a tavern license. I chartered all my men up and I started up. I went over a year or so doing that. The way this AMVET went, your charter was protecting you with the city and state and everything. But you really should have certain hours to open and close—and certain people to let in. Everybody should have a membership card. You're supposed to know everybody. It's more like a family. You're supposed to know your members and know everybody. You don't carry it like a public operation. Now, what I would do, I'd feed the people. They paid for their food. If one of the members wanted a birthday party or anniversary or whatever else, I would help 'em out and whatever they needed.

But to tell you the truth, Steve, it got so big and so fast that I just opened wide open! Just like a straight nightclub or something. And then I kept getting complaints. This is where the complaints came. And, as usual, you know what the police would do. They say, "You're making too much money now. You better take out a tavern license." And I thanked 'em. I said, "Thank you very much, sir. I'm able to do it." And I let 'em know I been successful that far. I said, "I thank you." And I went on and got a straight nightclub license. I went on to operating right!

And in the town I come from everybody call me Baby Eatmon. E-a-t-m-o-n— Baby Eatmon. How it came to be a change, I been here four or five—or six years. I bought a new Cadillac, a black Cadillac. There was very few Cadillacs on the South Side, pretty ones. I like a pretty car. I ain't able to afford one now. But my car was so pretty, Steve. I worked midnight. After working midnight most people thought I wasn't working. Even the police thought I wasn't working. But I really worked. Usually I would stop around some of the hangouts where a lot of the wineheads, they were thirsty with their tongues hanging out. They need a drink. Well, I done worked. I got money, a little money. I can buy the fellas—sold wine then by the jug—I'd buy 'em a jug of wine, my friends. They appreciated it so much, Steve, I'm not kidding. They would come up to my car. I didn't know who Allah was. "Allah, Allah. You must be the man from God!" Sure, when you're drinking and having a good time you'll say anything. 'Cause didn't nobody else give 'em nothing. They say, "*Allah, Allah. You the man from God!*" They'd get napkins and handkerchiefs out of their pockets and keep my car shining while I stand there and buy 'em wine. I love to show out and help people. So what they did—they knew I was Baby—they forgot "Baby," and they say, "You are Cadillac Baby!" And, boy, that did me good! They said, "You are Cadillac Baby!" Everywhere I went, "Cadillac Baby coming! Cadillac Baby coming!" They knowed they get a gallon of wine. (*laughs*) I'd have said "Cadillac Baby," too, if I needed a drink. So, now, that's how I got the name Cadillac Baby—seriously—from the winehead, and you're nice, and you know you're not able to afford it. I think twenty of them couldn't get a pint. So I'd say, "Fellas, here's a gallon. Wipe my car off." They say, "Allah!" They got down on their knees and bowed down to the ground. They said, "Allah, Allah. You must be the man from God!" And that's how I got the name, being nice to 'em.

I started off tending bar. After I got able to hire somebody, my wife and a fella named Jimmy Robinson and my wife's sister. Oh, I had Clara, Glory—I had about eight or ten waitresses and barmaids—the place was so big. I could seat five hundred people after it got stretched out. Maybe six hundred, maybe eight hundred people after I got it all laid out. On the west side of the club, the building was a frame building—it wasn't brick. And on the west end of the building—not on the Dearborn side—on the west side I had a swinging door where a car could drive in. On that side was a stage, anyway—round just like your table. So we put the stage on tracks just like a railroad or streetcar run. So after building this stage where the stage would revolve, then I built a ramp where I could drive a car up on the stage. But you could remove your ramp. Now, this was the stage where the musicianers played. I liked convertible Cadillacs at the time, and I owned three Cadillacs, brand-new, in one year. I was in the parade business—the Bud Billiken Parade, the West Side Parade. So I bring my car through the west side door, drive it on the stage, up in the tavern, and I could drive the car off of the stage up to the bar. I had a ramp, I could drive up to the bar and there where I could sit and watch my musicianers and see what the help was doing right from the car. I could emcee from the car. I was on radio, and sometimes I would do my radio show from the car. That was a novelty—nobody had that going then. And the show was over, or maybe next day I'd take the car out and use the same car on the streets. But the car was a showroom and the tavern was so big. That's what I used it for. And that's how I made the money. I'd step out in my high hat and tails on and salute my people. And I either had my walking cane or what else. At that time you could wear spats if you wanna.

Comedian—I'm a comedian and I'd tell a few jokes. I'd tell the people I'm the Chiseler from Manchester. (*laughs*) They enjoyed that, and I had different jokes I liked to tell. (*laughs*) I had several comedians, like Clyde Lasley—and Red Bobby. He was a good comedian. He told about the room was so small that every time he wanted to turn over in his bed he had to get up and walk outside, turn over, and come back in. (*laughs*) He stayed in a room so small he had to walk outside his room and turn over and come back and lay down! I had some good jokes, man, I'm telling you! And that's what give me the idea to work with musicianers.

But I started off with little local stuff. People learning how to play, and some guys couldn't hit a lick! Little ole L. T., and Shakey Jake, and all them kinda fellas wasn't doing too much, but I fooled around with 'em till I got a regular band going. Little Mack [Simmons] was the house band, and we had guests. We'd announce we had guests for that night, they'd play. In later days everybody dropped in—B. B. King, Bobby Bland, all the big bands—from time to time after they did their regular show someplace. Little Walter and the other people would come in and join us. But Little Mack was standard after he got situated. He had bass—Little Bobby [Anderson]. I gave him a nickname: Pygmy-Head Bob. Little Mack was harmonica. Most of the time we had [Fred] Below on drums. Sometimes this fella [Robert] Whitehead would drum. Little Mack had eight or ten different drummers. Every once in a while we'd have a couple of saxes come in, but that wasn't standard. Sometimes Robert Jr. Lockwood would play guitar, Eddie Taylor—we had different guitar players. There were always four or five standard players. And sometimes we'd have as much as eight or ten different players, 'cause what would happen, we'd keep so many guests we'd have to give 'em a little chance and they'd sit in. But we'd usually keep the regular rhythm section to keep it real tight.

I had the best—I'm not lying—I had the best entertainment in Chicago at the time. The 708 Club had folded. A lot of big entertainment clubs had folded. McKie Fitzhugh, he was trying to get going. He was on Cottage Grove. See, he used to do a show in his window on King Drive, but he had a club there on Sixty-third and Cottage Grove. So he said, "Man, how can you do it?" I said, "'I'm playing the blues." He had jazz. I say, "I'm playing the blues. Listening to my records." He said, "You sure are making the money." He said, "I'm only selling a bottle of beer." I said, "I'm selling fifths of whiskey." (*laughs*) He said, "I can't live selling a bottle of beer." I said, "I know you can't—you got the wrong crowd!" Well, the jazz crowd, they like their dark glasses, and smoke they stuff, and sip on a beer, stuff like that—rock with the music and get all up in the air!

They feel like they floating in the air, you know! And a blues guy, they're heavy. He sit there with money in his pocket. He say, "Bring me and set my friends up!" (*laughs*) That's the difference between jazz and blues, you see. It took me a long time to explain that to people, but I knew it because just like I'm telling you, I had that experience from down South!

I broadcast a program each night just as the club would open. The main part of the club would open at ten or eleven—near twelve o'clock. So I had a spot on WOPA. I had a spot going—Jimmy Harrison, Val's Boulevard Lounge at Fifty-fifth. We had a ring—one club come on, the next club come on, the next club come on, all in the same night. We paid for that time. My spot was about 11:30—something like that—right at the big-time entertaining. I was on about thirty-five to forty-five minutes each night. We hardly ever had a whole hour for a live band. But the club wouldn't close until two or three o'clock. The broadcasting didn't last too long. By the time the broadcasting came on, the house was rocking and everybody was hot and everybody was jumping anyway. We didn't have to do no rehearsing. All you had to do was tune in, 'cause we're already going, you know. Lot of times the place would be kinda slow. It might be raining or storming, and folks riding around in their car hear the broadcast and be nearby, they'd come in, really, for shelter. What few people was there would be so lively [it would] sound like the house was really packed, and sometimes it wasn't. That's the gimmick of it. (*chuckles*)

Well, Steve, I'd go on the air and I'd talk about the club, and entertainers, and what I got to offer there—and drinks was cheap and whatever else. And it was just a come-on, because everybody wanna save money. That made 'em feel like they come there and they knew they'd be treated right. If they come there, they come for little or nothing, or they might come and even ask for a favor. "Could I get a little credit tonight?" They'd still get it, make me no difference. That's the way I built up business. I built the business being friendly and doing favors and folks satisfied. I open up with the band. I first do an intro with the band, and I might hold the band and do a few announcements. Then I'd give the band a motion to come back on. But I gave 'em more entertaining from the band than I did talking, 'cause most people, they don't want to hear too much talk. They really wanna hear the band. They wanna hear records. They want something to make 'em feel good. Okay, too much talk is boring. I'd give 'em just enough at one time. If you give too much talking at one time, people say, "Awww, I don't hear nothing—guy talking too much." I give a little talk and more music, and it kept a lively show. See, I had a control cut the band down, but the band steady kept moving. If I wanted to be real clear, I'd

Cadillac Baby and family outside of Cadillac Baby's Show Lounge.
Photo courtesy of Jim O'Neal.

cut the band practically all the way out. But at all times I could turn 'em back in. It wasn't no problem. I didn't get too many complaints. Once in a while somebody say, "Say, man, you talk like a Southerner, you got too much accent." I say, "I know it. I'm doing the best I can. I ain't got no degree. I'm a Southern man, no education—I'm doing well!" You understand me—they want me to talk like I'm some kinda—I wasn't cut out for that. But anyway, I got the point over. So that's how we got started broadcasting.

When I came into the Billiken, the Billiken was a big going thing. This is how this Bud Billiken Parade started. And each summer it grew and grew and grew until it got to be a national-known thing. Every year people look forward to it now. But way back it started small, more like a neighborhood thing. And as it grew, people come from all around now. So I happened to get in it after it was very well started. I had a good alderman, Alderman Ralph H. Metcalf. During his election I'd campaign for him. It's really what kept me operating, because I open in a residential neighborhood and I had a lot of knocks, so I had to get close with the alderman to keep going. I had to participate in these parades, because the public asked for it, to tell the truth. "Why don't you do this—?" "We like your program—" "Let's parade it around." And I said, "Okay." I went out here on South Chicago to rent a float, and I wound up building my own float. I wasn't able to quite pay that much for a float. It was three or four or five hundred dollars a day. I said to have a standard float I could use from now on, it'd be cheaper to build my own float. So I built me a float. It only cost four or five thousand dollars, which was better than renting a float four or five times each summer. You practically pay that much for the use of the float. So I got together and started way up in the spring, and by parade time I had built a float. That's how I got started in the Bud Billiken Parade. Herb Kent and I worked together as a unit. He'd be in front and I'd be right behind, and each year we sorta led that parade during those years, back in the fifties. I had shake dancers and I had the band playing, electrotized amps playing, 'cause my float unit generated electricty. For years after I got out of the parade people said, "It don't seem like old times. You are not in that Bud Billiken Parade!" For the first two or three years after I quit—I'm not just bragging on myself—but it look like it went down and under. This was back in the sixties, but it picked up nice again!

Steve, I didn't have any way to get my money out of the musicianers. I got so stuck with the musicians. They owed me money—for food, for clothes, for rent, for shelter, for transportation—I even bought 'em cars. They owed me so much money till I decided if I made a good record on each musicianer, I could break even or even get some of my money back. So some I lost, some I made money on. I really didn't get the idea. Some musicians gave me the idea on himself. He said, "Why don't you take us and record us, and you might get some of your money." He didn't say "definite"; he said "you might." And I had no other alternative, 'cause, okay, I'm stuck! What little money I had I had invested in the musicianers. I like 'em and I like the sound. I like what was going on. So I said, "If there's a chance for me to get some of my money, I'll go into recording." But I told 'em the truth: "I know nothing about the business and the legal end of it." After I got into it, I found out it was the big fish eating up the little, and ooh I got scared! Now there's no way for me to get my money. People who's been in it for years and know all the ins and outs and outlets and how to promote it. See, your business is in promoting. If you ain't got no outlet on promoting, there's no need of having a good record. You can't handle it. So this is what happened to me.

I think the first record I made was on a group called the Sweet Teens. I picked up a group—they were young—and I recorded them. It was a West Side group. The first blues band was L. C. McKinley, the first blues. Then Eddie Boyd, then Little Mack, and then Detroit Jr., and then Bobby Saxton and Earl Hooker— and on and on like that. Detroit, he hung around and was so depressed for money and wanted to make a record. I said, "Detroit, I can't spend no money on you." He said, "Aw, you can do it!" I said, "Yeah, I guess I will." His name was Williams—it wasn't Detroit. I listened to him talk all the time. "When I was in Detroit I was a big shot!" I knowed that was a lie and on and on. So we get the band together with Detroit on the vocals and piano; he could play some piano. He's good on piano now. I take him in and I say, "I can't give you but one side!" Now, that's cutting the man down so low. I hate to do 'em like that, but the studio time and tape and the union was down on me. I had to pay them something. He did this record in the studio.

I liked the record myself, so—I always figure the name of the artist along with the record can make a better sale. Something catchy! But he didn't know this. I didn't talk this over with him. Instead of asking his consent, could I give him a new name, I put his name on the record [as] "Detroit Jr.," because he had bragged about Detroit, see. I released his record, and about a week or two later he was at the club and I showed him the record. He played it on the jukebox. He knew that was his record and he knew that was his voice, but he didn't know who this Detroit Jr. was! He said, "What you done done—give my record to someone else?" Little Mack was there and a lot of the other musicians. Didn't nobody say nothing. That man got so mad. He said, "I'm ready to fight! You done did me wrong!" I didn't tell him—wouldn't nobody else tell 'im. He walked around there huffed up half the night, ready to kill somebody. Finally I told somebody, "Go get that fool and let's explain things to him!" He was too mad at first—you couldn't explain nothing. So I just let him cool off a little bit. I said, "This is your record, and I'll tell you why. Didn't you say you was from Detroit? I just decided that would be a better gimmick to say you are Detroit Jr. I put your name on here—your name ain't saying nothing!" We finally got him to understand, and even today, man, he's so proud of that. I should make him pay me for giving him such a great name! (*laughs*)

The way I wrote "The Big Boat," Steve, Eddie Boyd needed transportation. He had nobody else to take him We were going to Joliet or someplace out of town. We left that evening about four or five o'clock. And just as we get to the outskirt of town and there was a skat of woods. The sun was sinking down through the trees. It was a beautiful scenery. I'm just driving along. I'm think-ing. I look through those trees and it look like a body of clear water looking through to the other side through those trees. Now, suppose there was a big boat on this body of water—an excursion boat or something—and it's leaving. So I said, "Eddie, that's a beautiful scenery. I imagine there's a boat on the other side. We can't see this boat, but suppose you was in love and your woman was over there getting ready to catch this boat. We got a distance of three or four miles to get there and this boat's getting ready to leave. Your woman's getting ready to run off and leave you—and we can't catch her. At this moment she's ready to step on board." So that's why I named it "The Big Boat"—" . . . *is at the landing and my baby's getting ready to step on board.*" Then we went on and put the rest of the words with it, Eddie and I. We both sort of visioned it at the same time. "*The big boat is at the landing and my baby's waiting to step on board. Oh, people, what's the reason, what's the reason—I just don't know.*"

Richard **Stamz**

"Open the Door" Richard Stamz was one of Chicago's most popular black radio hosts in the years from 1951 to 1961, billing himself as the "Crown Prince of Soul." However, as a white kid who grew up in the suburbs listening to Top 40 rock 'n' roll radio, I had no idea who Richard Stamz was. It was the production manager at our radio station, Claude Cunningham, who suggested that Richard might be an interesting person to interview, and that he knew how to get in touch with Richard if I was interested. Claude grew up

Richard Stamz, "The Crown Prince of Soul," with Al Benson. Photo courtesy of Robert Pruter.

in the Englewood District on Chicago's South Side, where Richard Stamz—twenty years retired from radio—was still very much a celebrity. I thought it was a great idea, so Claude went ahead and made the arrangements. Richard came down to our station, WBEZ, one weekday afternoon.

The first thing we did was to record Richard hosting his own radio program, attempting to re-create his program as it was heard during the 1950s. We then sat down and did the one-on-one interview. I asked only two questions—"Tell me your story" and "Tell me about payola"—both of which were edited out for the sake of continuity. When it was broadcast we opened with Richard doing his program, and then as the first record started to play we faded into his reminiscence, with Richard speaking of his career in radio. The focus of this interview is strictly on Richard's career in broadcasting.

In recent years a handful of researchers, including Robert Pruter and Patrick Roberts, have uncovered a more complete Richard Stamz biography revealing the amazing stories of his early years. These stories remain unpublished.

When I interviewed Richard Stamz in 1982 he was seventy-five years old. Between the time I received Richard's permission to publish this interview and the manuscript actually went to press, Richard passed away. He died on June 14, 2007, at the age of 101.

■ ■ ■

I started out working sound trucks, that's how the whole thing started. You know what a sound truck is? A vehicle that you use, you put signs on it and you use it to sell people's merchandise and whatnot and go up and down the street. Half the time you're ducking the police, 'cause they wanna either shake you down or shut you up, one of the two things. But I was pretty successful with my sound truck business.

It was in '51 I was working my sound truck, and the people who own radio station WGES, it was a five-thousand-watt station, located at 2800 West Washington Boulevard—that's where we broadcasted from. It was in nineteen and fifty-one when the radio station actually sent for me and asked me if I'd like to work. I told them no, I wasn't interested in working in radio, 'cause I told them there wasn't enough money in it. I was making a pretty good buck with my sound trucks. And they sent for me the second time and I still told them the same thing. So the third time they called me, a lady by the name of Mrs. Heinzman, she said, "Let's talk about the finance." So I said, "Okay, we'll talk about the finance. You've called me three times and you tell me I can make more money than I'm making on the sound trucks. I want you to prove it to me." She said, "Okay, this is the way we'll do it." She wanted to start me out on one hour. She says, "Each hour grosses"—it was 1951—"grosses fifteen hundred dollars, and you'll get thirty-three percent of that." That's five hundred dollars—that's a nice buck, you know. So (*laughs*) since I was doing a good buck on my sound truck, I said I'll combine the two and make a nice buck!

So I went to work for WGES. Mrs. Heinzman had told me, "Richard, talk to Herb Rudoff." "We gonna put you on," Herb Rudoff said. He was interviewing me, you know. "How many words can you say per minute and ra-ra-ra—" It was just a bunch of baloney—it didn't mean nothing. He said, "Well, I'll tell you, have you picked your name for the air yet?" All black dudes had a name for the air—Jam with Sam. Al Benson's name wasn't Al Benson. You know what his name was? Arthur Leaner—L-e-a-n-e-r. Arthur Leaner. That was his name. But, see, Rock with Rick, Jam with Sam, all that—the Real McCoy—everybody had a name! They did that to black disc jockeys, I don't know why. Down South they had Hot Papa, and Dizzy Baloney, and all that kinda stuff. They still do it down there. I'll tell you what I think it stemmed from—I think it stemmed from a white guy, when he wanted to get some black listeners, he'd go down to the shoeshine boy that shined his shoes and say, "Say, boy, you wanna go on the air?" And he take 'im and put 'im on the air! Down South that's the way that happened! And he'd say, "I got a name." But they owned the name, see. Rockin' Doc and all that, the station *owned those names!* And all they did, they go find a guy and put him on there and he had to fit the name! But we didn't—we picked our own.

So Herb said, "Man, lookee here. You coming in fast and everything—I'm gonna suggest something to you." He said, "Call yourself 'Open the Door Richard,' and I'll come up with a theme for you." We wasn't using [the song] "Open the Door" then; we didn't use Dusty Fletcher. Tell you what we did—we went into a room and took "Midnight in the Barrelhouse." At WGES we had all those sound effects—telephone bells and all that—so he did some door-opening tricks [*makes a creaking sound*], and then he come on with the music and it says, "And now we bring you Open the Door Richard!" Well, after wasn't no more than a month of that, I said, "Lookee here, man, I don't like this." "Well, what do you wanna do?" So I picked my theme song and that's what it was.

And I'll tell you what happened. Savoy heard about it. They [had] stopped selling this record in 1949—they were getting orders for this record *all over again!* So the first thing he did, he sent me about five hundred "Open the Door, Richard" records, and I took 'em to the record shops and sold 'em. And he kept doing that as long as I was on the air! He kept sending me those records, and people kept buying 'em. Even though the record had been dead—I revived it!

At that time there were three prime movers on the station—that was Al Benson; Sam Evans, which was on at night, called Jam with Sam; and Ric Riccardo, who came on at one o'clock. Now, I gotta say it like this—Ric wasn't doing too good. Somehow the radio station owners thought that I would heat the seat up for Ric. So they put me on. The first show I had on WGES was twelve to one. And I took it and I worked it, and I worked it hard. Within a year and a half's time it was hot—hotter than cayenne pepper—*and* I was heating up the seat for Ric. Ric came on behind me and Ric had three hours. This went on real good—I mean *real good.* I really began to make a buck. Fact is, I sold out the hour. Don't forget that I said the hour grossed for fifteen hundred dollars. The station would take a thousand and I would take five hundred.

Then—we'd had problems on the morning show from six to seven. They tried four or five fellows on there and they couldn't sell. And so Mrs. Heinzman asked me if I would take six to seven. So I took the six-to-seven hour and inside of three months I had *it* hot. I didn't quite sell it out at fifteen hundred, but I averaged a thousand to eleven hundred, and one-third of that was around four hundred dollars. Now, the noon show is netting me five hundred, so I'm hitting nine hundred dollars a week. I say, "Geeze, this *is* a good buck!" and I'm still working my sound trucks. I'm getting a little greedy now! (*laughs*) Well, that rocked along for a while, and then Mrs. Heinzman said, "Richard, you're doing pretty good. Can you think of anything else you'd like to do?" So I said, "Yeah, I'd like to try another half hour," which was unheard of at WGES. They never opened up the station at that time; they opened it up at five thirty and rolled along till seven o'clock. I sold that whole half an hour to one automobile dealer, and he was doing so good, he just loved it and he wanted some *more* time! Then I had a number one sponsor came in with me. This came out of the Urban League. I had a good friend over to the Urban League, and he called me and said he had some calls from Mr. Joyce, who owned 7Up, and said he like to have a live person for ratings—so he called me! So I went out and talked to Mr. Joyce. And Mr. Joyce said that in that year he agreed to spend seventy-five hundred dollars with me, advertising-wise, on the station. Okay, that was good. At the end of the year he called me and said he was doing good but he'd like to heat it up some.

So I started to doing promotions on the street. I set up a crew. One fellow that's in the record business today, Leroy Phillips, at that time he was in Wendell Phillips High School. He was in his second year and I started him in to work with me spinning records. I had two girls who would demonstrate 7Up—on Friday and Saturday only! After about a month of doing this I began selling sixty and seventy cases of 7Up *on the spot.* Well, that interested the 7Up people.

After a year of that they called me in and we reevaluated the whole show results and that settlement, and they almost knocked me off my feet. They said, "We are ready to double the amount of money we are spending with you, or even do better!" Gee, whiz, that scared me, now. Fact is, I'm beginning to make *too* much money now! Here I got an hour and a half in the morning that is netting me $1000 a week—I got the noontime show that's netting $500. Now Mr. Joyce wants to pay me $250 a week for two days, Fridays and Saturdays alone. It was a fantastic era, really fantastic!

We was the largest black radio station in the United States, and we were the first black radio station to acquire national advertisers. The first one that came on was Coca-Cola, then Pepsi-Cola, then all the flours. Then all the breads began to come on, then the beers began to come on, then the automobiles began to come on. This thing mushroomed and that was primarily [due] to Al Benson's efforts. To tell the truth, I saw Al Benson earn one million dollars as a disc jockey in three years working on three stations. Even today with the fabulous salaries they're supposed to pay disc jockeys, they came nowhere near what we made on those brokerage and percentage deals. See, there are no opportunities like that today, in radio. And on top of it, I think the key to the whole thing was the fact that we played music that black folks at that time were hungry to hear. We played the blues! At that time we were beginning to get some black competition. We had one little station down south, one on the West Side. But none of those stations— I mean the jockeys had the freedom to work like we did, and play the type of music we did. We picked our music and we were the whole radio station for the time we were on the air. Nobody told us what we couldn't play; nobody told us how to program the show; nobody even told us how to set up a log. We set up our own logs! Fact is, we didn't even have any log.

Almost everything we did was from memory, merchandising-wise. That was all from memory. I can sit right here now and give you—which I haven't done in eighteen, nineteen years—give you an automobile commercial. You see, I have absolutely nothing in front of me. First I gotta find me a name. Okay, I'll call it Starwars Automobile Company. "Okay! Listen here, friends, I gotta tell you this. Starwars Automobile Company right today has the most fabulous deals that you have ever heard! These are not *used* cars, as you'd call it a used car—these are *pre-owned* cars! Hey, look at those tires! Look like brand-new— whitewalls! Beautiful steering wheel! Alligator cover on it. Ha! Boy, you'd look awfully good in that ride! Picking up little girls down on the corner of King Drive! Better come and get it. And on top of it, you can get this—if you have *any* credit, absolutely *any* credit at all! We'll give you this car—*oh, no,* not for ten hundred down, not for five hundred down, not for a *hundred* down! We'll give you this car for the low, low price—now, you listen to me—for the low, low price, if you have any credit, for—ten—dollars—down! So come on out to 551 West on every boulevard today and pick up this beautiful 1979 Buick automobile from Starwars! See you later. Let's get back to music!" We had no script, you know. (*laughs*)

I had a thing called Orange Tonic, a screwdriver in a bottle—it's not even on the market anymore. And I used to go around taverns at night—it came in a six-pack, a little seven-ounce bottle—and I'd say, "Hey, lookee here. I know you're tired—you been dancing all night, discoing, you and your boyfriend. In order to ensure that you enjoy the evening, take home a six-pack of Orange Tonic, screwdriver in a bottle." You know, it was connotations—all the time it was connotations!

Beers, the same thing. Wines, we had all kinda wines. I guess all four of us, each one had two wines. You couldn't have more that one beer, 'cause the advertiser would object if you put another beer in a time slot. But that was an advantageous thing at that time, money-wise, and I'll tell you why. Okay, you're on two hours, and you can only carry one beer. This guy *got* to spend a *lot of* money, you understand? To keep the other beers off he's got to spend money. You're not gonna let him come on and buy one minute or two minutes! We sold slots—we sold fifteen-minute slots, see, and for every hour we try and sell an outfit like a beer, we'd sell 'em a fifteen-minute slot, a minimum of ten minutes, see. We wouldn't *take* 'em if it was less than that, 'cause we didn't *have* to. There was always another beer standing in line. Like automobile dealers—if we fired an automobile dealer, there was another one ready to come on, and sometimes, I believe, we'd get a little arrogant about that. But we were professionals in the business and we knew how to make a "come-on" with the advertisers. Sometimes we'd deal with the advertising agencies—they'd deal direct with us. Now, we had a real good beer and the beer was popular, and we would ask for a talent fee, see. You guys can't do that today. Jocks on the air at commercial stations, they can't do that today; they can't ask for a talent fee. They can ask for it, but we *demanded it!*

I'm gonna tell you what I saw Benson do—this is the most fabulous thing in the world. Benson had one beer company that was gonna cancel out. So Benson called the beer company directly; he wouldn't even call the agency. He told the beer company, "I understand you give me a cancellation notice?" The beer company said, "Yes, Al, you're not getting the results in certain areas." It might be on the West Side; it might be on the South Side. Benson says, "So where is this place you're not selling none of this beer? I'll tell you what I'll do. I'll give you a deal. If you'll take out a new yearlong contract, I'll sell *five thousand* cases in one week!" *And he did it!* He did it. He got on the phone at the radio station and he'd call taverns, over the phone, and liquor stores—right on the air! And he'd say, "Lookee here, so-and-so. You running such-and-such liquor store located at so-and-so corner?" And the guy would say, "Yeah, I'm the owner." And Benson would say, "Will you take five hundred cases of beer, of so-and-so's beer?" And the guy would say, "Why I wanna take that beer?" Benson would say, "Haven't I got you on the air? You're getting free advertisement now, and I'm gonna give you some *more!*" And the guy would say, "Send me the beer!" (*laughs*) That's right! That's the way we did it! I was calling all my own shots.

I'm gonna tell you exactly how far I was calling my own shots. I had an account by the name of Meister Brau beer—they just went out of business. I kept Meister Brau for five years. On the South Side annually the *Defender,* which is a black newspaper, would have a show called the Defender Home Show. And we would all work that show. Okay, Meister Brau had a big booth over there and they had Fahey Flynn over there. Jesse Owens was working for Meister Brau at that time, too. They had this big booth, and photographers came out for the beer company and they wanted to make pictures of Jesse Owens, myself, and Fahey Flynn. So I let 'em make the pictures, and the next morning I called up the beer company. I called the advertising manager and the marketing manager—I called 'em all. I had a conference call going and told them I wanted to come over and talk to them about the pictures they wanted to use and they wanted to use in the *Chicago Defender.*

Okay, so I went over to the Meister Brau company, which was on North Avenue, and I asked 'em why is it that every week they had some big pictures, full pages there—they put all the white celebrities in there, but they'd never put a black one in the *Tribune.* I asked 'em, "Why is it you don't put Jesse Owens and myself in the *Tribune?*" "Naw, we wanna keep you all in the *Defender,* 'cause that's where you are on the South Side—blah-blah-blah-blah-blah." So I said, "How come you're putting Fahey Flynn down there? He's a North Sider." You ask Fahey about this, he'll tell you about this today! And they said, "No, you can't tell us how to run our business." I said, "If I can't tell you how to run your business, you can't tell me how to run mine. Now, I'm giving you a thirty-day notice, as of the first day of the month. You are off of Open the Door Richard's radio show!" And I got up and walked out.

The next day everybody that was at that meeting was at the station and talked to the owners—Mrs. Heinzman—and say, "We're off the air!" And Mrs. Heizman said, "Let's call him upstairs." I was on the air—they knew that. They came over at one o'clock as I was coming off the air. So I came upstairs and we went through this *whole* thing again! And they said, "Mrs. Heinzman, can he fire us off the air?" Mrs. Heinzman said, "Sure, if he says you're fired, you're fired." The phone rang in Mrs. Heinzman's office. Mrs. Heinzman says, "It's for you, Richard." I picked up the phone. It was Champale from New York saying, "Yes, we'll take the same amount of time Meister Brau had at the same time on the air." That's right! The guys from Meister Brau say, "Now, he sold our time!" She says, "It's not your time anymore! Didn't he give you a thirty-day notice, which was in your contract?" "Yep!" "Well, that's it." I fired them guys, man! And Champale came on and stayed with me until I went off the air. That's the power, that's the clout we had! We sold 'em, and we fired 'em if they didn't do right! (*laughs*)

We had some automobile dealers that didn't do right—we *had* to get rid of 'em! They'd rip the people off, you know. Hey, we were the people that put 'em in that bag! You know, I worked in the stockyards when I was a youngster. Do you know what the black sheep did in the stockyards? He led all the white sheeps to the slaughter. They had a black sheep with a bell around his neck, and he'd lead the sheeps up this ramp. See, nobody hit him, but after he passes by there's two guys standing there with sledge hammers and they hit the sheep in the head. And the treadmill took the dad-blamed sheeps down to the skinning pen. But the black sheep, next day he came around and did the same identical thing. Actually we were black sheep leading people to the slaughter! (*laughs*) So—the results—when people got misused—and we *gotta* say this, misused—everybody that buys a used car is abused—but you don't wanna *misuse* 'em, see! (*laughs*)

So they would call us up. Man, I came up with a thousand gimmicks for these automobile dealers, but this one ripped off three people. One of these dealers, I know you remember, got shot up. That's right! A guy that bought a Cadillac from 'em and they wouldn't fix it, he went in with a shotgun and killed *two*—and was gonna shoot up the whole joint, but somebody caught him and knocked the shotgun outta his hands. But he actually killed two of the car dealers! Those people closed up that place and moved out of town. They didn't want no part of black people with shotguns! *Therefore,* we had to be careful ourselves if we led the sheep to the slaughter and the car dealer didn't treat 'em right! We were the ones on the spot, not the car dealers. So-and-so would call up and say, "Richard, you told me to use your name and he gave me credit, and then after I had the car a week he came and took it back!" (*laughs*) "He had a garnishee on me and all that business," you know, and that's the way it went. And we'd feel guilty sometimes. And sometimes we'd get em off.

I'll tell you something else we had to fire two or three times—in fact, we fired so many of these people, we fired enough of 'em that we wouldn't take 'em no more—that was gypsies. Fortune tellers! And this boy on the old WOPA station, he would take 'em all. He got 'em all! We had a mob of 'em up until the time we decided we weren't gonna take those turkeys no more! You know, *ripping people off!* (*laughs*) And on top of it, besides taking their money for nothing, they'd go in your house and steal from you! We were the bearers of all kinda problems, man! (*laughs*) We made a little money, but, my goodness, we got a lot of people in trouble! You had to be careful.

In nineteen and fifty-five I picked up this account. It was a chain of stores—they're out of business now. You might remember them, they were Martin Clothing Stores. Now, he wanted me only a few minutes on radio, but he wanted me a lots—like five hours a week—on the sound truck. Well, I did that for 'em and, boy, I charged him a big buck, 'cause he had some beautiful big stores. After I had worked with him about two months, he called me and says, "Here's what I wanna do. I wanna put you on television." Well, the top of my head was shaking—"Television, I don't wanna go on no television!"—'cause I had the same idea about television as I had about radio, 'cause both approaches were the same. He says, "No, I want you to go on television and sell these clothes." Okay, so we decided what kind of show we're gonna have and how we're gonna set it up. He had an agency, which is still in existence over on Chicago Avenue—still the same location, I think. But we set up this show—part interview, part talent show—*we're gonna do it all.*

The first show we had—I'll never forget this—we had Edith Sampson. She was the first black appointed to the U.N., and she came home on her first visit. And I scooped all the newspapers. Well, the newspapers didn't know her anyway, and I had her on my Saturday night TV show. It was called *Richard's Open Door.* Now, the show on radio was called *Open the Door Richard,* and they changed the TV show to *Richard's Open Door.* We were on channel seven for thirteen weeks. We'd have interview for five minutes and the rest was a variety show, and we featured live artists. We used to broadcast from over there on State Street—right where they are now, State and Lake—and we broadcast for thirteen weeks. They had the fellow who managed the station, he didn't like me from the first time I went on. I don't wanna call his name—he's dead now. He didn't like me. He said that I was too forward and I was too fast! Well, being the first black on that type of a thing and writing my own shows, he *didn't* like it! See, everybody else at the station was a station employee, except the advertising guy that was with me and the fellow that helped me write the shows and set 'em up and manage 'em. Everybody else was just like a regular television show today, same thing. But he just couldn't feel me—I don't know, I guess I was a little arrogant, 'cause I had all this going and nobody ever heard of a black dude with this kind of money, with this kinda clout, calling all his own shots!

Cushing, I'm glad you asked me this, because I don't believe that there has ever been the truth told about this payola business—there's never been the truth! I can say all I want about payola, because I was the very first victim of payola. You see, payola not only was given to disc jockeys; payola was given to program directors, was given to station owners—even some of the record promoters put payola in their pocket. So it was a big thing. See, payola was not the dangerous thing. The dangerous thing was where did the money come from to finance the payola? Now, that's the gimmick, and that's what confused the government to such an extent that they could only hit disc jockeys! They never punished a record company—never punished a record company.

You talk about Chess and his payola. Chess had many unique methods of payola—he didn't have just one, giving cash. Chess gave automobiles. I know a couple of guys who got houses. That's right, he gave him a house! A home! *Do you hear what I'm saying to you? A home!* Chess, man, Leonard Chess was the worst in the record business. Now, there were others that were bad, but he was worst! There was one disc jockey that had a yacht given to him. I don't wanna name him, because he might sue me. I still got about four or five bucks hidden up under the bushes and he might find 'em. But this turkey got a yacht—and named the yacht after the company that gave him the yacht. He named it the Mercury! That was the name of the yacht, the Mercury! So you go to talking about payola—I know one turkey in town here, he's still on the air, and he was charging a hundred dollars a record! He later got to the point where he was charging five hundred dollars a record.

Oh, I'll tell you another form of payola it was hard for them to catch. Sam Evans, Al Benson, and I made regular trips to New York to sell Madison Avenue. Now, nobody else ever did this. We did this on a regular basis, and here's how we did it. You learn fast, you know. A record company would call up and say, "You boys coming to Madison Avenue to sell?" "Yeah." "When you think you'll be up here?" "Well, we'd like to come next Thursday and stay over the weekend." "Okay, we'll have your airplane tickets at the station at such-and-such a time, and you'll stay at the Waldorf-Astoria." See? We didn't do no cheap ones, baby, no cheap ones! Here we'd have a car waiting for us when we got there to take us to the hotel. You get in the hotel and— *(laughs)* Lord have mercy, this thing got ridiculous!

I never will forget we had a big promoter, we had a guy, we're trying to get a guy to give us some accounts out of Batten, Barton, Durstine & Osborn, and this guy came over and brought his little girlfriend. He says, "Gee, whiz, I'm hungry!" So we went ahead and got something to eat. I don't know what kinda salary he was on, but it couldn't have been that large—he didn't have on any three-piece suits, handmade suits, regardless of working for this big-name, international-name advertising company. So I said, "Okay." I picked up the phone and ordered wines and lobsters and whatnot, you know. And when all that stuff came up, it just knocked this cat on out, man! He had never in his life been the guest of anybody that just gave him carte blanche on ordering whatever he wanted for his company and everything. So as a result, we kinda partied—well, it was more like a conference, really, than a party. But what we wanted to do was get some business out of BBD&O. Norm Spaulding was with me that night (*laughs*), and that meal that night ran about $175! See, when we left we didn't even sign our tab—that tab would go to the record company. Whatever! That was a form of payola that the government couldn't keep up with, because it was marked off as promotion. Eighty percent of payola was marked off as promotion.

Now, I know that one time, Leonard Chess—I'll tell you about this, too—you shouldn't *never* have brought up his name. I could talk about him for a year! When I had my sound trucks and Howlin' Wolf and Muddy Waters was first started to making records, I used to go by Leonard Chess and pick up records to play in my sound trucks.He was using payola then! And I'm just working sound trucks—that was before I was on the radio—he didn't have any idea I was going on the radio, and I didn't either! I wasn't even thinking about it, you know. But, man, Leonard Chess was one hundred percent crook! All the rest of 'em were just as bad—Capitol, Mercury, Columbia—you name 'em. In fact, Columbia was the only company that ever got cited about payola. That's why Clive Davis lost his job, you know. He was the president of Columbia and they fired him because of payola. And, boy, he was spending it! But at that stage of the game payola had left money and had gone into narcotics. That's what they were using for payola when Clive Davis got fired. Now, I don't say that he's responsible for it—his promotion men were the ones that did this maneuvering, see.

I played Joe Brown's records just because Joe Brown [owner and operator of the J.O.B. Record label] made good records. He made *real good* records, and I wouldn't have charged Joe Brown two bucks. Joe Brown didn't have a quarter! Now, I'm gonna tell you what Joe Brown used to do. Joe Brown would come up to the station, and he'd reach up under his coat and pull out a half pint of alcohol (*laughs*)—that was the extent of Joe Brown's payola! I wouldn't let Joe Brown give me any whiskey, man! Fact is, I didn't charge no local people. Now, some of the guys did. I know they'd make 'em go out there and scrape up a hundred dollars, fifty dollars, a hundred and fifty dollars, whatever they could get. And they'd play the record ten or twelve days.

One thing about it—if a jock on WGES played their record twelve days, the guys who made the record were gonna make their money back! Because, heck, you didn't put but four, five, or six hundred dollars into a record. It's not like today, where you put ten to thirty thousand into an LP—you didn't have to do that. That's a game I'd like to talk about. Anytime a local distributor would order two new records, and he'd come to us and say, "Hey, man, I got ten thousand "Make Love to Me on the Floor." He'd give you records to get on a record and sell out the remainder of what he had left after a record got cold. We used to do it. You could pop a record like that. Play it three or four times and talk about it. See, we could do what we wanna do—it wasn't like it is today! It wasn't nothing but payola. Any way you take it, it's payola!

See, you gotta look at it like that. It was payola. It was as dirty as dirty could be! (*laughs*) Bribery was dirty then. Bribery is dirty now! There ain't no difference in it—that's all it is! Payola was just a form of bribery, that's all! A lot of people get out on the street and clean it up and say, "Hey, man, a guy works, he's supposed to get paid." But that was illegal, man, you were getting paid otherwise! Now, you got enough about payola, or you want me to do some more?

After they sold WGES I pure quit, and then they brought in all these modernized disc jockeys. That was 1963. All right! Benson, myself, and Ric [Riccardo], we had a conference with this guy that bought the station out of Texas. He was a white guy, and I have to put it like this, 'cause he was the guy who had beat the American League. He had been illegally broadcasting the American League's games—you know, rebroadcasting 'em. I can't think of his name right now—it'll come to me. Anyway, they sued him for three million dollars. *He countersued them* for three million dollars for invasion and he *won* the suit. Well, he took that money and bought WGES.

He called us all in and told us he was gonna make some changes. He was gonna modernize the station. But that wasn't the point. We told him that we brokered our own shows. 'Course he was aware of all that, but he wasn't gonna give us any money like we made when we brokered our own shows. Hey, man, we're making *big money—big, big money!* And *he* was gonna pay those jocks $175 or $180 a week. We couldn't even hear that, so we tried to make a deal with him. Here's what we told him: "Look, we will sell for you and control all those sales, and you will keep all these accounts on the air." "Oh, no!" And can I use the lowest connotation, it ain't so low today? He said, "Lookee here, I ain't gonna let no niggers tell me nothing!" So Benson, Riccardo, and I walked out!

At that time we had a million and a half dollars on 'GES—black jocks! We took it all and farmed it out everywhere for five cents. Now, remember we're making over thirty percent. We farmed it out for a nickel on the dollar, whatever we could get! We put some on WAAF, some on WMPP, put some on WBEE—we put it everywhere! And as a result they never—WYNR—never, never got over a hundred thousand dollars a year. They went broke! Remember, they went broke? They even let all the jockeys go and tried talk. They were the first ones to try all-talk. Then they tried the good-music station, then they tried the all-news station. They tried everything, but they still went broke!

Hosting *Blues Before Sunrise*

When *Blues Before Sunrise* first hit the air in June 1980, I didn't know what to expect. The program covered several music genres from 1900 to about 1965. Some of it was pretty creaky stuff, way off the path of mainstream tastes. To my surprise, reaction to the program was positive. After a few months on the air I began to hear more and more and *more* from the listeners. Jazz fans liked it. College kids liked it. But most surprising to me, the program was enthusiastically embraced by a large listening audience of African American seniors, from fifty to ninety-five years of age. These were the people who grew up with the music I was presenting, and it had been twenty years since any radio station in Chicago had broadcast this music.

The buzz I received from audience feedback was all positive. Of course, this can be misleading. People who don't like you generally don't stick around to tell you so—they turn the dial to another station or turn the radio off altogether—so you tend not to get negative feedback. But there were other ways to gauge the program's popularity. As a public radio station we held regular fund-raisers during which the program hosts would beg the listeners for donations. An accepted rule of thumb in estimating the number of listeners in late-night radio audiences is that you have 10 percent of the daytime audience. Yet we were raising money at the rate of one thousand dollars an hour, which was rare even during many daytime slots. Also, the only time I'm aware that the station ever used Arbitron ratings for the overnight, *Blues Before Sunrise* was the second most-listened-to program in its time slot—second only to Chicago radio behemoth WGN. So in addition to the firsthand buzz I was receiving from listeners, we confirmed the acceptance of the program through more professional standards.

There were several things that made *Blues Before Sunrise* different from the average blues radio program. First, I had a large block of time—five hours—so I could stretch out and play heaping helpings from each genre. Second, I presented a large, uncompromising dose—most weeks about ninety minutes' worth of prewar recordings, including classic blues singers. And I presented them as valid entertainment, not feeling as though I had to make excuses for old, scratchy recordings or beg the audience's indulgence. And, third, I presented and mixed several different genres of music in each program—most notably, the jazz-influenced side of blues played alongside the sounds of down-home blues. This is unusual because the jazz-influenced side of blues and the down-home blues are two separate and distinct camps. Oddly enough, the fans of the jazz-influenced blues would readily listen to down-home blues with no complaint. But down-home fans were extremely intolerant of the jazz-influenced sounds.

Interaction with the audience grew steadily over the months. One thing I received from black listeners were requests for certain tunes or artists. I *never* took requests—the programs were carefully planned in advance, so I knew what I wanted to play. This prevented well-lubricated listeners from requesting the same records week after week—*and* my records were at home, so it was unlikely I would have the specific requested record. But a strange thing happened: I got requests for artists I *didn't know!* And so began my education.

It's hard for me to imagine today, but when I started the program back in 1980 I didn't know anything about Buddy and Ella Johnson, the King Cole Trio, JoJo Adams, Joe Carroll, or Dusty Fletcher and dozens of other artists who today are heard regularly on *Blues Before Sunrise*. It took the old-timers, the black seniors who grew up with this music, to pull my coat about so many artists. Many was the time I'd get a phone call: "Hey, I know you don't take requests, but do you have any records by so-and-so? We used to listen to him or her all the time when we were teenagers. It'd be great to hear something by them again!" My reply would be: "Wow, that's a new one on me. What was that name again? Let me see what I can find in the next week or two." And I'd be on the hunt, asking Bob Koester over at Jazz Record Mart or other fellow blues enthusiasts if they knew the artist and what records did he or she have. Veteran listeners introduced me to many wonderful artists down through the years. Not only did they introduce me to new artists, but they would also check in with scads of personal information about the artists that wasn't in any history book—personal information obtained firsthand: where artists performed, where they lived, who they were married to. Even today my LPs and CDs are filled with handwritten notes, nuggets of information. I remember many years ago playing a record by an obscure prewar pianist, Piano Kid Edwards. As the record was playing, a listener called to tell me that Piano Kid Edwards had retired from music, become a medical doctor, and had moved to Minneapolis. This was long before these facts showed up in any liner notes. And this education wasn't limited strictly to musicians' bios. Listeners would explain terms of slang or cultural references heard on the records. One memorable example was from a record by Slim and Slam, "A Tip on the Numbers." In the lyrics a man placed a bet for a "gas meter." Listeners explained that the term "gas meter" meant twenty-five cents—so named because in that day and age people would rent a single room that was equipped with a coin-operated gas burner to cook or heat their meals. It operated on quarters; therefore, twenty-five cents became a "gas meter." In another cryptic cultural reference, Ma Rainey sang: "*He ain't good-lookin.' He ain't got Poroed hair.*" Listeners explained this was a reference to the Poro School of Beauty, Chicago's leading black beauty school. In other words, his hair was not processed. So each week I brought back the music of their past and they, in turn, set about educating me in regard to the musicians and their work and about African American culture in general. And this informal education was a continuing process. As long as I was on the air live—sixteen years in all—as long as I was in the studio doing the program, taking phone calls, listeners continued to call with valuable biographical and cultural information. It was an amazing, invaluable experience—a true education. I refer to it today as attending the University of Bronzeville (referring to the black section of Chicago that for many years was known as "Bronzeville.")

Since we were on Saturday overnights, I heard from a lot of musicians who were on the way home from gigs. I also heard from veteran bluesmen, including Blind John, Billy Boy Arnold, and Floyd McDaniel. There was a cast of regulars, people who would call each week. Some called early, some called late, but they all checked in to say hi and let me know they were listening.

Steve Cushing at WBEZ studios, 1980s. Photo by Bruce Powell.

To list them all here would be meaningless to everyone but me. However, a handful of callers are worth mentioning. Dave Thomas is a cab driver from the South Side whose uncle, Alfred Elkins, played bass on literally hundreds of blues records. Dave made arrangements for me to meet and interview his uncle. Thomas Palmer was a regular listener who for years sent me tapes of collectible records to play on the show. He did this under the pseudonym of the "Unknown Record Collector." It must have been eight or ten years before he told me his real name. Harrel Jones was a Chicago policeman who retired and moved to Louisiana, where he continues to listen to the show. Another regular was Walter Anderson, who called himself the "Black Leprechun." Dale Dickson is a middle-aged white guy, a fellow record collector, and good company. His calls were always welcome. Perhaps the most memorable listener was Robert Little. Robert was a senior citizen and blind. When he learned that I stayed awake on the overnights by drinking Coca-Cola, he had his brother deliver a case of Coke to me at the studio each month. He also made arrangements for me to interview the pastor of his local church, the Rev. F. W. McGee Jr., whose father recorded a series of sermons for the Victor label during the 1920s. And then there was Claire Foster.

For seventeen years I was paid a fair salary at public radio and spent it all on records. While others my age were buying houses and raising families, I was intent on building a record collection: LPs, CDs, foreign imports, you name it. But I made a conscious decision *not* to buy 78s. Even the cheapest 78s cost as much as a CD, and you only got two songs! And I stood by my guns—until I ran across Claire Foster. Claire lived at Forty-sixth and Evans. She was blind and in her eighties. Like many senior citizens, she didn't sleep at night, and my program provided good company and brought back many memories. I didn't hear from Claire directly. I heard from Chicago blues pianist Jimmy Walker, who was her neighbor. Jimmy called to let me know that his friend Claire had some records she wanted me to have. I generally declined record offers from listeners. They were usually sides I already had—and usually beat to hell—and in the event there was a record I was interested in, you ran the risk that the record owner would be disappointed in what you were willing to pay, generating hard feelings with someone who had been a devoted listener. So I generally declined record offers from listeners. But Jimmy was a good friend and this was his friend, so I made an exception and went on down to Forty-sixth and Evans.

When I arrived, we sat at the dining room table. Claire was friendly and frail, and after a bit of small talk she went to the closet and pulled out several 78 record albums. She handed them to me and said to see if there was anything in there that I might be interested in. *God have mercy!* She had records on the

Black Swan and Paramount and the Emerson labels—and all in mint condition! It was the Aladdin's Cavern of classic blues records: Trixie Smith, Ethel Waters, Alberta Hunter—and their earliest recordings at that. After I picked my jaw up off the floor, I told her what wonderful records they were, what great shape they were in—and how valuable they were. I also said that as much as I liked them, I couldn't possibly pay her what they were worth. She told me that whatever I offered would be enough, that they'd been in the closet for fifty years untouched, and that she knew they'd have a good home with me. So I changed my mind and bought 78s. Three different times she called with more records—all great artists and titles, all in great shape. And I've done my best to give them a good home and to share them with listeners over the years. Thanks, Claire!

Sadly, this audience interaction slowed down over the years. There were two reasons. First, in 1990 *Blues Before Sunrise* went into national distribution, and I stopped making reference to local listeners and local events in an effort not to alienate listeners in other parts of the country. It really flattened the free-wheeling atmosphere of the old local-only program. And, second, many of the senior citizen listeners started dying. One week I would talk to a person, and the next week a son or daughter, a niece or nephew would phone to let me know that their father/mother/aunt/uncle had passed away. It was terribly sad and disheartening, like the passing of an era. From 1990 to 1996 there was still contact with listeners, but it had slowed considerably and it was from listeners on various stations throughout the country.

In 1996, with new management in place at the Chicago public radio station, I was given a choice: stay in house at WBEZ as a local-only program once again—pulling the plug on the national distribution of *Blues Before Sunrise*—or continue to distribute the program nationally but as an independent production, no longer employed by WBEZ but with the program still broadcast on that station. National distribution was what I had been working for all along, and at that time I had fifty stations taking the program, so I took a chance and became an independent producer. Under the new setup as an independent producer and program host, I was required to record the program in advance, which meant I was no longer available to talk with listeners while they heard the program. So my days at the University of Bronzeville came to a close. Many of the listeners who had been my best friends over the years had gone on to the next phase of their journeys, and I was about to begin mine. National syndication as an independent production was the start of an entirely new adventure and new era for the *Blues Before Sunrise* radio program.

Index

Five O'Clock Supper Club (Atlanta), 158
Flame Showbar (Detroit), 162, 168
Fletcher, Dusty, 196, 230
Flynn, Fahey, 234
Foot's Place Club (Birmingham), 160
Fortune Record Label, 71, 84, 87
Foster, Babyface Leroy, 128, 129
Foster, Ervin, 128
Foster, Little Willie, 128, 131, 143
Foster, Nat, 164
Fowler, Jesse, 147
Foxx, Redd, 174, 181
Franklin, Flossie, 75
Franklin, Guitar Pete, 17, 73, 74, 85
Franklin, Sammy, 193, 194
Frank Pandy's Tavern (New Orleans),
  186
Freddie and Flo, 174
Freedom Record Label, 33
Freeman, George, 94
Freeman, Von, 94
Fullbright, John R., 33
Fuller, Blind Boy, 216
Fulson, Lowell, 28, 146

Gaither, Bill, 76, 84
Garner, Errol, 203, 204
Gayles, Billy, 119
Gennett Record Label, 46
Gibson, Danny, 187
Gibson, Lacey, *190*
Gillespie, Dizzy, 194
Gillum, Jazz, 79, 138
Glaser, Joe, 210
Gleason's Lounge (Cleveland), 167, 168
Glenn, Lloyd, 27, 28, 31, 33
Glover, Henry, 170, 208
Goodman, Benny, 28, 107
Goodman, Gene, 107
Gordon, Dexter, 190, 201
Graham, Marty, 174, 175
Gray, Henry, 94, 109, 111, 115, 146
Gray, Wardell, 190, 201

Gray-Haired Bill, 128, 129
Green, Cora, 42
Green, Slim, 48
Green, Sugarfoot, 59
Gregory, Dick, 210
Grey Ghost. *See* Williams, R. T. "Grey
  Ghost"
Griffin, Jimmy, 165
Griffin Brothers, 165, 166, 167
Griffith, Shirley, 17
Guitar Slim, 115
Guy, Buddy, 80
Gypsy Room (Atlanta), 188

Hall, George, 42
Hammond, John, 37
Hampton, Lionel, 173, 195
H & T Club, 79, 84, 138
Happy Home Lounge, 99
Harmonica Hotel Lounge, 151, 152
Harmonicats, 93
Harrington, Hamtree, 42
Harris, Shakey Jake, 102, 131, 222
Hawkins, Coleman, 36
Hawkins, Roy, 163, 164
Hayes, Gus, 164
Hayes, P. T., 131, 135
Hegamin, Lucille, 49
Heinzman, Mrs., 229, 230, 231, 234, 235
Henderson, Fletcher, 36, 44, 47
Henderson, Rosa, 48
High Chaparral, 183, 214
Hill, Big Bill, 147
Hill, Raymond, 177
Hilltop Tavern, 110
Hines, Earl, 54, 55
Hines, Eddie Porkchop, 152
Hite, Les, 30
Hite, Mattie, 42
Hob-Knob Tavern, 147
Hogg, Smokey, 19
Holley, Buddy, 171
Hollis, Edward, 76

STEVE CUSHING has been the host of *Blues Before Sunrise* for thirty years. He has served as anchor of WBEZ's nationwide broadcast of the Chicago Blues Festival, performs frequently as a drummer, and has produced several recordings by Magic Slim, Lurrie Bell, and Smokey Smothers.

The University of Illinois Press
is a founding member of the
Association of American University Presses.

———————————————————

Composed in 10/13.25 Adobe Minion Pro
by Celia Shapland
at the University of Illinois Press
Designed by Kelly Gray
Manufactured by Thomson-Shore, Inc.

University of Illinois Press
1325 South Oak Street
Champaign, IL 61820-6903
www.press.uillinois.edu